Anthony Neilson
Plays: 3

Relocated; Get Santa!; Narrative;
Unreachable; The Prudes

Relocated: A sinister mystery. 'Not an experience for the faint-hearted . . . morally challenging and riveting . . . leaves an indelible stain on the memory.' (*The Times*)

Get Santa!: It's Christmas Eve but Holly isn't happy. All she's ever wanted from Santa is to meet her real dad for the first time. And every time, Santa's failed to deliver, bringing lots of useless presents instead. Well, Holly's had enough. This year she has a plan. 'A hilariously inventive and unconventional extravaganza. A hoot . . . vivid, stylish . . . witty. Warmly recommended.' (*Independent*)

Narrative: Devised throughout rehearsal with a seven-strong cast it's a play about storytelling and the narratives of our everyday lives. 'A drama for an age of stories and friendships stored in the cloud . . . It's a sharply written, coolly constructed and laudably ambitious piece of theatre.' (*Exeunt*)

Unreachable: 'Intoxicatingly chaotic comedy' (*Time Out*) following a film director on an obsessive quest to capture the perfect light.

The Prudes: A comedy about relationships in the current sexual climate, and a vicious satire on the male response to it. 'It's a damning, riotous and occasionally raw glimpse of the upheaving dynamics of men and women today.' (*WhatsOnStage*)

Anthony Neilson (b. 1967, Edinburgh) is a playwright and director. His breakthrough play *Normal: The Dusseldorf Ripper* was produced at the Edinburgh Theatre Festival in 1991. Other plays include *The Censor* (1997), *Stitching* (2002), *The Wonderful World of Dissocia* (2004), *Realism* (2006), *Edward Gant's Amazing Feats of Loneliness* (2009) and an adaptation of Poe's *The Tell-Tale Heart* (2018).

T0347791

Anthony Neilson

Plays: 3

Relocated

Get Santa!

Narrative

Unreachable

The Prudes

With an introduction by the author

methuen | drama

LONDON • NEW YORK • OXFORD • NEW DELHI • SYDNEY

METHUEN DRAMA
Bloomsbury Publishing Plc
50 Bedford Square, London, WC1B 3DP, UK
1385 Broadway, New York, NY 10018, USA

BLOOMSBURY, METHUEN DRAMA and the Methuen Drama logo are
trademarks of Bloomsbury Publishing Plc

First published in Great Britain 2019

A catalogue record for this book is available from the British Library.

A catalog record for this book is available from the Library of Congress.

ISBN: PB: 978-1-3501-0079-4
ePDF: 978-1-3501-0080-0
eBook: 978-1-3501-0081-7

Series: Contemporary Dramatists

Typeset by Mark Heslington Ltd, Scarborough, North Yorkshire

To find out more about our authors and books visit
www.bloomsbury.com and sign up for our *newsletters*.

This volume of plays is dedicated to my father,
Sandy Neilson, who read to me as a child.
His love of stories, and of the theatre, lives on in me.

Contents

Introduction

As I write this, in 2018, I feel there are two great challenges ahead for all storytellers.

The first is a matter of responsibility. In this fractured and divisive time, I believe it is vital that we position ourselves as guardians of empathy. Journalists can document lives but we have the unique ability to allow audiences to experience those lives from an emotional perspective. If we can do this, truthfully and without judgement, there seems to me no better antidote to the increasingly cruel and dangerous culture of tribalism now sweeping the globe.

There is currently a huge demand for escapism. There's nothing wrong with that, per se – we all need to forget reality sometimes – but that cannot be the bulk of our diet. I'm not suggesting that we should all be writing grittily realistic stories about the refugee experience; but I do believe we have a duty to represent those whose stories are so seldom told: the weak, the sick, the dispossessed. Sport is the celebration of success: art is the celebration of frailty. We must address that frailty with clear eyes and compassion; even if the form of that frailty repels us morally.

If we shirk that responsibility – if we abandon the voiceless – they will be forced to turn elsewhere: to unscrupulous players who will exploit their fears to nefarious ends. Artists are not the solution to the problem; but we are not bystanders either. It is not good enough, in days like these, to hide behind the fig-leaf of false humility. We have a duty to truth and we must honour it.

Our second challenge is more esoteric but in some ways more challenging: we need to find a new way to tell stories.

The shape of life has changed dramatically in recent decades but the shape, or structure, of stories has not. The 'hermetically sealed' narrative – one that begins and ends neatly – no longer corresponds to our increasingly episodic lives; and I suspect this may partly explain the cultural shift towards serialized cinema and television.

In the twenty-first century, we can expect to have multiple careers and several significant relationships in our ever-longer lives. Our partners may be of various sexes and we may have children with more than one of them, achieved by various means. The post-war models of narrative structure no longer make sense. Even death is not as final as it was: generations of the future will live on in a digital afterlife so detailed that only those closest to them will feel their loss in any real sense. Even the concept of 'end' is in flux.

We are also undergoing, as a species, a dizzyingly rapid cognitive evolution. Audiences are now so sophisticated that they can switch back and forwards between layers of reality and artifice without dropping a narrative stitch. They can switch tonally from the banal to the profound, from the deeply silly to the deeply serious, with the same ease they skip between tabs on a browser. Even five-year-old children can process meta-narrative.

The ubiquity of the internet – itself modelled on our neurology – is rewiring our brains by the day. A browsing session has no structure; instead, it operates as our brains do – forging new connections and pathways with every click. I recently adapted *Alice in Wonderland* for the stage and was amazed by how modern its free-associative structure feels, even if its content hasn't dated so well. It left me wondering if perhaps Carrol is a better template for future narratives than Shakespeare will ever be.

I suggest then, for discussion at least, that the stories of the future will have no discernible beginning or end, except in their duration; that they will be more collage than story; that they will have no need for tonal or structural coherence; that they will employ multiple forms and techniques; and that plays – whilst they cannot logistically embrace the episodic – are well-placed to push the envelope of story if they embrace their 'liveness'. The proverbial 'well-made play' of the future might look more like cabaret or circus than a Rattigan or a Miller.

My play *Narrative*, included in this volume, was my first baby-step towards testing these ideas. Though it struck some critics as an inconsequential piece, it is in some ways the play I am most proud of, in that – despite its deeply odd structure – the general audience seemed to have no difficulty assimilating it.

I stress that because the challenge is not to be 'experimental' for the sake of it: we already have 'anti-narratives'. The challenge is to find a new structure that is easily accessible to all – a new *mainstream*, if you will – and it was both gratifying and liberating to feel that audiences might be ready for that. To some extent, *Unreachable* continued in that vein, albeit in a way that will be less obvious on the page than in performance, where the actors really played with different levels of reality, breaking not only the fourth wall but also the fifth and sixth occasionally. Even I was slightly concerned we would run the risk of losing the audience, but no; they were with us all the way and generally delighted to be let in. The important thing, in retrospect, is that all of the ad-libs and asides were real and spontaneous and truthful on some level. Audiences can smell it when they're not. It's well-known that I suggested the greatest theatrical sin was boring an audience; but lying to them is a close second.

All the plays in this volume are, to some extent, adventures in form: *Get Santa!* was my first play written specifically for children, particularly for those in dysfunctional families; *Relocated* uses the horror genre to convey the emotional state of long-term trauma (the 'condition of horror'); *The Prudes* is a two-hander about impotence, both sexual and political, in which the audience is a third character. To paraphrase The Dude, that's the best I can do to really tie this collection together. My analyst could probably do a better job but her hourly rate is considerably higher.

In closing, I should also mention that every one of these five plays was commissioned and produced, sight unseen, by the Royal Court Theatre in London. It is one of the very few theatres that will allow me to work as I prefer, creating the play from scratch in rehearsals, and it is no understatement to say that I would not exist as the artist I am without their patronage. My deepest thanks go to Dominic Cooke and Vicky Featherstone, the artistic directors of the Court during this period, and to all the staff that worked on and supported these shows.

As ever, I must also thank all the actors and design teams credited, without whom these plays would be entirely different and very possibly much worse. Many of the best ideas in here are theirs but I have deliberately forgotten which ones they were.

Finally, I should also thank my family – my mother, Beth; my dear brother Ranald; my nephew Nicholas – and my partner, Lucy, all of whom bear the brunt of my strange working methods and get their personal lives plundered as a reward; my agent, Julia Tyrell, and everyone at Methuen Drama; and lastly, all of you out there that pay to see and read and occasionally perform these plays. Without you, I could never afford the therapy.

Anthony Neilson, 2018

Relocated

Relocated was first performed at the Royal Court Theatre, London, on 6 June 2008 with the following cast and creative team:

Connie	Frances Grey
John/Schinkel	Phil McKee
Man/Liam	Stuart McQuarrie
Molly	Katie Novak
Marjorie	Jan Pearson
Kerry	Nicola Walker

Director Anthony Neilson
Designer Miriam Buether
Lighting Designer Chahine Yavroyan
Sound Designer Nick Powell

Characters

Marjorie
Man
Kerry
John
Liam
Connie
Schinkel
Molly

Notes

As ever, what follows is a transcript of the show as performed. Though details of the production are included, they are only intended to provide an impression of the atmosphere created for a play in which sound, lighting and set design are as important as the text.

In the set design, our aim was to create as complete a black-out as possible in the auditorium. To this end, the playing area was painted black and black carpet was laid. The audience was separated from the stage by a gauze screen which imposed strict parameters on the lighting used. Single sources were used where possible.

The gauze had the further effect of 'sealing' the audience into a box. The gauze screen would become opaque during scene changes.

The ceiling was lowered, at a skewed angle, for the full length of the auditorium to achieve a feeling of claustrophobia. The audience 'box' was set at an angle to the stage so as to create further disorientation.

Speakers were placed in the audience enclosure and at the far end of the stage. No speakers were deployed at the front of the stage or at mid-distance. Speakers were also placed directly above the audience, behind the ceiling piece.

Relocated is, by design, one of my more opaque plays. To gain a more detailed understanding of the piece, research the Soham murders of 2002, with particular emphasis on Maxine Carr's involvement, and the 2008 case of Josef Fritzl, which was just breaking as the play was being written. *Relocated* is a work of fiction and metaphor and not based specifically on these crimes; but they informed the premise.

As the audience enters the auditorium, the radio news of the day is playing. There is a strong smell of disinfectant. **Marjorie** *is vacuuming, oblivious to the audience filing in.*

When the audience is seated, she rubs her arm, puzzled by the feeling. Suddenly, she clutches her chest and falls to her knees, then pitches forward face-down onto the floor. All sound ceases.

The lights fade to black and the play begins.

Prologue

In the thick darkness, the audience hear the names repeatedly, as if whispered in their ears:

Kerry. Marjorie. Connie.

The sound collage fades. And then, suddenly, there is a deafening, ugly buzz. The buzz travels from the audience area to the stage where the source is revealed as an intercom system.

In one fluid movement, as if her collapse had not occurred, **Marjorie** *gets to her feet, and walks to the intercom system.*

Marjorie   Yes?

Pause.

Intercom   Miss Charles?

Marjorie   Yes?

Pause.

Intercom   Could you come downstairs, please?

Marjorie   Why?

Pause.

Intercom   It's time to move on.

Pause. She looks at the vacuum cleaner, then at her watch. She brings the watch up to her ear, listens to it. It seems to have broken. She presses the intercom again.

Marjorie   Will I need my coat?

But she can only hear whispering.

Pause. She walks over to the vacuum cleaner, looks down at it. Behind a door, a dog whimpers and scrapes to be let in.

Mummy will be back for you. Be a good girl.

She remains still. The lights fade to pitch black. The sound of rain.

Scene One

Marjorie   Hello?

Smoke curls out of the darkness. A man appears, holding an umbrella in one hand, a cigarette in the other.

What's going on?

The man exhales a plume of smoke.

It's past midnight.

Man   Were you doing something?

Marjorie   No, I was just . . . cleaning.

In retrospect, this puzzles her. Pause.

Man   What's wrong?

Pause.

Marjorie   I don't think I left the dog any water.

Man   The German Shepherd?

She nods.

What's she called these days?

Marjorie   Still Priscilla.

Man   Nice dogs. Obedient. Blindly faithful.

Marjorie   Yes, she's good as gold.

Pause.

She gets anxious when I leave her.

Man   Isn't your boyfriend with her?

Pause.

Marjorie   No, he's at home.

Pause.

Man   How's all that going for you?

Marjorie   It's fine; it's not . . . serious.

Pause.

I know you don't approve. But I get lonely.

Man   Does it help?

Marjorie   Sometimes.

Pause.

Is it over then?

Man   Oh yes.

She drops her head.

Marjorie   What's happened?

Man   This.

He takes an A4 envelope from his pocket.

Marjorie   What's that?

Man   Photographs.

Marjorie   Of what?

Man   Of you.

Marjorie   Of me? Who took them?

Man   Your boyfriend. I hope.

Marjorie   I don't understand . . .

Man   They're what we in the trade call dirty. Dirty photographs.

Marjorie   Oh no . . .

She smirks involuntarily. Her hand covers her mouth.

Man   I'm glad you find it funny.

Marjorie   I'm embarrassed, aren't I?

Pause.

Where did you get them? Did you steal them from my house?

Pause.

Look – I know. It was just a silly thing. We were drunk. He wanted some photographs.

Man   How romantic.

Marjorie   You wouldn't understand.

Man   Try me.

Marjorie   It didn't feel dirty. It was nice – to be wanted. To be fancied. I felt . . . normal.

Man   Normal.

Pause.

Marjorie   You've got no right to be searching my house.

Man   We didn't.

Pause.

Marjorie   Then where . . .?

Man   We found them. On a charming little site called fuckmywife.com

Pause.

Marjorie   What?

Man   He posted them. On the internet.

Pause.

Marjorie   Oh no . . .

Man   Did you agree to that?

Marjorie   No, of course not!

Pause.

He said he'd keep them private! He swore he would!

Man   Sorry – what's your name again?

Marjorie   My – ?

Man   Simple question, isn't it?

Marjorie   You know my name.

Man   Remind me.

Pause.

What's your fucking name?!

Marjorie   Marj – Marjorie.

Man   Marj-Marjorie?

Marjorie   Marjorie.

Man   Marjorie what?

Pause.

What are you smirking at?

Marjorie   You're scaring me!

Man   What's your fucking name?!

Marjorie   Marjorie Charles! My name is Marjorie Charles!

Man   And who can you *trust*, Marjorie Charles?!

Pause.

Marjorie   You.

Man   Me. And who else?

Marjorie   No one.

Man   *Who else*?!

Marjorie   Nobody, no one! Just you. Only you.

Long pause.

Man   Who's the other man? We need to know.

Marjorie   The other man?

Man   Your boyfriend took the photographs –

Marjorie   Yes . . .?

Man   So who's the other man?

Pause.

Marjorie   I don't know what you're talking about – what man?

Man   The *man* with his *dick* inside you! The *man* you are fucking. Is it coming *back* to you now?

Marjorie   Please, just stop it – there was me and there was Ben, there was no one else there –

Man   Don't believe my lying eyes?

Marjorie   You've made a mistake.

She takes the envelope, slides out the photographs. Pause. What she sees stuns her.

This is impossible.

Pause.

No. These are not the photographs. That is not Ben's house – I don't know this man – that's not me.

Man   The resemblance is remarkable, wouldn't you say?

Pause.

Marjorie   Well, then, they're fake. These have been made by someone. They've cut my head out and stuck it on. They can do that; you know fine well they can.

Man   They've been authenticated. They're not fakes.

Marjorie   You're wrong.

She pushes the photographs back to him.

Marjorie   Test them again.

Pause.

Man   Look – what's done is done –

Marjorie   No! It's not. I would not do these things – with anyone – and I swear to you – I have never seen or met the man in these photographs *ever*. You need to test them again.

Pause.

That *thing* in the photographs is not me, I swear. On my mother's life. I swear.

Pause.

Man   Pack your things.

He exits.

Marjorie   Where am I going? Where are you going to send me?

Snap to black. The audience is 'sealed' into their box. The sound of the rain intensifies.

Scene Two

Darkness.

Marjorie (*V/O*)   I don't know this place. The shadows fall in different ways. Make different shapes. I don't know where the switches are.

A candle lights, illuminating **Marjorie**, *now in a dressing gown. Faintly, we hear the sound of children playing in a playground. She looks at her watch.*

A faint illumination of the window pane, as if her eyes have adjusted to the darkness. The sound of the children playing builds.

Slowly, she walks to the window and looks out, the moonlight on her face. She inhales sharply.

Pause.

She tries to open the window but to no avail.

Marjorie   What are you doing? It's four in the morning!

She taps at the window. The sound continues.

Hello, can you hear me?! What are you doing in school?!

The sound of the children playing stops.

Pause. Now she looks scared – she backs away from the window. Slowly, she turns to look at the audience.

She walks towards them, shaking with fear. She walks right up to the gauze, stares at them.

Then she screams, a nerve-shredding scream, terrifying, dragged up from the depths of her soul.

Scene Three

Kerry   Hello?

The lights change.

Marjorie   Hello?

Kerry   Is it all right to come in? I just wanted to say hello.

Kerry *is a frightfully posh-sounding woman. She carries a black plastic bag and a small orange cake box. Her lipstick is too red.*

Marjorie   Hello?

Kerry   Hello! I couldn't help noticing you'd moved in. I'm from downstairs. My name's Kerry.

Pause.

Marjorie   I'm – Marjorie.

Kerry   Ooops – you don't seem too sure?

Marjorie   No, I'm Marjorie.

Kerry   Pleased to meet you. I brought you something.

She gives **Marjorie** *a box, tied with a ribbon.*

Kerry   Just to say hello.

Marjorie   Oh that's very nice of you, thank you. Come in.

Kerry   It's just a piece of cake.

Marjorie   Oh, lovely.

Kerry   Just a sponge I'm afraid. They do a lovely Black Forest but they were all out of that.

Marjorie   No, actually sponge is my favourite.

Kerry   Oh that's lucky.

Marjorie   Yes, it is, it's perfect.

Kerry   How are you settling in?

Marjorie   Oh, fine. Just unpacking, you know.

Kerry   Have you got a lot of stuff?

Marjorie   No, not really – I travel light.

Kerry   Do you do a lot of travelling?

Pause.

Marjorie   No – well – I'm a classroom assistant so, you know – I go where the work takes me.

Kerry   Oh I see. So where did you come from?

Pause. The voice on the intercom (the **Man***'s voice):*

Intercom   Petersgate Infant School.

Marjorie   Petersgate Infant School.

Intercom   It's in Hampshire.

Marjorie   It's in Hampshire.

Intercom   You were there for eighteen months.

Marjorie   I was there for a year and a bit.

Kerry   Oh, I see – Well, you're handy enough, aren't you?

She indicates the window.

For the school.

Marjorie   Oh – yes, I know – I won't be getting much exercise, will I?

Kerry   You could just about do the job from here, couldn't you?

Marjorie   Yes, I suppose – I could shout over the roll-call.

Kerry   In your nightie!

Marjorie   Yes, imagine!

They laugh.

Kerry   The girl that lived here before was a teacher.

Marjorie   Yes, so I'm told.

Kerry   That was all very strange.

Marjorie   What do you mean?

Kerry   Didn't you hear?

Marjorie   No?

Kerry   Well, she just disappeared one day.

Marjorie   Did she?

Kerry   Upped and left, middle of term, without a
by-your-leave.

Marjorie   Goodness . . .

Kerry   They even called in the police at one point; that's
how worried they were. But then I think they got some letter
from her, saying she was in, I don't know – Ibiza or Goa or
somewhere, you know; wherever it is people go to 'find'
themselves.

Marjorie   Oh, well . . .

Kerry   Course, as I said at the time, that letter could have
come from anyone. But nobody seemed much bothered
about that.

Marjorie   Oh . . . well . . .

Kerry   I know. I'm such an armchair detective. Actually,
that's one of the reasons I'm here; to give you this.

She passes the carrier bag to **Marjorie**.

Marjorie   What's this?

Kerry   It's just some stuff she left at my house. She'd
forgotten her keys one day and I meant to bring them back
but then she . . .

Marjorie *lifts out a rolled-up piece of paper.*

Kerry   I don't really know what's there. A notebook, I
think. Some underwear. Some you-know-whats.

Marjorie *looks at her.* **Kerry** *mouths 'tampons'.*

Marjorie   Oh . . .

Kerry   And this is a painting, look.

She takes the paper and unfurls it.

I think it's by one of the children at the school. I thought
maybe you could take it back.

The painting, obviously by a child, shows children playing in a playground.

Marjorie*'s hand goes to her mouth.*

Kerry   It's quite sweet, isn't it?

Pause.

Marjorie?

Marjorie   Oh – sorry.

Kerry   What's wrong?

Pause.

Marjorie   Nothing, it's just – it reminds me of a dream I had.

Kerry   What dream?

Marjorie   Oh really, it was nothing.

Pause.

Kerry   Did this dream involve . . . children?

Pause.

Marjorie   Yes.

Kerry   In a playground?

Marjorie   Yes. How did you know that?

Kerry   Well – it's a picture of children in a playground.

Marjorie   Oh – yes.

Kerry   I told you I was a detective!

Marjorie   Yes, you did.

Kerry   So what were they doing, these children?

Marjorie   Oh really . . . I don't want to bore you.

Kerry   You wouldn't be boring me at all. I'm very good on dreams.

Marjorie   Well . . . they were all in the playground, running around and laughing.

She retraces her steps, as in Scene Two.

Kerry   Like they do.

Marjorie   Yes, except it was the middle of the night. And they looked . . . pale. Their hands and faces were . . . chalk white, like they'd never seen a day of sun in their lives.

So I tried to shout over to them, you know – find out what was going on – and then they just stopped . . .

Kerry   Stopped?

Marjorie   Yes. Stopped running, stopped shouting. And then slowly . . . they all turned to look at me. All these little white faces, just . . . staring at me.

Pause.

That's all I remember.

Kerry   Goodness. How marvellously creepy. And then I give you this painting?

Marjorie   I'm sure it's just coincidence. I mean, I work in a school and I've got a school across the road. What else am I going to dream about?

Kerry   Well, exactly. Except for one thing – and I always thought this was a bit odd, look –

She holds up the painting again and points to a crescent shape.

It's the moon!

Pause.

The sound of the dog scraping and whining outside the door.

Marjorie   Oh that's the dog. It's all right, Priscilla – Mummy'll take you out soon.

Kerry *is staring intensely at her. Pause.*

Marjorie   Well – I'll see all that stuff gets to its . . . respective owners.

Kerry   Thank you so much.

The dog.

Marjorie   I should take her out, I think.

Pause.

Kerry   You know, I hope you don't mind me saying; but there's something very familiar about you.

Pause.

Marjorie   Really?

Kerry   I'm sure I recognise you from somewhere, or that we've met or something.

Slowly, **Marjorie***'s face darkens to invisibility.*

Marjorie   I don't think so . . .

Kerry   No, I'm not sure.

Marjorie   I think I've just got one of those faces. Nondescript, I suppose.

Pause.

Anyway . . . I really should take the dog out.

Kerry   Oh, try some of the cake first!

Marjorie   Oh I will, I'm looking forward to it; but I better take her out first, the poor thing's –

Kerry   Oh go on. It's from the most wonderful little cake stall, down at the market. That's me, you see – if I find something I like, I have to convert everyone. It's a good job I'm not religious.

Pause.

Go on. Just a mouthful.

Pause.

Marjorie   All right . . .

She opens the box, looks inside. **Kerry** *is still staring at her.*

Marjorie   Mmm, it does look lovely.

She takes the cake out. **Kerry** *obligingly takes the box.*

Pause. **Marjorie** *takes a bite, catching the crumbs with her hand. Whilst she does so,* **Kerry** *– still fixedly staring at her – softly sings:*

Kerry
Hush, little baby, don't say a word,
Mummy's going to buy you a mockingbird.

Marjorie *nods, humouring her.*

Kerry
And if that mockingbird don't sing
Mummy's going to buy you a diamond ring.

The lights begin to fade.

And if that diamond turns to brass,

Dark now, and **Marjorie** *joins in.*

Both
Mummy's going to buy you a looking glass.
And if that looking glass gets broke,
Mummy's going to buy you a billy goat.
And if that billy goat won't pull,

And now just **Marjorie***:*

Marjorie
Mummy's going to buy you a cart and bull.
And if that cart and bull fall down,
You'll still be the sweetest little baby in town.

Now fully lit again, it is **Kerry** *who holds the cake. Pause.*

When **Kerry** *speaks, she is no longer posh-sounding, but softly accented, like* **Marjorie***.*

Kerry   You're right, it's delicious. Very moist.

Marjorie   It is, isn't it?

Kerry   I should really take the dog out now.

Marjorie   Yes, I've got to be going too. But listen – it was lovely to meet you. And remember, I'm downstairs if you need me. Anything at all, I'll always be in. Just ask for Marjorie.

Kerry   Thank you, I will. That's very kind.

Marjorie   Oh – just one more thing – the dog: you should call her Sasha from now on.

Kerry   Why?

Marjorie   You know why: it's time to move on.

Pause. **Kerry** *nods.* **Marjorie** *hugs her, then disappears into the dark.*

Kerry *crams the rest of the cake into her mouth, crumbs spilling everywhere. She stares at the painting.*

Scene Four

At the school:

John   Hey . . . no eating in class.

Kerry *turns to him.*

John   I don't remember giving you detention, young lady. What was the name again?

She blushes at his patter.

Kerry   Balfour. Kerry Balfour. I'm the new classroom assistant.

John   Yes, I've seen you around.

He extends his hand.

I'm John Hickleson, the very old art teacher.

She shakes his hand.

You don't want to model for the life class, do you?

Kerry   Oh – is there a life class on?

John   No. But I'm game if you are.

She shakes her head, laughing. **John***'s a joker – the kind of man who has a revolving bow tie in a bottom drawer somewhere.*

You walked into that one.

Kerry   I did.

John   Right – enough of that, Hickleson! How can I assist the assistant?

Kerry   Oh – well . . . it's about this –

She gives him the rolled-up painting.

John   Ah – my diploma's come through at last!

Kerry   No, I believe it's by a girl here . . .

John   Really?

He unfurls it.

Kerry   I can't make out the name. I think it's Molly someone. Molly Cams?

He stares at the painting, his mood changing. Pause.

John   Cairns.

Kerry   Do you know her?

Pause.

John   Where did you get this?

Kerry   Um, it was . . . in the flat that I moved into.

John   Are you across the street?

Kerry Yes.

Pause.

John Thank you.

Kerry I thought she should have it back.

He nods.

Kerry I think it's quite good actually. What year is she in?

John She would be in . . . Year Five now.

Pause.

Kerry Year Five?

Pause.

John I'm afraid . . . that Molly Cairns died; two years ago.

Kerry Oh my God.

He nods.

I'm so sorry.

John Yes, it was very sad. She was a sweet little girl.

Pause.

Kerry What happened?

Pause.

I'm sorry – that's none of my business.

John No, it's all right. She was murdered, as it happens.

She smirks.

Is that amusing to you?

Kerry No, please – not at all – I've got this weird thing where I look like I'm smirking when I get upset, I can't help it. Please don't think that. It's terrible – it's a terrible thing.

Pause.

Do they know who . . .?

John (*shakes head*)   A couple of people were questioned but no one was charged. I don't think there was enough evidence. They didn't find the body.

Pause.

Kerry   But if they didn't find the body . . .?

John   They found some . . . of the body.

Kerry   Oh my God. That's awful.

John   Yes, it is.

Pause.

But look – thanks for this. I might run it by the police . . . see if it's of any interest.

Pause.

Kerry   Do you have other paintings by her?

John   A few, yes. Why?

Kerry   I don't suppose I could see them . . . could I?

John   Um . . .

Pause.

I'm actually not that comfortable with that. Do you mind?

Kerry   No, not at all –

John   I know it's silly, it's just . . . people can be a bit ghoulish about these things.

Kerry   I understand, totally . . .

John   I'm sure not you, but . . . we had a lot of reporters snooping around.

She nods.

Maybe when I know you a little better . . .

Kerry   I really understand, believe me. I was just . . . interested.

Pause.

John   Well, that's not got us off to a very good start, has it?

Kerry   No, listen – you're right. I could be anybody.

John   It's the small-town mentality. It creeps up on you. Don't stay here too long, that's my advice.

Kerry   Oh – speaking of advice, I don't suppose you know of a good car mechanic, do you?

John   A what?

Kerry   A car mechanic.

Pause.

John   What's that?

Pause.

Kerry   A car mechanic?

Pause.

John   I'm sorry, I don't know what you're saying . . .

Kerry   A car mechanic – someone who fixes cars.

John   Oh – a *car* mechanic?!

Kerry   Yes.

John   Sorry – I thought you'd got all New Age on me. A car mechanic – well, there's a garage I use that's reasonable.

Kerry   You don't have a number for it, do you?

John   Uh well . . . to be honest . . . I'm not that comfortable with that either.

Kerry   Oh. Ok . . .

John   I'm pulling your leg!

He laughs. She joins in with the joke.

It's written on my manual. Walk me to my car and I'll get it.

They walk into the darkness.

The audience is sealed in again. Above them, they can hear this, muffled (it is not important that they can make out the words):

John   So do you know your way around yet?

Kerry   Not really. I went down to the market on Saturday.

John   Yeah, that's nice; it gets a bit samey though. There's a farmers' market every month. That's a bit better. Do you cook?

Kerry   Not much. I'm a bit dependent on ready meals, I'm afraid.

John   Oh that's not good. You need some home cooking once in a while.

Kerry   Why, do you cook?

John   Why do I cook? Good question.

Kerry   You know what I mean.

John   I do cook. I try. I'm not Heston Blumenthal but I'm not rock-bottom. I'll cook for you one day and you can give me your opinion. Are you a veggie?

Kerry   Not full-blown but – chicken mostly.

John   Chicken is good. Chicken is the prawn of the land. Did you know that?

Scene Five

A smoke alarm sounds, horribly shrill.

Liam *enters, wearing a towelling robe. He is wet from the shower and steaming slightly. He carries a sodden newspaper and leaves wet footprints as he walks.*

He reaches up to the smoke alarm and turns it off.

He sits down at the table – the tablecloth is a deep red colour – and attempts to open his soaked newspaper.

Kerry *enters, eating a stick of celery.*

The paper is coming to pieces in his hands.

Liam   Fucking hell.

Kerry   What happened?

Liam   It fell in the bath.

Pause.

Suddenly, **Liam**'s *face changes (achieved using ultraviolet light) and* **Kerry** *screams, just as* **Marjorie** *had done, over and over – a horrifying sound.*

Lights snap to black. The audience is sealed in again. They hear this, muffled, from directly above:

Schinkel *(V/O)*   Shut the fuck up, down there! No one can hear you! You make that noise again, I'll come down there and pull your fucking teeth out, do you understand? Now shut the fuck up!

Scene Six

Lights fade up. **Liam** *is still sitting there, in his bathrobe.* **Connie** *enters, eating a stick of celery.*

She notices the sodden paper.

Connie   Oh, what happened to the paper? I was in the middle of the crossword.

Liam   You'd given up.

Connie   I hadn't given up. I was stuck on an anagram. What happened to it?

Liam   It fell in the bath.

Connie   *It* fell in the bath? You mean you *dropped* it in the bath.

Liam   If I meant that I'd have said it, wouldn't I?

Connie   It just magically fell into the bath?

Liam   No, maybe not. But I didn't 'drop' it into the bath. That sounds deliberate. I didn't think 'Oh, I'll just drop this paper into the bath'. It was an accident. It fell in.

Connie   Right. So when something's an accident, *it* did it?

Liam   Well, what would you say? If I said 'what happened to the paper?', you'd say –

Connie   'I dropped it in the bath.'

Liam   *You* dropped it in the bath? Well, that was stupid of you.

Connie   *You* dropped it in the bath.

Liam   No, you said *you* dropped it in the bath.

Connie   No, I said –

Liam   You can't take it back.

Connie   I was saying what / I would say –

Liam   No, no, can't take it back. You dropped it in, you said so.

Pause.

Connie   What age are you?

Liam   What age are you?

Connie   Well, I'm a good bit younger than you –

Liam   And that's why –

Connie   – but I still don't –

Liam   And that's why you think –

Connie   – but I still don't think –

Liam   – that it's all right –

Connie   – that that's the way to win –

Liam   – that it's all right to cop off –

Connie   – that's the way to win an –

Liam   – to *cop off* with a teenager!

Connie   – that that's the way to win an argument!

Liam   With a fucking *teenager, in a fucking disco*!

Connie   Fuck off, Liam.

Pause.

I had one anagram to finish.

Liam   So what do you want? Do you want me to put my clothes on and miss the start of (*name of TV show*) so I can drive down to the village and get you a paper so you can finish one shitty anagram?

Connie   What I'd like is an apology.

Liam   For what?

Connie   For ruining my crossword.

Liam   Connie – you're on dangerous ground.

Connie   Why? Because I want an apology?

Pause.

Oh, I see – because I've given up my right to any kind of an apology ever again, is that it?

Pause.

I was pissed, I snogged some kid. I know it hurt you but it's not the worst sin in the world, is it?

Pause.

Liam   I left the water in the bath.

Connie   I'm not having a bath in second-hand water.

Liam   It's not dirty.

Connie   It's not dirty?

Liam   Not really, no.

Connie   Why did you have a bath then?

Liam   Eh?

Pause.

Anyway, I didn't mean for you. I meant for the kids.

Connie   For the kids?

Liam   They're all muddy. Their legs, anyway.

Pause.

Connie   What are you talking about?

Liam   They've been down by the stream or something. They're filthy.

Connie   Liam – we don't have any children.

Liam   Right. I wish you'd told me that sooner. Would've saved us a lot of money.

Pause.

Connie   I don't get it.

Liam   Get what?

Connie   Are you trying to be funny or nasty or what?

Liam   Neither.

Connie   So what are you trying to say?

Liam   I'm not trying to say anything. I'm saying the kids are muddy, they might as well use the bath water.

Connie   Liam, we don't have any children! Have you gone completely mad?

Pause.

Liam   Are you being serious?

Connie   Am *I* being serious?

Pause.

Stop it. It's cruel. It doesn't matter what I've done.

Liam   *What's* cruel?

Pause.

Christ, you know – I will never understand you.

Connie   Liam – I'm being deadly serious now. Please don't try to wind me up because I'm getting very freaked out. Do you seriously think we have children?

Pause. He gets up.

Liam   I'm going to watch the telly.

Connie   Answer me, Liam. Please.

Liam   If we don't have children, Connie – then who the fuck is that upstairs?!

Pause. She looks up. The sound of squealing, of thumping around.

You're fucked in the head, you know that?

He exits.

Connie *sits there, listening to the noise of children playing. She suddenly looks terribly sad. A drip of water squeezes from the ceiling and splashes on the floor.*

Noticing this, she gets up and walks to the spot. She puts out her hand to catch the drops.

She looks at the water in her palm.

Connie   Something's happened . . .

Scene Seven

Marjorie *forms from the darkness.*

Marjorie   Yes.

Connie   But what?

Marjorie   I don't know.

Connie   Are we asleep?

Marjorie   No. It's something else.

Connie   Weren't we . . . cleaning?

Marjorie   Yes, that's right. And . . .

Connie   The news . . .

Marjorie   Yes . . .

Connie   That thing . . . on the news.

Marjorie   That poor girl. In the basement.

Connie   And her children.

Marjorie   And the wife.

Connie   They say she didn't know.

Marjorie   They won't believe her.

Connie   How could she not know?

The sound of children playing in the playground.

Marjorie   They're back.

Kerry *appears out of the darkness, holding a lit candle.*

Connie   Who's this?

Marjorie   It's Kerry. She's new.

Kerry *looks at her watch.*

Connie   Can she hear us?

Marjorie   Only faintly, now and then.

Kerry *goes to the window, looks out.*

Connie   Do you think she can save us?

Marjorie   She's smart and she's brave. She's like you.

Kerry *turns and looks at the audience.*

Connie   He's too powerful. He'll trap her here like us.

Marjorie   We'll see.

Kerry *walks to the audience and stares at them. Pause.*

Kerry   What do you want? Why are you staring at me? Go away! Go home!

Fade to black.

Scene Eight

The sound of the sea, and seagulls squawking above. The wind is howling. The man appears. Again, he carries an umbrella.

Kerry *turns to him.*

Kerry   I'm not moving. Not again. Let them find me, I don't care.

Man   Who said anything about moving?

Pause.

Kerry   I'm just saying. That's what I've decided.

Man   Fine. I'll be able to retire and move to the city.

Pause.

So who's the new boyfriend?

Pause.

Kerry   He's not a boyfriend. Not really.

Man   You're always so coy. Like I'll be hurt somehow.

Pause.

Kerry   I don't think you'll be hurt.

Man   What's his name?

Kerry   Like you don't know.

He smiles.

Kerry   Does he check out?

Man   So far, yes. That's not why I'm here.

Pause.

We looked into that website you . . . inadvertently appeared on; it's registered to a German company called Magdala, which fronts itself as a construction firm. Its managing director is one Johan Schinkel. Have you heard that name before?

Kerry   I don't think so.

Man   About four years ago, German police raided his house. In a hidden bunker under the house, they found three people. The oldest was Schinkel's daughter, who'd been missing for fifteen years. The other two were her children. Schinkel was their father too.

Pause.

Kerry   That's horrific.

Man   Schinkel left the country before they could arrest him. No one knows where he went.

Or if they do, they're not saying.

Pause.

Kerry   Why are you telling me this?

Man   This is Johan Schinkel.

He hands her a small photograph.

Kerry   I've told you – I don't know this man. I've never met him.

Man   Connie – we've got photographs of you fucking him. Can you understand why we're having trouble believing you?

Kerry   Yes, I can understand. And no, I can't explain those photographs. All I can tell you is that I do not know this man, I have never met him, and I have never had any form of sex with him.

Pause.

And my name is Kerry. Connie Johnson died six years ago.

Man   I don't know how you keep track. You just put them out of your head?

Pause.

Kerry   They're in there somewhere, doing their thing. I don't pay them any mind.

Pause.

Man   Look, if you know anything at all that could help us find this man –

Kerry   Then I'd tell you! Don't you even believe that?

Pause.

Man   Schinkel's smart, Kerry. He seems to have some kind of power over people. He'd been a suspect in several cases of rape and child abuse before they even found the basement.

Not one conviction. And even his daughter – who he raped and kept in a dungeon for fifteen years – even she won't testify against him. Do you know why?

Kerry (*shrugs*)   Probably because she's frightened.

Man   No. Because she loves him. Because she wants him to come home.

Lights fade on him. The wind howls.

Scene Nine

From above, the sound of water pipes creaking and juddering.
Kerry *opens the fridge and kneels down, staring into the light.*
John *enters, bleary-eyed, in shorts and a t-shirt.*

John   Kerry?

She remains transfixed.

Kerry, what are you doing?

Kerry   Oh – sorry, I was just . . . getting a glass of milk.

Pause.

John   Did you go out somewhere?

Kerry   When?

John   Just now. I thought I heard the door.

Pause.

Kerry   Oh, yes – I took Priscilla down.

John   Who's Priscilla?

Pause.

Kerry   Sasha. Sorry. The dog. She needed a pee.

Pause. He's puzzled but chooses to move on.

John   Are you all right?

She rubs her chest.

Kerry   I'm fine.

Pause. He turns, about to go back to bed.

John?

John   What?

Kerry   When you've stayed here – have you ever . . . heard anything? At night. In the middle of the night. Has anything woken you up?

John   Do you mean snoring?

Kerry   No – do I snore?

He shrugs.

No, I meant . . . children. Playing.

John   Children? I don't think so. From next door, do you mean?

Kerry   No – I mean . . . maybe, yes. Maybe that's it.

Pause.

John   *I* know what it is . . .

Kerry   What?

John   Why you're acting so shifty. You're having a bit of cake!

Kerry   I'm not . . .

John   You are so busted – you're eating cake at five in the morning, admit it.

Kerry   Well . . . just a little bit.

John   You're going to turn into a cake, my girl.

Kerry   It wouldn't surprise me.

John   You shouldn't eat cake at this time of night. The calories just turn to fat.

Kerry   I know . . .

Pause.

John   Well, with any luck it'll go to your breasts.

Pause. She nods, somewhat hurt.

I mean – I didn't mean it like that. I meant, it's better it goes there than . . . to your stomach or something, right? You'd prefer that.

Kerry   I suppose.

John   I didn't mean there's anything wrong with your breasts. I love your breasts – you know I do!

She nods. Pause.

Are you . . .?

Kerry   I'll be there in a minute.

Pause.

John   I didn't mean anything by it, honestly.

Kerry   I know. I believe you.

Pause. He goes.

The sound of the children playing gets louder and louder. She covers her ears. Fade to black.

Scene Ten

A smoke alarm sounds, horribly shrill.

Liam *enters, wearing a towelling robe. He is wet from the shower and steaming slightly. He leaves wet footprints as he walks.*

He reaches up to the smoke alarm and turns it off.

He sits down at the table. The tablecloth is white. Water drips from the ceiling. **Connie** *enters and sits down beside him. She eats a stick of celery.*

Pause.

Liam   I left the water in the bath, if you want it.

Connie   I'm not having a bath in second-hand water.

Liam   It's not dirty.

Connie   It's not dirty?

Liam   Not really, no.

Connie   Why did you have a bath then?

Liam   Eh?

Connie   Why did you have a bath if you're not dirty?

Pause.

Liam   Anyway, I didn't mean for you. I meant for the kids.

Connie   For the kids?

Liam   They're all muddy. Their legs, anyway.

Pause.

Connie   What are you talking about?

Liam   They've been down by the stream or something. They're filthy.

Connie   Liam – we don't have any children.

Pause.

Liam   No, I know we don't have any children. I meant for the girls.

Connie   What girls?

Liam   I don't know their names. The girls from the school.

Connie   There aren't any girls here.

Pause.

Liam   Then who's that upstairs?

They look up to the ceiling. They look at each other.

Connie   I don't hear anyone.

Liam   I just saw them. I thought they were friends of yours.

Connie   How old are they?

Liam   I don't know. Twelve-ish?

Connie   Why would I have twelve-year-old friends?

Liam   Not friends – pupils, whatever. I thought they'd just come round – you being Miss Popular and everything.

Connie   I didn't let anybody in. Are you sure you saw them?

Liam   Yes I'm sure. They were in the bedroom.

Connie   In the bedroom?

Liam   I know – I nearly walked in there with just a towel on. They were sat on the bed, looking at the photo album. And one of them said 'Look how young Connie looks'.

Pause.

Seriously – you didn't let any girls in?

Connie   No.

Pause.

Go and see.

Liam   Go and see what?

Connie   See who they are.

Pause. He looks up.

Liam   Me?

Pause.

Liam   They're your friends.

Connie   Liam, go and see. They might be robbing us or God knows what!

Pause. He gets up. Pause.

Liam   Maybe we should just call the police.

Connie   For a couple of twelve-year-old girls? Be a man, for Christ's sake.

Pause.

Fade to black – the audience sealed in. The muffled bass of **Liam**'s *voice as he talks. Then the voice raises, as if he's shouting.*

The sound of thumping, a struggle, something falling.

Then we can hear his voice, still muffled but now distressed, stricken: '*Oh my God! Oh my God!*'

Connie   Liam?

Pause. Eventually **Liam** *enters. He is wet now. He sits back down at the table. He looks like he's been in a struggle – his hair is messed, his face scuffed. He is trembling and doing his very best to hold back tears.*

Connie   What happened? Where are the girls?

He doesn't reply.

Liam – answer me!

Liam   There weren't any.

Connie   There weren't any?

Pause.

Liam   No, I – made a mistake. I thought there were girls in the bedroom but there weren't. It was just a pile of old coats.

Connie   Old coats?

Liam   There's a pile of old coats on the bed and I don't know, I just – I passed the door and I thought I'd seen two girls in there, but I was wrong.

Pause.

Connie   How could you think a pile of old coats . . .?

Liam   Connie, please – I feel stupid enough as it is. Let's just leave it shall we?

Pause.

Connie   But I heard voices . . . and the water – why's there water dripping through the ceiling?

Pause.

Liam   Oh, that's the . . . bath. I overfilled it. It must have seeped through the bathmat.

Have we got any pickle? I fancy a sandwich. Do you want a sandwich?

Pause.

Connie   I just don't see how you could mistake a pile of old coats for two girls. You said they were muddy. You said they were looking through the *photo* album!

Liam   Look – I'd had . . . a very hot bath. I walked very quickly past the bedroom door, I saw a vague shape . . .

Connie   And you thought it was two twelve-year-old girls?

Liam   Well, I'd probably been thinking about . . .

Connie   Twelve-year-old girls?

Liam   No – about school. About what I've got to do this week. We're doing all the boiler inspections this week, so . . .

Pause.

What time's (*name of TV show*) on?

Connie   And what coats? I didn't leave coats on the bed.

Liam   Clothes then.

Connie   Or clothes.

Pause.

Liam – what's going on?

Liam   Why don't you make us a sandwich?

Connie   I don't want a fucking sandwich! I want to know what's going on!

Liam   Jesus Christ, woman! I've told you what's going on! I made a mistake!

Why would I lie about it? What is it you think I'm lying about?!

Connie   I don't know.

Pause. She walks to the drip and puts her hand out. It splashes blood red on her open palm.

Connie   Oh my God, Liam – it's blood! What have you done?

He gets up and goes to her.

Liam   Connie, calm down – I haven't done anything. You know me – what could I do?

Connie   I heard the noises, Liam – I heard you shouting –

Liam   You didn't. You didn't hear anything.

Connie   I did.

He shakes her violently.

Liam   No! You didn't! You didn't hear a fucking thing! What do you think you heard?

You think there are girls up there, do you? Girls you've never met, that just wandered in off the streets, that just wandered out of their houses, that just wander about looking for strange houses to walk into?! Do you think that's more likely than me just making a mistake, like I said? Because go ahead – if you think I'm a liar, go upstairs, right now. Go and look in the bathroom and tell me if you see a couple of twelve-year-old girls up there that I've been lying about!

Pause.

Connie   I'm not saying you're lying – I just –

Liam   Right. Good. Because we need to move on, Connie, and I'm willing to do that.

As he talks, the blood from above drips down onto his back, blossoming across his damp bath robe.

I'm willing to say right now, from this moment here, we start again. And maybe we're not the people we thought we were, or the people we want each other to be. But we love each other, don't we? Don't we?

Pause. She nods.

And that doesn't just happen everyday. Not to people like us. I mean – I might walk out on you for what you've done . Or you might leave me for what you think I've done. And we might walk out that door, Connie, and never meet anyone that loves us again, ever. Not if they knew us. Not if they knew who we really were.

Pause.

Now come on. You know me inside out, right? You know I wouldn't hurt a fly. You're a woman. Women know these things. What's your heart telling you? It's telling you whatever's happened, it can't be that bad. You wouldn't love a man who could do anything that bad, would you?

Pause. She shakes her head, scared.

Course you couldn't. So you're going to make us some sandwiches – and go and turn the telly on. And I'm going to go upstairs . . . and fix the bath. And that's what we'll have done . . . with our Sunday night. All right?

Pause. She tries to regain her composure.

Connie   All right.

Liam   Ok?

She nods. Pause.

Connie   Do you um . . . do you want . . . ham . . . or
. . . cheese?

Pause.

Liam   Both. Ham and cheese.

She nods. He exits.

Scene Eleven

Connie *slumps back into the chair.* **Marjorie** *appears from
the darkness.*

Connie   That's not what happened . . .

Marjorie   I know.

Connie   But that's what they think.

Marjorie   It doesn't matter what they think.

Connie   But it does, though, doesn't it? It's the only thing
that matters. We're the proof of that.

Pause.

Marjorie . . .

Marjorie   Yes?

Connie   Why didn't we finish cleaning?

Marjorie   I don't know. I'm wondering that myself.

Connie   We always finish.

Marjorie   I think . . . I fell.

Connie   And then what?

Marjorie   Then I got up again.

Connie   But you didn't hurt yourself?

Marjorie   No.

Pause.

Connie   I can't go on like this; living it over and over again.

Marjorie   I know. But there's still Kerry. He doesn't know about Kerry.

Connie   She doesn't know about us.

Marjorie   No. But we're not the only ones here.

They look behind them, into the darkness, where something scuttles. Lights fade to black. The audience is sealed in.

Scene Twelve

John   Kerry – it's very sad – but Molly Cairns is dead . . .

Kerry   But they didn't find the body!

John   I told you, they found parts –

Kerry   And what parts did they find, John?

John   I don't remember.

Kerry   They found her *right* arm; and her *left* hand. Didn't they?

John   I don't know. I think they found an arm, yes. I didn't linger on the details, believe it or not.

Kerry   They did – I read the reports. They found her *right* arm and her *left* hand. They found the parts of her she needed to *paint*!

John   To paint?

Kerry   What if her paintings – what if this painting – isn't just a painting? What if it's some kind of . . . beacon or transmitter. A distress call that comes alive at night – saying she's out there somewhere, calling us – begging us to rescue her.

Pause. He shakes his head, at a loss for words.

I know how it sounds. But she's alive, John. Molly's alive. I can feel it.

Pause.

John   So why you, Kerry? Why's she sending this message to you? What makes you the saviour of little lost children?

Pause.

Kerry   Maybe I'm not the first. I mean, the girl that lived here before, the teacher that disappeared –

John   No, no, no – she didn't disappear, she went to India. She was a stoner. That's what stoners do.

Kerry   We don't know that for sure. Maybe she tried to find Molly and was kidnapped or killed or something . . .

John   Kerry, I knew her. She was brain-dead. She spent two hours telling me 9/11 was part of a global conspiracy against hemp!

Kerry   We should talk to her parents –

John   Absolutely not.

Kerry   Why not?

John   Because they've suffered enough!

Kerry   They might believe me.

John   Yes, Kerry, they might. People in despair will believe just about anything.

Pause.

Why am I even discussing this?! What you're saying is crazy, it's insane. And you actually believe it –

Pause.

I think I should go.

Kerry   Why?

John   Because I just . . . should.

Kerry   John . . .

Pause.

John   What?

Kerry   Has a German man . . . moved here? In the last few years?

John   A what?

Kerry   A German man.

Pause.

John   I'm sorry, I don't know what you're saying.

Kerry   A man. From Germany. A German man.

John   Oh, a German man?! I don't think so – why?

Kerry   Because there's a man called . . . Johan Schinkel . . . he's a criminal. A very bad man. And I think he might be in this country. Somewhere.

Pause.

It doesn't matter. It's stupid. You're right. She's dead. Molly's dead. I can't change that.

She begins to weep. It is a quite disproportionate reaction.

Everything is lost.

Her voice echoes, as do her sobs.

Everything is lost!

Fade to black.

Scene Thirteen

Marjorie *appears in the shadows, barely lit. She looks odd and there is a gradual realisation that her arms are far too long. Her hands hang beside her knees.*

Marjorie (*posh voice*)   I thought we were friends.

Kerry   Oh – Marjorie, isn't it?

Marjorie   Is it?

Pause.

Kerry   From downstairs?

Marjorie   Don't act like butter wouldn't melt. I know what you're up to.

Pause.

Kerry   I don't understand . . .

Marjorie   You keep your hands off Mr Schinkel. It's my turn. Mine.

Kerry   Is he here?

Marjorie (*mimics her*)   'Is he here?'

Pause.

Now you listen to me. If you think you can just turn up here and jump the queue, you've got another think coming. He's fucking that slag Jemima at the moment but it's my turn next, do you understand?

Kerry   Your turn on what?

Marjorie   What do you think?

Pause.

Look at you anyway. You're not ready for it. It'd rip you in half. I've spent three years working up to this and I'm not going to let you spoil it.

Kerry   Look – I don't want to have anything to do with him . . .

Marjorie   No of course not. How silly of me. So why have you been asking about him?

Kerry   Because of what he's done. Don't you know what he's done?

Marjorie   I don't give a tuppenny fuck what he's done. I just want to drink his cum from a shotglass. And I'm not sharing it with anyone.

Pause.

Anyway, he's already had you, hasn't he? According to the photographs.

Kerry   That wasn't me.

Marjorie   No. It wasn't.

Pause.

His penis has a barb in it, you know . . .

Kerry   A what?

Marjorie   A barb. Like a hook. Some animals have it.

Fade to black on **Marjorie**.

Scene Fourteen

John (*V/O – whispered*)   Kerry?

Kerry *answers her mobile phone.*

Kerry   Yes?

John   It's John.

Kerry   John – I'm sorry about yesterday . . .

She opens the fridge and takes out a piece of cake.

John   Just listen to me: I'm not saying I believe you. But a German did move here, three years ago. I did some interior design for him. He was building an extension on his house.

Kerry   Yes – that makes sense – he had a construction company! That must be him.

John   But his name wasn't the name you said. His name was Schoonj.

Kerry   Skoonj?

John   That's what it says on the invoice. Heinkl Schoonj.

It sounds a little like **John** *is suppressing laughter.*

Kerry   How do you spell it?

John   H – E – I – N – K – L

Kerry   Heinkl . . .

John   Schoonj. S–C–H–O–O–N–J.

Kerry   That's not even a name.

John   It's German, isn't it?

Kerry   It can't be a real name. It's ridiculous . . . unless –

Pause.

No wait. It's not ridiculous – it's an anagram! John, it's an anagram!

Pause.

John   Are you sure?

Kerry   Yes. It's a terrible anagram but that's what it is. Heinkl Schoonj – Johan Schinkel. Except there's no 'a'. But it's close enough.

Pause.

Where's this house? We need to go there, John, right now!

John   No, no but that's the thing. He sold it. He was building the extension so he could sell it.

Then he was moving on.

Kerry   No, he's still there – I just had some woman, some mad . . .

Pause.

John   Some woman?

Pause.

Kerry?

She looks faint. She rubs her head.

Kerry   I was . . . cleaning. I fell.

She drops to her knees and falls flat on her face.

John   Kerry?

Pause.

Kerry, are you all right?

Pause.

Kerry!

Blackness.

Scene Fifteen

The sound of a storm.

The **Man** *stands with his back to us. His umbrella has been turned inside out, the spokes twisted and splayed.*

Kerry   He's here. In this town. Schinkel is here.

Pause. He neither turns, nor answers.

I think he's holding a little girl – Molly Cairns. She's been presumed dead but I don't think she is. I think Schinkel's kidnapped her.

Pause.

Do you hear me? Johan Schinkel is here.

Man (*V/O*)   We know.

Pause.

Kerry   You know?

Pause.

Kerry   Is the girl there? Is Molly with him?

Pause.

Answer me!

Pause.

Man (*V/O*)   We had him all wrong, Connie. He just wanted to protect his family. He just wanted to keep them safe.

Kerry   What are you talking about?

Pause.

Kerry   What has he done to you?

Man (*V/O*)   He's helped me. He's shown me – what it is to be a man. A man the way a man should be.

Kerry   This isn't you talking. He's manipulating you. He's evil.

Man (*V/O*)   You're so ungrateful. Do you know what I would give to have him take care of me? To have him take me into his home?

Pause.

Kerry   Tell me what he's done.

He turns, bringing down the gnarled umbrella. His face is gone, replaced by male genitals.

Man (*V/O*)   How do I look?

Pause.

Kerry   Not that good.

He nods.

Man (*V/O*)   I'm relaxed about it. But it's hard to breathe.

Pause. She is in tears.

Kerry   Where is he? I'll find him. I'll make him change you back.

Man (*V/O*)   This is his house. He makes the rules.

Kerry   No. You protected me all these years. And I'm going to help you.

Man (*V/O*)   You don't know what's happened, do you? It's only been seconds since you fell.

Kerry   Since I fell?

Man (*V/O*)   You can't save me. But you can save the girl.

Kerry   How, though? How do I save her?

Man (*V/O*)   You'll know when the time comes.

Pause. He turns away again.

Man (*V/O*)   You should go now.

Kerry   No – I'm not leaving you. I know you didn't love me. But you protected me and that's the only thing that matters.

Man (*V/O*)   No. Please go. I don't want you to see . . . what happens next.

Pause. He's starting to breathe very heavily, as if building to a sneeze.

Save the girl.

Fade to black. In the darkness.

John   Kerry? Kerry, it's me. It's John.

Scene Fifteen

Lights up.

John *is standing over* **Kerry**, *shaking her awake.*

Kerry   John . . . .

John   What happened?

Pause.

Kerry   I don't know . . . I fell.

John   Look, I think we should take you to a doctor . . .

Kerry   No – there's no time –

John   Kerry – you have to calm down. Your heart's racing.

Kerry   We have to go to the house. Schinkel's house.

John   I told you – he sold it.

Kerry   Well, where else? It's the only place she can be.

John   No, just ssshh – the car's outside. We can drive to the hospital. And then we can go wherever you like. Just to put your mind at rest.

Kerry   Don't you understand?! Molly could be dying!

Pause.

John   Listen to me, Kerry – please – none of this is real. Molly Cairns is dead. This Schinkel character doesn't exist.

Kerry   No, don't say that. You told me that man's name. It's a perfect anagram. Now you explain that!

John   But who is this Schinkel? How do you know he's a 'dangerous man'? Kerry, you're a classroom assistant! How would you know any of this?!

Pause.

Kerry   My name's not Kerry Balfour.

Pause.

My name's Connie Johnson.

Pause. He can't help but laugh.

John   Of course it is.

Pause. She looks completely serious.

Kerry   Why – would I lie about it?

Pause.

John   I don't think you're lying.

Kerry   No, you think I'm mad. I might as well say I'm Queen Victoria.

She laughs bitterly.

There *are* people who say they're me. Mad people. And there's people that get mistaken for me, and they get . . . petrol bombs, and bricks thrown through their window!

Pause.

Maybe I'm not me. Maybe I just think I am. I honestly don't know any more.

This strikes her as very funny. **John** *looks serious.*

Kerry   No but come on – it's funny isn't it? I've spent all these years running and hiding . . . and then when I finally get up the courage to tell someone . . . they don't believe me.

I should just go round telling everybody who I am – they'd never suspect!

John   Oh but I do believe you.

She laughs. Pause.

Kerry   You're going to humour me now?

John   I thought you were clever. I thought you were good with anagrams.

Kerry   I am . . . I knew it the minute I heard it. Heinkl . . .

John   Schoonj. It's clumsy don't you think?

He smiles.

Kerry   It's awful. He should have gone for something simpler. I mean, Johan . . . you've got –

Pause.

John   You've got what?

Pause.

Kerry   You've got John right there . . .

John   Try John Hickleson.

Pause.

Kerry   There's still no 'a' . . .

John   I was never very good with anagrams.

And then, very faintly, the sound of a woman screaming. **Kerry** *looks confused.*

The tinny sound seems to be on a loop; a woman screaming and begging for mercy. It gets suddenly louder and she is unsure why. And then she realises –

It's because **John***'s taken out his mobile phone.*

She looks at him in horror. He shrugs, and in a German accent says:

John   I just have to take this.

Lights snap to black. The audience is sealed in.

Kerry (*V/O*)   By now you will know that I have left my position as classroom assistant.

I am so sorry to have done this without notice but due to personal circumstances I had no choice. Please accept my most heartfelt apologies for any inconvenience this has caused.

I am owed outstanding wages; but given the inconvenience caused to you, I feel it is right to forgo them. I cannot give you a forwarding address but if I have left any personal items please give them to Mr John Hickleson for safekeeping.

Once again, I must express my apologies for my actions. I hope you can find a replacement for me without too much trouble, and I wish you all the best of luck in the future.

Yours sincerely, Kerry Balfour

Scene Seventeen

The lights fade up.

Kerry *sits in the middle of the basement.*

One of her arms has been removed and lies beside her. She is shivering, soaked in blood, barely conscious.

Schinkel *enters. He is wearing a short-sleeved Hawaiian shirt, with shorts and sandals.*

His face is daubed with sun cream and he wears a tinfoil sun reflector round his neck. He speaks in a heavy, not entirely authentic German accent.

Schinkel   Ah – it is so hot outside! I think it is better to be here in the shade.

She picks up her severed arm and makes a feeble attempt to swipe at him with it.

You are wonderful, Connie. You so like to fight. So strong and full of life.

I would say it was a miracle you came to me but of course that would sound like God's doing. In fact we have Molly to thank for bringing us together.

He sets up a deckchair.

She is quite the fisher, no? You are not the first she has landed but this time . . . I think we will not be throwing you back into the water. No but really – quite the catch: Connie Johnson.

I didn't know at first. You look quite different from those terrible photographs. Is it surgery was done? The nose maybe, the lips – the lenses in? Anyway, it is very good. You are still very beautiful. Any man would be proud to have you, and I have had many; but not to have a big head about it.

He lies down in his deckchair.

We have both been unjustly treated, Connie. We have both been torn away from everything we knew and loved. And why? You because you were loyal; because you trusted; because you put love higher than everything. And me – because I protected my family, because I kept them safe from a world full of danger. But this what society thinks of duty now. It is a weakness. It is a sin.

Pause.

I know you will think we are not the same. And I do not expect you this instant to love me. But perhaps we have things we can both give to each other.

Pause. And now the words echo, fading in and out, overlapping, as time passes.

I can give you safety. Comfort, I can give you. No more having to run, to hide. I can give you things the same, every day, for as long as you live. The world will be small but then when you are hunted, the world *is* small, no? And I can give you the best thing of all: I can give you a child.

I know how you love children, Connie. It is what makes your life so tragic. When that monster killed those girls, he killed also any child you would have. Can you think of it? Such a wonderful mother you would be but what kind of life? Always moving, from place to place, always in fear of discovery. You could not even say who you were to your own child. You would always be strangers. It would be cruel; and you are not so cruel as that, Connie.

But here – here there are no secrets. Here you can be what you should always have been. A wife, a teacher, a mother. And Molly so badly needs a mother. You will see. I can give her much but I can never be that for her.

Pause. He sits up.

Well – I have said everything for now. You are here and of course I cannot be allowing you to go free now. So you will stay here, Connie. But I wish you will stay here for Molly and be happy staying here. I will promise that I will treat you fairly and I will treat you well and I will protect you. And we will eat together and we will watch the TV and uh . . . all will be normal. And maybe one day, you will come to feel something for me and it will surprise you.

Pause.

Good so – there is someone who wants to meet you of course. She is not so used to the light so take this . . .

He gives her a torch.

That's it – don't drop it. And I will come back in a while and see if everything is ok.

Good.

He exits. The lights turn out.

Even in her weakened state, **Kerry** *jumps, scrabbling for the torch, holding it unsteadily.*

Schinkel (*O/S*)   Molly?

Suddenly a noise from above – a sudden shuffling, covering lots of ground quickly – almost like a squirrel.

Kerry *looks up, torchlight darting across the ceiling. Whatever is there moves suddenly again, and then stops.*

And then, the shuffling noise is in the room with her, somewhere at the far back.

The torchlight catches only glimpses of this, the illumination made even more erratic by her fearful reaction:

Crouched in the furthest corner of the room is a completely white figure, its eyes and mouth crudely drawn with marker pen, its hair like black straw, its breasts and genitals crude scrubs of black; a child's drawing come to life.

It seems frail, hyperventilating, its chest and ribs rising and falling with frightening rapidity, like a bird in shock. It seems to only have one arm, and one hand.

*At first, **Kerry** and **Molly** are simply terrified of each other.*

*But then the light comes to rest on **Molly**'s oddly sympathetic face.*

Kerry   Ssshhh – Molly – it's all right. I'm not going to hurt you.

She tries valiantly to get to her feet and approach it.

It crashes from side to side the more frightened it gets and she modulates her approach accordingly.

It's all right. I came here to help you. Is there a way out?

Closer.

Do you know a way out, Molly? Don't be frightened.

Closer.

Oh, you poor thing – don't be scared.

*It's panting so hard it looks like it might expire there and then. And **Kerry** is not doing so well, either. She lies down.*

Kerry   Molly . . .

She drops the torch.

I'm here . . . to help you . . .

Pause.

My name's Connie . . .

Pause.

The torch clicks out. The audience are sealed in. In the darkness:

Kerry (*V/O*)   I know this place. I know where the switches are. I recognise the shadows.

How long have I been here? How many years, how many months – how many seconds since I fell?

Time has no meaning here. And because we are all damned, there is no condemnation. Forgiveness blossoms everywhere, like crimson flowers.

And when we sleep, it is deep, and dark, and silent.

Scene Eighteen

A smoke alarm sounds.

Schinkel *sits at the kitchen table, reading a paper. The same set-up as the scenes with* **Liam** *and* **Connie***.*

Schinkel *stands up and turns off the alarm.* **Kerry** *enters, eating a stick of celery. She sits down.*

Kerry   Sorry. Burnt the toast.

Pause.

It's very sensitive that alarm.

Schinkel   I'll pick up a new one in town.

Kerry *pours him some tea. The sound of a baby crying.* **Schinkel** *lowers his paper.*

Kerry   It's all right. I'll see to him. He's teething.

Pause.

Will you be staying down here tonight?

Schinkel   Not tonight. Tomorrow maybe.

Kerry *nods. She kisses him on the head.*

Kerry   Molly? – come and help me with your brother!

She exits. **Schinkel** *continues reading his paper. Fade to black.*

Kerry *(V/O)*   They will tell you we were evil, my darling. And you will come to believe them. They will show our house to the world and say it was a place of torture.

Never say there was kindness, Molly. Never say there was love or laughter. It's not what they want to hear.

Scene Nineteen

The smoke alarm sounds again but this time it doesn't stop. **Schinkel** *is pitched forward, his head on the table.*

Kerry *enters, looks at him for a time. She feels for a pulse in him. Nothing.*

Pause.

Kerry   Molly? Get your coat.

Pause.

It's time to move on.

Scene Twenty

Kerry, **Marjorie**, **Connie** *and* **Molly** *walk outside. It is night.* **Molly** *is a normal-looking girl, blonde hair, wearing a white top. She's eating a piece of cake.*

Kerry *(V/O)*   Walk with your head hung down. Flinch when the cameras flash. Cry when they ask you to talk.

They need that from you. They need the world to make sense. My name is Connie Johnson, and I won't live to see you die. And at least in that, I have been lucky.

They all look up into the sky. **Molly** *looks awestruck. Crumbs fall from her mouth.*

Molly   What's that?

Marjorie   It's the moon.

Molly   That's the moon?

Marjorie   That's the moon.

Pause. **Molly** *squeezes* **Marjorie***'s hand.*

Molly   Mum?

Marjorie   Yes, darling?

Pause.

Molly   You didn't do anything, you know. It was the man.

Marjorie*'s hand squeezes hers tighter than ever. She fights back tears.*

Marjorie   Thank you, my darling. Thank you.

Lights slowly fade. And again we hear the voices, speaking the names:

Connie Johnson, Kerry Balfour, Marjorie Charles.

The words fade to silence.

Coda

The audience are sealed into the box. On the ceiling of the box are stars and planets and moons, like the ones you see on children's ceilings.

When the stage is visible again, they see what they first saw: **Marjorie** *face down on the floor, the vacuum cleaner whining beside her. The radio plays, picking up where last we heard it.*

One last time, the lights fade to black.

Get Santa!

Get Santa! was first performed at the Royal Court Theatre, London, on 1 December 2010 with the following cast and creative team:

Newsman/Thomas	Bill Buckhurst
Holly	Imogen Doel
Bumblehole	Tom Godwin
Gran/Jenny	Amanda Hadingue
Mum	Gabriel Quigley
Santa	David Sterne
Bernard	Robert Stocks

Teddy operated and voiced by Chand Martinez

All other parts played by the cast

Story Anthony Neilson and Nick Powell
Music Nick Powell
Lyrics Anthony Neilson and Nick Powell
Director Anthony Neilson
Designer Miriam Buether
Lighting Designer Chahine Yavroyan
Sound Designer Nick Powell
Puppetry Mervyn Millar

Characters

Holly
Bernard
Gran
Mum
Santa
Bumblehole
Teddy
Newsman
Jenny
Thomas

Notes

Please note that the music composed for this production must be used in any subsequent productions and the play will not be licenced separately. Basic notation is available, though arrangements are at the producer's discretion.

Also, if at all possible, please use puppetry to animate a teddy bear of normal size, rather than putting an actor into a teddy-bear suit. The children's delight will make the effort worthwhile.

Prologue

The **Caroller Chorus** *takes its place and sings:*

Song: Christmas Intro

Christmas (Christmas, Christmas, Christmas) Christmas
(Christmas, Christmas, Christmas) Stuffing (Stuffing,
stuffing, stuffing) Turkeys

Hanging (Hanging, hanging, hanging) Baubles (Baubles)
Pulling (Pulling, pulling, pulling) Crackers

Killing (Killing, killing) time till Father Christmas comes

Holly*, a feisty ten-year-old, pushes through them, to address the
audience:*

Holly   Christmas is rubbish!

The lights on the Christmas tree short-out in a shower of sparks.

That's what Holly Finnegan thinks, and I should know. Cos
I'm Holly Finnegan! And this is Teddy!

She holds up her raggy old bear.

And he thinks Christmas is rubbish too! I bet you're saying
'Don't be mad, Christmas is great – you get loads of brilliant
presents!' But look:

She holds up a letter.

This is my letter to Santa. Every year I send a letter to Santa
and it always says the same thing:

'Dear Santa

This year I would like *no* presents. I don't want an iPod or
an iPad or an iPhone. I don't need any dolls or ponies or
pigs or princesses and I definitely don't need a Wii! (I
thought that was quite funny that bit.)

All I want for Christmas is to meet my Real Dad. I'm ten
years old and I've never even met him because nobody
knows where he is, not even my mum.

But you're Santa and you must know where everyone in the world is so please help me to find my dad so I can have a happy Christmas this year, instead of a rubbish one like usual. In return, I will be a very good girl.

Yours hopefully, Holly Finnegan'

So – every year I'm really good – I tidy my room and do my homework and eat all dinner even when it's got horrible green things in it – and every year I wake up on Christmas Day with lots of presents but no dad. And I wait all day, hoping he'll turn up, but he never, ever does.

Bernard *enters to fix the tree.*

Holly   What's that, Teddy?

*She looks behind at **Bernard**.*

Holly   Teddy says you're probably thinking that's my dad there. But it's not. That's Bernard. He's my stepdad. That means my mum got married to him even though I told her not to. And maybe you'll notice something else about Bernard – he's a dog!

Seriously, look! Look at his ears and his nose. He's even got a tail! My mum married a dog! How embarrassing is that?!

Bernard *gets a shock from the Christmas tree lights.* **Holly** *snickers.*

Holly   Well, I've had enough. That's the last straw. Tonight, it's Christmas Eve. And when Santa comes down that chimney, he's in for a *big* surprise! Tonight, me and Teddy, we're going to get Santa!

Bernard   Get Santa?

Holly   Get Santa!

*The **Chorus** appear from everywhere.*

Chorus   Get Santa?!

Holly *punches the air.*

Holly   GET SANTA!

The **Chorus** *enter, and decorate the room, to this tune:*

Song: Christmas Intro (Uptempo Reprise)

Christmas (Christmas, Christmas, Christmas)

Christmas (Christmas, Christmas, Christmas)

Giving (Giving, giving)

Holly   Stupid presents!

(Batteries not included) Singing (Singing, singing)

Holly   Rubbish songs!

Deck the halls with boughs of holly/'tis the season to
be jolly

Playing (Playing, playing)

Holly   Boring board games!

Wishing (Wishing, wishing)

Holly   That my real dad was here!

She leaves, slamming the door behind her.

Act One

The Christmas tree lights snap back on.

Bernard I've done it! Look everyone, I've finished the tree! What do you think? Gran – what do you think of the tree?

Gran The tree? The tree is . . . it's *resplendent*, that's what it is! I've not seen such a majestic Christmas Tree since your father sawed me in half at the White House.

Bernard What about you, poopy? Do you like the tree?

The serving hatch opens to reveal **Holly***'s* **Mum***, with a tray of cakes.*

Mum I do. It's perfect.

Bernard That's brilliant! Genuinely – that's – I'm chuffed, that's what I am! I'm absolutely chuffed to pieces!

Mum *brings the cakes in.* **Bernard** *hugs her.*

Bernard I'm chuffed chuffed chuffed! Chuffed chuffed chuffed!

Mum All right, that's good. But listen –

Bernard Get Holly down, get Holly down!

Mum What?

Bernard Get Holly down to see the tree! She'll go absolutely mad for it! She'll love it.

Mum She doesn't really like Christmas.

Bernard Oh but come on – when she sees that tree, she'll be totally chuffed. Chuffed, chuffed, chuffed! Chuffed, chuffed, chuffed! Chuffed, chuffed –

Mum All right . . .

She looks upwards.

Holly!

Pause. Nothing.

Holly!

Still nothing.

Put your ears down.

Bernard *does. The next shout is like a foghorn, shaking the room:*

Holl-eeeeeeeeeeeeeeeey!

From above:

Holly (*O/S*)   What?!

Mum   Come down for a minute!

Holly (*O/S*)   I'm busy!

Mum   Just for a minute!

Holly (*O/S*)   Why?!

Mum   Do as you're told!

Holly (*O/S*)   All right!

The sound of angry clumping.

Mum   She doesn't sound happy.

Holly *arrives, carrying her teddy.*

Holly   What do you want? We were busy!

Bernard   We've got a surprise for you.

Holly   What?

He steps to one side to reveal the tree.

Bernard   Ta-daa!

Pause.

Holly   What?

Bernard   Well – the Christmas tree.

Holly   What about it?

Mum   Bernard decorated it.

Holly   So?

Mum   So don't be so ungrateful, young lady.

Holly   You said it was a surprise. That's not a surprise. It's Christmas. Everyone decorates their Christmas tree. And most of them do it before Christmas Eve.

Bernard   Well, yes but – well – I think it's an especially well-decorated tree, don't you? I mean – don't you? Or do you not? You don't, obviously.

Holly   What's that smell?

Bernard (*sniffs the air*)   Which one?

Holly   Like – bacon or something . . .?

She approaches the tree.

Bernard   Ah yes – I know what that is.

Holly   What?

Bernard   It's bacon.

Holly *picks something off the tree.*

Holly   Oh my God! It's bacon! He's put bacon on the tree!

Bernard   Not just bacon. There's roast beef there and – this is smoked ham – and look: sausages!

Holly   But you don't put meat on a Christmas tree!

Bernard   Don't you?

Holly   No! You put chocolate on it!

Bernard   I can't eat chocolate.

Holly   The tree isn't just for you, you know! Mum – tell him!

Mum   You can decorate anything with anything you like.

Holly   Oh that's right – take his side! You always take his side, all the time!

Bernard   Don't you like the lights? You must like the lights . . .

Holly   No, I don't! The lights are cooking the meat! This is the most revolting Christmas tree I've ever seen, ever, and I hate it!

Bernard *looks hurt.*

Mum   Holly – you apologise right now.

Holly   Why? It's true, you know it is!

Bernard   It's all right. I think I'll – go for my walk. Get some air.

Mum   Bernard . . .

Bernard *takes a plastic bag and leaves.*

Gran (*to* **Holly**)   Oh, Holly, dear – You know your dad's still a bit confused by Christmas.

Holly   Stop saying that! How can he be my dad?! He's a dog!

Mum   Oh that's it – you see if you can talk some sense into her! I've got things to do.

She leaves.

Holly   It's not fair, Gran! How come nobody else thinks it's weird that my mum married a dog?!

Gran   Oh, don't be so old fashioned. You could do a lot worse than Bernard for a stepdad. He's loyal, he's faithful and he's very family orientated.

Holly   It's not normal though!

Gran   Oh, normal: is that what you want to be?

Holly   Yes!

Gran   Ah well – as my tattooist often says – the problem with normal is that everyone's got a different idea of what normal is. I mean – you love Teddy, don't you?

Holly   Yes.

Gran   And you take him with you everywhere you go?

Holly   Yes. But that's different! Teddy was a present – wait a minute, I should tell them this –

She approaches the audience.

Right, I told you that I've never met my Real Dad? But one Christmas Eve, when I was little, I mean – much littler than I am now, about five or something, there was a knock at the door and I heard it and I had to reach up to open it and there – sat there on the doorstep, in the snow – was Teddy. And he had a note on him, look –

She opens a locket on a chain around her neck and takes out a note.

You probably can't read this but it says 'Look After Me' and there it says 'Dad'. That's his actual handwriting there. So it's not just any teddy. My dad actually held him; in his own, actual hands.

Gran   Yes, but nobody'll care about that, not when you're grown up. A grown-up girl who carries a teddy around with her all the time? That's not normal, they'll say.

Holly   I don't care what they say.

Gran   No. And neither you should . . .

And she sings a song, that goes like this:

Song: Don't Let Anybody Tell You Who to Love

Don't let anybody tell you who to love!
If you love your teddy bear,
Who's to say you shouldn't share
Your lives together,
However people stare? Oh –
If you want some happiness in life
You must be brave:
If a penguin makes you smile
Why not take him up the aisle?
Pay no mind to those that tell you
It's depraved;
And never care
What normal people say –
Don't let anybody tell you who to love
And let everybody love the ones they may!
Don't let anybody tell you who to love
And let everybody love the ones they may!

If you love an axolotl
I can tell you tying the knot'll
Do an awful axolotl for your esteem!
Or going down on bended knee
To a handsome chimpanzee;
Or going on a honeymoon
With a honeybee!

Don't let anybody tell you who to love
Love's a funny thing
And no one knows what it will bring
You've no control over the song
Your heart will sing!
If you want some beauty in your life
Then be courageous: Take up with a porpoise; Better yet,
a kindly tortoise (They may be slow
But they can go
For ages!);
And pay no mind

To what the neighbours say!
Don't let anybody tell you who to love
And let everybody love the ones they may
Don't let anybody tell you who to love
And let everybody love the ones they may! (In the way
they want to love them!)
Don't let anybody tell you who to love
And let everybody love the ones they may!

So – what do you think?

Holly   I still think it's weird.

Mum *enters.*

Mum   Well, all I'll say is this: I wouldn't count on Santa
visiting you tonight.

Holly   What do you mean?

Mum   I don't think he visits naughty children, does
he, Gran?

Gran   No, I don't think he does.

Holly   That's not true. He visits Billy Gribbins and he
flooded the toilets. You're just saying that as a system of
control.

Gran   Where did you hear that?

Mum   You believe what you like. We'll see what's true and
what's not.

We hear the door open.

That's Bernard back now.

Gran   Why don't you say sorry anyway? Just in case Santa's
listening?

Pause.

Holly   I'll have to talk to Teddy.

*She takes **Teddy** to one side.*

We've got a difficult decision to make, Teddy. We don't want to say sorry, because we didn't say anything wrong. But we can't take the risk that Santa won't come or our plan to catch him won't work. So there's only one thing to do in a situation like this: We have to say sorry but just not really mean it. Do you agree?

She nods.

Good. Just keep your paws crossed when we do it.

Bernard *enters.*

Bernard   Hello, everyone, I'm back! And guess what, guess what –

Mum   What, dear?

Bernard   There's snow coming!

Gran   Really?

Bernard   Definitely. And tonight. It's going to be a white Christmas! Isn't that brilliant?! Holly – isn't that great?!

Holly   Yes, Bernard, it is. And can I also say that I'm sorry for saying the tree is disgusting.

Bernard   When did you say that?

Pause.

Holly   Just before you went out?

Bernard   Oh, right – yes – well; you're probably right. I shouldn't use meat as a decoration. It's just – it's so pretty.

He approaches the tree and gears up for a song . . .

Song: Meat

   Meat!

And that's it.

Mum   Right, well – on that note – I believe it's time for your bed, my girl.

Holly   Ok.

Stunned . . .

Bernard   Goodness . . .

Mum   Did she just say ok?

Gran   I believe she did.

Mum   Is that it? I say it's time for bed and you're not going to put up a fight?

Holly   Well, Santa doesn't come until you're asleep, does he?

Bernard   Hmm. Hmm.

Gran   What is it, Bernard?

Bernard   That's the bit I don't like. Some stranger coming into the house.

Mum   It's not a stranger – it's Santa.

Bernard   But why can't he just leave the presents in the wheelie bin; like the postman does?

Holly   Mum!

Mum   What, darling?

Holly   Can I sleep down here tonight?

Mum   Here in the living room?

Holly   I can sleep on the couch.

Bernard   That sounds brilliant!

Mum   What's wrong with your bedroom?

Holly   I don't know – just makes it more . . . special.

Gran   I don't see the harm in it.

Mum   That doesn't mean there isn't any.

Bernard   Come on, poopy, why not? It's Christmas Eve, after all.

Mum   Fine, do what you like.

Holly   Thanks, Mum!

She jumps onto the couch.

Mum   If it was down to me, I wouldn't. It's Bernard you should thank.

Gran *enters with a sleeping bag. She helps* **Holly** *into it.*

Gran   Here you go.

Mum   I said: It's Bernard you should thank.

Holly   Thanks.

Bernard   No, no, well – thank you for saying thank you. I'm chuffed that you're pleased. I'm chuffed, chuffed, chuffed! Chuffed, chuffed, chuffed!

Mum   All right, come on.

She and **Bernard** *leave.* **Gran** *kisses* **Holly** *goodnight.*

Gran   I'll see you in the morning, Chicken Slippers!

She turns the light out and leaves.

Holly   G'night, Duck Boots.

She contains herself until they've gone – then throws the sheets off, sits up and turns the light back on.

All right, Teddy. It's time for the plan. This is how we're going to get Santa.

She climbs out of her sleeping bag.

Now – the first thing is – I'm going to block up the chimney with this –

She stuffs her sleeping bag into the fireplace.

That'll force Santa to come through the skylight! Now –

She retrieves a bag full of things from behind the couch.

The second problem is we have to be asleep otherwise Santa won't come. So how are we going to know when he's here? Answer – crisps!

She pulls a bag of crisps out, opens them and dumps them on the floor.

I tried lots of different crisps and these are the loudest, crunchiest ones you can buy.

She eats a crisp.

Sure enough it makes a very loud crunch. They're quite nice, so she has another, then another.

Then she remembers what she's doing.

So – he'll come down and he'll land right in the crisps – they'll make a big crunch and we'll wake up!

She takes a camera from the bag.

Then we need to give him a fright so he's confused. So I'll set off the flash on this camera – like this –

She fires off the flash.

That'll make his eyes go funny and he'll stagger back and he'll fall over this chair –

She mimes blindly staggering.

– where he'll get his head stuck in this bucket –

She brings out a tin bucket and places it behind the armchair.

Now he'll be, like, 'I can't see, I can't see', and he'll grope around and he'll put his hands on the mantelpiece where they'll get stuck – !

She squeezes glue along the mantelpiece.

– because of all this glue! Then – (*She takes out an umbrella.*)

I'll give him this umbrella and it'll get stuck to his hand and then I'll throw this chilli powder in his face – !

She produces a small canister, puffs out a cloud of chilli powder.

And he'll go 'Aah, it burns, it burns, I need some water!' and he'll run up here for some water –

She runs to the breakfast bar, where she produces a glass.

But it'll be whisky!

She produces a bottle of whiskey and pours some in. A lot.

And he'll get really drunk and he'll be, like, 'Oh I'm so drunk, I feel ill, I don't knew where I am', and he'll fall over the couch, like this.

She mimes him falling face first over the couch arm, legs up in the air.

And that's when I'll tie his legs with this tinsel and he'll stand up and I'll push him into the tree where he'll get all tangled up and he'll be trapped! What do you think?

Paws.

Thank you, Teddy. I think you're a genius too. All we have to do now is go to sleep. Come on.

She takes Teddy and lies down on the couch.

Right. Just go to sleep and Santa will come.

Pause. She's not sleeping. She gets up to turn off the light. Then goes back to the couch.

Sleep sleep sleep.

Pause. She sits up.

Oh, this is no good! I can't sleep because I'm excited about Santa coming. But if I don't go to sleep, Santa won't come. Who thought up a stupid rule like that?!

Pause.

I know. Maybe if I make up a song, that'll help us go to sleep.

And she sings a monotonous lullaby of her own invention:

Song: Holly's Lullaby

Outside the snow is falling
Inside what's falling is me
Into a sea of dreaming
Into the sea that is me
Inside the dream I am falling
Falling down into the sea
Deeper and deeper and sleepier and sleepier
Hoping you're waiting for me
Deeper and deeper . . .
And sleepier and sleepier . . .
Hoping . . .
You're waiting . . .

She falls asleep.

Only the light from the skylight now. Then – a faint sound – could it be? Sleigh bells . . . getting nearer . . . and nearer . . .

Loud now and suddenly – light floods the room from the skylight!

Santa (*O/S*)   Whoah there! Whoah!

The noise reaches a pitch and then something clumps against the roof. The light blinks out. **Holly** *stirs but doesn't wake.*

Footsteps across the roof. Then voices from above:

Bumblehole (*O/S*)   Aren't we going down the chimney?

Santa (*O/S*)   It looks like the chimney's been blocked. You'll have to go through the skylight.

Bumblehole (*O/S*)   Who, me?

Santa (*O/S*)   Of course you! You haven't done a hand's turn all night. Now get over there!

Footsteps on the roof.

Torchlight through the skylight now, probing the room.

Bumblehole (*O/S*)   It's a long way down!

Santa (*O/S*)   Get on with it!

The skylight is opened.

Bumblehole (*O/S*)   All right – it's open.

Santa (*O/S*)   Line's secure. Go.

Bumblehole (*O/S*)   What, now?

Santa (*O/S*)   Yes, now.

Bumblehole (*O/S*)   Go now?

Santa (*O/S*)   Yes, go!

And suddenly, **Bumblehole** *descends quickly on a line into the living room. Just as he's reaching the floor –*

Santa (*O/S*)   Stop!

Bumblehole *jerks to a stop and hangs suspended, just above the floor.*

Bumblehole   Oooh, my sleigh bells!

Santa *surveys the ground with his torch.*

Bumblehole   Why did you stop me?

Santa (*O/S*)   Crisps.

Bumblehole   Crisps?!

Santa (*O/S*)   Yes, crisps. On the carpet.

Bumblehole   Oh yes . . . someone's a messy eater.

Santa (*O/S*)   It's a trap, you moron!

Bumblehole   A trap?

Santa (*O/S*)   What happens when you step on a crisp?

Bumblehole   Umm . . . you get . . . crispy foot disease?

Santa (*O/S*)   They crunch! The child hears them crunch. It wakes up.

Bumblehole   Oh . . . and that's bad . . .

Santa (*O/S*)   Of course it is, you bell-jingler! If the child wakes up, it'll see me. And I can't be seen by a child, not ever.

Bumblehole *unclips himself and avoids standing on the crisps.*

Bumblehole   All right, Dad, it's fine – I'm not standing on the crisps. I'll unblock the chimney.

He goes to the fireplace.

That's funny. This is a sleeping bag. Why would anyone block a chimney with a sleeping bag?

He shouts up the chimney.

All clear now, Dad. You can come down.

Dust and stones fall. **Santa** *crawls out of the chimney.*

Bumblehole   Dad?

Santa   What?

Bumblehole   I'm hungry!

Santa   What, again? You ate just after Australia!

Bumblehole   I know but I threw it up over Wales.

Santa   Well, you'll just have to wait. We're behind schedule as it is, thanks to you.

He pulls a sack of presents out of the chimney.

Bumblehole   Dad?

Santa   What is it now?

Bumblehole   Why is it bad if we get seen by a child?

Santa   It's not bad if *you* get seen. Well – apart from the fact that you're an ugly geek! But they can't ever see me. If a child sees me, that's it – I'm trapped.

Bumblehole   Trapped?

Santa   Frozen. Can't move a muscle. Not until they fall back to sleep.

Bumblehole   You've never told me that!

Santa   It's not the sort of thing you spread around. I mean, look at this – the whole room's one big trap. The crisps, the bucket – oh yes, the glue – that's a classic. Who is this little monster?

Bumblehole *takes out a notebook.*

Bumblehole   Um – this is Billy Gribbins.

Santa *looks at* **Holly**.

Santa   What's in the sack?

Bumblehole   Um – a rocket launcher, a screaming sword, a monster truck –

Santa   Is this Billy Gribbins a boy?

Bumblehole   Um –

Santa   Let me see that!

He takes the notebook.

Follow the Thames till Orion's in view, take a left at –

Pause. He looks at **Bumblehole**.

Santa   You stupid boy. This is the wrong house!! Can't you even read a map?! This is a girl called – Holly Finnegan. Billy Gribbins is four bobbing streets away!

Bumblehole   I'm sorry, Dad – it's hard to read that map and hold on to the sledge at the same time.

Santa   I've told you – you won't fall off! You can't!

Bumblehole   I know but it feels like you will. This is my first time out, remember? You've never taught me what to do. How can I learn to be Santa if I'm mucking out the reindeers every day?

Santa   Bumblehole, you may be my son but you're not cut out for this work! It's time you accepted the fact – you'll never wear the beard.

Bumblehole   Don't say that, Dad. I can be the Santa, I know I can. I just need a bit of practice.

Santa *looks at his watch.*

Santa   Oh this is a right baubles-up. Right – I'm going to do Scotland. Is the body armour packed?

Bumblehole   Yes, and I've reinforced the sledge.

Santa   Savages. Now – you get these presents to Billy Gribbins.

Bumblehole   Why can't I come with you?

Santa   Because you're slowing me down, that's why.

Bumblehole   I won't, I promise.

Santa   Just deliver those presents. Do you think you can do that without making a mess of it?

Bumblehole   Yes, totally. Not a problem. You can count on me.

Santa   Here, put this on in case someone sees you –

He takes a traditional Santa suit out of his bag.

Deliver those presents and be on the roof by the end of the day. I'll pick you up. And here –

Carefully, he pulls a single hair from his beard.

– one strand of the magic beard: only to be used in an extreme emergency, do you understand?

Bumblehole   Don't worry, Dad. I got a BH in Magic.

Santa   Those were your initials, not your exam mark!

Bumblehole   Were they?

Santa   BH – for Bumblehole. Your mark was a D – for dunderhead. Rudolph – up!

He ascends back up through the skylight.

Bumblehole   But what about presents for this girl?

Santa   Oh – just give her any old rubbish!

Bumblehole   I won't let you down, Dad! You'll see!

Pause. The sound of sleigh bells – a blast of light – as the sledge takes off into the night. He waves goodbye as it goes.

Leave everything to me!

He stuffs the sleeping bag up his suit and admires himself.

Ho ho ho!

He struts around.

Yes, that's right, I'm Santa! And what would you like for Christmas, little girl? Ho ho ho! Some rubbish? No – something nice. Something a girl would like.

He looks in the bag of presents.

Hmm – Girls don't like guns and trucks. I know – I'll use this strand of Magic Beard to make something more suitable. Now – if I can remember the spells . . . Elevation, that's 'Go up', yes – and Animation that's um – 'Wake up!', that's right – but what's Transformation? Oh come on, Bumblehole – try and remember! Elevation, Animation, Transformation. E.A.T. That spells EAT. Yes, well, I am hungry –

He picks up a crisp.

Oooh – turkey and stuffing flavour. My favourite!

He puts it in his mouth – and the crunch is deafening! **Holly** *sits up immediately!*

Holly   Got you!

She fires off the camera.

Blinded, **Bumblehole** *staggers backwards towards the chair – he falls over it and gets his head stuck in the bucket.*

He gropes his way to the mantelpiece, where his hands get stuck. He pulls one hand free and flails blindly –

Holly *gives him the umbrella, which sticks to his hand.*

He gets his other hand free and takes the bucket off his head – but the bucket gets stuck to his hand. He uses his foot to try and lever the bucket off his hand – it works, but his foot gets stuck in the bucket!

Then the umbrella opens dragging him back! **Holly** *throws chilli powder in his face.*

Bumblehole   Aaagh – it burns, it burns – I need some water!

He runs to the breakfast bar, where he swigs back the glass of . . .

Whisky!

Instantly drunk, he reels to the couch, singing – where he falls over the armrest face-first, his legs in the air.

Holly *wraps tinsel around his ankles and ties it. He stands and hops – she pushes him backwards into the tree, getting himself tangled in the lights – there's an explosion as the lights short-out again.*

Holly   All right, Santa – consider yourself *got*!

Bumblehole   No, no – you've got it wrong – I'm not Santa – !

Holly *uses the power cable to shock* **Bumblehole**.

Bumblehole   Naaaaaagh!

Holly   Don't lie! Don't you know it's naughty to lie?!

Bumblehole   I'm not lying!

Shock.

Naaaaaagh! This is torture! There's laws against this! Let me go right now!

Holly   You're not going anywhere, Santa! Not until you give me what I want!

Bumblehole   But I'm not Santa, look at me – I'm not wearing the beard –

Shock.

Holly   You're wearing the suit!

Bumblehole   Right, yes – but actually Santa doesn't wear this kind of –

Shock.

Naaaagh! No, no – listen – I'm not Santa – I'm his son. My name's Bum –

Shock.

Holly   Don't be rude!

Bumblehole   I'm not – that's my name – Bumblehole!

Holly   Bumblehole?!

Bumblehole   Bumblehole, yes.

Holly   You've just made that up.

She's about to shock him again –

Bumblehole   No, please – don't do that again – I'm telling the truth, I promise! I'm not Santa – he just gave me this suit because I've got to deliver some presents. Look – lots of presents, there – wouldn't you like some lovely presents?

Holly   Presents?! I'll show you what I think of presents!

Out of nowhere, she produces a massive sledgehammer.

I-TOLD-YOU-I-DON'T-WANT-ANY-PRESENTS!

She smashes all the toys to pieces.

Pause. **Bumblehole** *starts to cry.*

Holly   What are you crying about? Haven't you read any of my letters?! Every year I write to you and say I don't want any stinky presents!

Bumblehole   But those weren't your presents –

Pause.

Holly   Oh.

Bumblehole   I was supposed to deliver them. And my dad said – don't mess it up and I said I won't – but now I've messed it up and he's going to shout at me and call me names.

Holly *feels ashamed.*

Holly   Right, well – it's a bit pathetic crying cos you're going to get told off. I get told off all the time.

Bumblehole   Look – I don't know what you want –

Holly   I want to meet my Real Dad, that's what I want! If you'd read my letters, you'd know that!

Bumblehole   It's not my job to read the letters!

Holly   Whose job is it?

Bumblehole   Well – it's – the elves.

Holly   Not Santa?!

Bumblehole   He used to read them. But he's tired and grumpy all the time now and he doesn't like being Santa anymore. That's why he's retiring.

Holly   He's retiring?

Bumblehole Yes. This is his last one.

Holly What – the last Christmas ever?

Bumblehole Don't be stupid!

Holly I'm not being stupid. You're being stupid.

Bumblehole No, you are.

Holly No, you are.

Bumblehole I know you are but what am I?

Holly How am I being stupid? No Christmas, no Santa.

Bumblehole Yes, but there'll be another one.

Holly Another what?

Bumblehole Another Santa. Santa's not a person, you know. Santa's a title. It's a common misconception:

Song: Put the Beard in Me

> There are many people think
> That Santa's just one man
> But there have been close to a hundred through the years
> And now the time is coming
> For a new one to be named
> And for someone else to wear the Magic Beard . . .

Holly The Magic Beard?

Bumblehole Yes. The beard of the Santa. The most powerful beard in creation. It's like I sang – there's been lots of Santas but none of them were special in themselves. Not until they put on the Magic Beard. It's the Magic Beard that makes you Santa.

Holly What's magic about it?

Bumblehole Well – each hair can be crushed down to make a dust, and that dust can do all kinds of things – it can alter time, it can make things fly or come alive; all the things a Santa has to do. And when one Santa retires, he passes it on to the next.

Now I've always presumed
That when my dad had had enough
of being Santa, then the beard would come to me
But he thinks that I would muck it up
That somehow I would fudge it
I simply don't know how to make him see . . . that if he –

Puts the beard on me
I'd try my best to be
The greatest Santa that there's ever been!
I'd read every single letter
I'd knit everyone a sweater
I'd take the time to learn the name of every single elf. So –
Put your beard on me
I'll make history
And everyone will congregate to scream

Bumblehole! Ho-ho-ho, ho-hole!
The greatest Santa that there's ever been!
Bumblehole! Ho-ho-ho, three cheers for Bumblehole!
The greatest Santa that there's ever been – Bumblehole!
Ho-ho-ho-hole . . .

(*Spoken.*) The greatest Santa that there'll never . . . be.

Pause.

Holly   Well, I think you're being a bit defeatist. Has anybody actually said you won't be the next Santa?

Bumblehole   Yes, my dad, tonight. 'You'll never wear the beard,' he said.

Holly   Yeah but my mum says things like, 'Right, that's it, no TV for you' and stuff, but then she lets me watch it anyway. That's just stuff people say when they're annoyed.

Bumblehole   My dad's always annoyed with me. He says I'm a moron and that I look like a bogey.

Holly   Then you'll just have to prove him wrong.

Bumblehole   How though?

Holly   By doing the kind of thing that a good Santa should do. Like finding my Real Dad, for example. I don't know what he looks like but his name's Terry. I don't know his second name and my mum can't remember it.

Bumblehole   Oh no, no. We don't do that. We don't interfere with adult things. It's not allowed.

All we do is deliver toys.

Holly   Yes but you go to all the houses in the world – you must know where everyone is.

Bumblehole   No, just children. As soon as they become adults, they're taken off the list.

Holly   Well – but – you can travel all round the world, really fast – couldn't you find him for me?

Bumblehole   I'm sorry. I can't.

She sits down, upset.

Can you let me go now? I need to get back to the roof. My dad's picking me up.

Pause. Huffily, she cuts him loose.

Thank you.

Pause. He feels guilty now.

I like your Teddy, by the way.

She shrugs.

Did we give him to you?

Holly   No. My dad left him for me.

Bumblehole   Well – I better go and deliver these presents.

Holly   They're all broken.

Bumblehole   Oh no – that's right. You smashed them all up. But maybe I can fix them . . .

He takes something from the bag, holds it delicately.

Holly   How?

Bumblehole   You see this? This is a strand of the Magic Beard. If I rub it between my hands like this – it turns into a magic dust and you can use it for spells.

He begins to rub the hair vigorously in his hands as if trying to start a fire with twigs.

Holly   Wait a minute – you've got a bit of the Magic Beard?

Bumblehole   Yes.

Holly   Then you could use it to find my dad!

Bumblehole   I told you –

Holly   I know, you're not allowed. That doesn't mean you can't!

Bumblehole   No but I told you – it only does things a Santa needs to do. Santa doesn't have to find dads.

Holly   But just try – please?

Bumblehole   I can't. Little Billy Gribbins needs a Christmas too.

Holly   Billy Gribbins?!

Bumblehole   Do you know him?

Holly   He flooded the toilets! I've been good every year and I don't even have a dad!

She advances on him.

Bumblehole   No, now – keep away from me!

Holly   Give me that magic dust!

Bumblehole   No! Get back!

Holly   Give it to me!

She drops **Teddy** *and chases* **Bumblehole** *round the room.*

Bumblehole   Help! Dad!

Holly   Give it to me!

They struggle – he trying to keep the precious dust in his palm – but then – the dust flies everywhere! They watch as it disperses through the room.

Bumblehole   Oh no! Now you've done it!

Holly   Done what?

Bumblehole   I don't know. It depends what the last spell was.

Holly   What do you mean?

Bumblehole   You have to reset the spell otherwise it does whatever it did the last time someone used it!

Holly   Who was the last person to use it?

Bumblehole   My dad, probably!

Pause.

Have you got a watch?

Holly   Yes?

Bumblehole   Let me see!

She gives it to him. He stares at it – checks it against the night sky.

Right, well – it's not a time spell.

Holly   Why does Santa need a time spell?

Bumblehole   So he can deliver all the presents in one night. Is anything flying?

Holly   What?

Bumblehole   Can you see anything flying?

Holly   No.

Bumblehole   It's not a flying spell then. Maybe it was a repairing spell after all!

Holly   Ssshh!

Bumblehole   What?

Holly   Do you hear that?

Pause. The faint sound of an engine.

They turn to look at the bag of presents. It's moving slowly across the floor.

Holly   It's moving . . .

Bumblehole   Oh no . . .

He approaches the bag.

Holly   What is it?

Bumblehole   Animation!

He opens the bag and there's the noise of trucks revving and guns firing. He picks up the bag and struggles with it.

Help me!

She helps him – they struggle with it.

Holly   What's happening?!

Bumblehole   The toys have come to life!

Holly   What?!

Bumblehole   It's all right – the magic only lasts one day!

Holly   But they're making such a noise! It'll wake everyone up!

Bumblehole   So what do we do?

Holly   When something gets broken, you hide it! Don't you know anything?

Bumblehole   Hide it where?

Holly   Outside or something – into the garden!

She wraps the sleeping bag around them to muffle the noise. They carry the toys out of the living room. Silence for a while. Then something happens –

Teddy's *legs move . . . then his arms . . . then he stands up and runs across the room! Hearing the others, he drops to the floor again.* **Holly** *and* **Bumblehole** *enter.*

Holly   That was unreal! The sword-thing was trying to stab me! What does Santa need a spell like that for?

Bumblehole   Because he's got to get, like, a bazillion toys onto sledges. Do you know how long that would take, even with all the elves?

Holly   So they get on the sledges themselves?

Bumblehole   The cars drive on, soldiers walk on – the toy planes fly alongside.

Holly   Wow! That's amazing!

Bumblehole   Don't look so happy. I was meant to deliver those toys. Maybe my dad's right – I'm not cut out for this work.

Holly   Hey, where's Teddy?

Bumblehole   He's there.

Holly   But . . .

Bumblehole   But what?

Holly's *sure he's moved from where he was. Pause.*

Holly   Nothing.

Bumblehole   Listen – have you got anything to eat? I'm really hungry.

Holly   Sure, there's some cakes – there's biscuits –

Bumblehole   Anything else?

Holly   There's some meat on the tree, if you want that.

Bumblehole   Yes, I noticed that.

They go to the kitchen hatch.

Teddy *sits up, looks around.*

Bumblehole   Who puts meat on a tree?

Holly   My stepdad, Bernard.

Teddy *waves his arms then walks back where he came from.*

Holly   He's a dog.

Bumblehole   Ah, well – that explains it.

Holly   That explains it?

Bumblehole   Well, they can't eat chocolate. Apart from that dog stuff; and that tastes of bacon anyway.

Holly   Why does nobody think it's –

Back now, she realises:

Wait a minute – Teddy was there a minute ago, wasn't he?

Bumblehole   I don't think so.

Holly   He was, I'm sure he was!

Bumblehole   Have you got anything to drink?

She sighs.

Not alcohol! Just milk or something.

Holly   Yeah, we've got some milk. Or orange juice, if you want.

She goes to the fridge.

Teddy *lifts his bum up and farts really loudly.*

Holly   Oh, that's disgusting!

Bumblehole   What?

Holly   You know what.

Bumblehole   That wasn't me!

Holly   Well, it wasn't me.

Bumblehole   He who smelt it, dealt it.

Holly   Who said the rhyme committed the crime.

Another fart.

Oh my God!

Bumblehole   That wasn't me!

Teddy   Sorry.

Bumblehole   Well – apology accepted.

Holly   What?

Bumblehole   I accept your apology. Which means it must have been you.

Holly   I didn't apologise for anything.

Teddy   No, I did.

Pause. They turn, slowly, to look at **Teddy**.

It's been building up for a long time. Sorry.

Pause.

Bumblehole   Oh no! My dad is going to kill me!

Holly   You can talk!

Bumblehole   That's not all he can do . . .

He wafts away the fart smell. **Teddy** *stands.*

Holly   Oh my God – you can stand!

Teddy *seems to have a Russian accent.*

Teddy   Yes! It's a miracle, Holly! I have life! I am alive!

Bumblehole   Not for long!

He tears the wrapping paper off a present and uses the box to cover **Teddy**.

Holly   No, what are you doing?!

Bumblehole   We have to throw him out with all the other toys!

Holly   No but he's my teddy!

Bumblehole   Holly, believe me – I've worked with toys all my life –

Holly   I don't care – get off of him!

Teddy   Let me out of this box! Let me out!

She pushes **Bumblehole** *away and takes* **Teddy** *out of the box.*

Holly   Are you all right?

Teddy   Yes – I am ok – I am alive, Holly! Look at me! I'm alive!

Bumblehole   Yes, well don't get used to it, toy.

Holly   That's a horrid thing to say.

Bumblehole   It's true. Beard spells only last for one day.

Teddy   One day? I will only be alive for one day?

Holly *picks him up.*

Bumblehole   That's what my dad says. It's a fail-safe – you can't have animated toys running around. They've got no principles.

Teddy   Be quiet! I will show you who has principles, elf!

Bumblehole   I'm not an elf!

Teddy   You look like elf. I think maybe Santa's been mixing with the workers, no?

Holly Oh, it's so weird. I can feel you breathing! Where's that accent from?

Teddy I'm from Russia.

Holly A Russian bear! Oh that's so cute! I'm going to make a little Russian hat for you.

Do you like it when I dress you up?

Teddy Eh . . .

Pause.

Holly You don't like it?

Teddy I do like it! I love it.

Holly And dancing too.

Teddy Yes, I like to dance . . .

Holly Justin Bieber's your favourite, isn't he?

Pause.

Teddy Yes. He is great. But Holly – I must tell you something else, that is very important.

Holly Ok –

Teddy Let us sit down first.

She sits down with him on her lap.

Holly What do you want to tell me?

Teddy Well, you see – I am not a bear.

Holly You look like a bear . . .

Teddy Yes, but I am not. I am – your father.

Pause. She punches him on the nose.

Oww!

Holly Oh – did you feel that?

Teddy   Yes! What is that feeling? I don't like it!

Holly   That's pain. I'm sorry. Usually you don't feel things. But you shouldn't make jokes like that.

Teddy   Like what?

Holly   Like saying you're my dad.

Bumblehole   I told you – no principles, toys.

Teddy   You be quiet, stinkweed! It is the truth! I am your father, Holly – not this bear that you see, but inside. Let me tell you the story –

Pause.

It was many years ago – at Christmas –

The hatch slides back to reveal a shadow-puppet enactment of the following:

The winter was hard as any I've known. This bear you see here now, I had worked my fingers to the bone to buy him, as a present for you, my daughter. I made my way to you across Eastern Europe. It was a time of great danger. Dark things occurred in the hearts of men and all manner of black magical creatures walked the ragged roads.

Bumblehole   Black magical creatures?

Teddy   Yes.

Bumblehole   Like what?

Teddy   Like – werewolves.

Werewolves appear, howling.

Bumblehole   Baubles! There's no such thing as werewolves.

Teddy   Well – vampire bats then!

Vampire bats appear, squeaking.

Bumblehole   In South America, maybe. Not Eastern Europe.

Teddy   Not bats then, em . . . penguins!

Penguins appear, squawking.

Bumblehole   Penguins?!

Teddy   Yes – forest penguins – it doesn't matter! Let me tell the story.

I stopped for a night with a troupe of travellers. I was hungry and, like a fool, I agreed to a game of chance with a gypsy fortune teller, a crone with one staring eye. She beat me in every game and I accused her of cheating. She did not take kindly to this and she cast a dreadful spell: she imprisoned me here, inside this toy, with no power to speak or to move. She wrote the note that you keep with you, and she laughed as she pinned it to my chest.

As the final humiliation, she had me delivered to your door, as I had intended. I have lived these many years, always hearing your sorrow, your loss but unable to comfort you – to tell you that the father for which you search has been with you all this time. And I had resigned myself to live inside this fluffy tomb for the rest of eternity. Until today. Until this . . . miraculous day. And now – I am free.

The hatch slides shut. **Holly** *is strangely silent.*

Teddy   You are very quiet, Holly? Are you not glad to see me?

Holly   Yes, I am, I'm just –

Pause. Her face lights up.

I'm so surprised that you're Russian! I mean, that's brilliant, isn't it?! That means I'm half-Russian!

Teddy   Yes. And you look like many Russian girls.

Bumblehole   Holly –

Holly   That's so amazing! I mean, I imagined so many different things – that you were a pilot, or a millionaire, or a secret agent or something. But I never thought you'd be Russian!

Bumblehole   Holly – listen to me –

She suddenly hugs **Bumblehole***!*

Holly   And you! You did it, Bumblehole! You found my dad! You're not an idiot at all! You totally should be the next Santa and you're right – you would be the greatest Santa there's ever been ever!

Bumblehole   Well, that's nice but Holly – you can't trust a toy, believe me. I mean, they're fine to play with but they're basically liars and cheats.

Teddy   I am not a toy! I am a human being!

From upstairs:

Mum (*O/S*)   Holly!

Holly   Oh no – sshh – that's my mum!

Mum (*O/S*)   Holly, is that you making that noise?!

Teddy   You see what you have done, elf?

Bumblehole   I'm not an elf !

Mum (*O/S*)   What was that?!

Holly   It's nothing, Mum!

Mum (*O/S*)   Have you got somebody down there?

Holly   No, Mum!

Pause.

Wait a minute, I'll come up!

Listen – both of you – stop it! I don't want my mum finding you here. So be quiet, all right?

Bumblehole   I'm being quiet. It's him –

Holly   I don't care who's being quiet. I mean – as long as it's both of you. I'll be back in a minute.

She goes.

Bumblehole   You are such a liar! You're not Holly's dad!

Teddy   What do you know about it?

Bumblehole   Gypsy spells – Gypsies can't even do imprisonment spells! Why are you pretending to be Holly's dad?

Teddy   I'm not.

Bumblehole   You're not Holly's dad?

Teddy   Yes –

Bumblehole   I'm right?

Teddy   No –

Bumblehole   You're not Holly's dad?

Teddy   No –

Bumblehole   So you're not.

Teddy   I am!

Bumblehole   You're not.

Teddy   I am!

Bumblehole   You are.

Teddy   What?

Bumblehole   You so are!

Teddy   No, I – I'm not.

Bumblehole   You are!

Teddy   I'm not, I'm not!

Bumblehole   Ah – so you're not! You said it.

Teddy   Curse you and your word games! All right! I admit – I am not Holly's father!

Bumblehole   But that's the most terrible, most awfullest lie ever! Why would you tell such a horrible lie?

Teddy   Why? I'll tell you why!

Song: I Want to Live

> I want to live
> I want to go and see the real bears at the zoo
> I want to press the buttons on the telephone
> I want to put my paws into a pot of paint
> I want to be alone sometimes
> I want to choose
> When I dance and who I'm dancing to
> And what colour dress I wear when entertaining
> And run about outside the moment it starts raining
> And go on the wobbly bridge

Pause.

Bumblehole   Is that it?

Teddy   No! That is just what I can think of right now. The main thing is –

> I want to live –

Bumblehole   Yes, yes – I get it. You want to live. But why do you have to pretend to be Holly's dad?

Teddy   All right – as you will soon be unconscious, I will tell you: I am going to steal the Magic Beard of the Santa! And when I have crushed it down, I will have enough magic dust to live for all eternity!

Bumblehole   My dad'll never let you take the beard.

Teddy   Ah but you forget – I have the one thing he is afraid of. A child that is awake. When Holly sees him, he will be trapped here – frozen – and at our mercy!

Bumblehole   You can't do that! The Magic Beard is what gives Santa his powers! Without a Santa – Christmas will cease to exist! Holly will never help you do that!

Teddy   She would not help a teddy bear no. But she will do what her father tells her!

Bumblehole   You fiend! I'm going to tell her the truth!

Teddy   No you will not – you idiot! You long, green bogey!

Bumblehole   Don't call me that!

Teddy   The Santa is right! You are only good to clean up the dung from the reindeers!

Look at you – look at your stupid little beard!

Bumblehole   Be quiet!

Teddy   Your feet are like boats but your head is small, like a pea! Because your brain is so tiny!

Bumblehole   I'm warning you – !

Teddy   What are you warning me of, Tinkerbell? Soon Christmas will be gone and you will be on the scrapheap with your stupid elves and your reindeers and your rotten dad!

Bumblehole   Don't call my dad rotten!

And he grabs **Teddy***'s nose. They struggle.* **Holly** *enters.*

Teddy   Holly – help me – help – !

Holly   Bumblehole! What are you doing?!

Teddy   Help – !

Holly   Leave him alone!

Bumblehole   He's evil, Holly – !

Holly   Leave my dad alone!

She hits **Bumblehole** *on the head with a frying pan – clang! He reels then turns to her:*

Bumblehole   Ooh, what was that?

Holly   A frying pan. Sorry.

Bumblehole   No, it's fine.

Pause. He collapses.

Teddy *is gasping.*

Teddy   Thank you, Holly – I thought he was going to kill me!

Holly   Why was he doing that?

Teddy   I don't know. He just went completely mad!

Holly   But why though? It doesn't make sense.

Teddy   This is how it is with elves – they are all crazy madmen!

Pause.

Holly   I won't let anyone hurt you, not ever. You're my dad.

She hugs him. A moment.

Teddy   Holly –

Holly   Yes?

Teddy   It is good that we are together again. But for now we must act.

Holly   Yes, of course. We have to find this – witchy-gypsy woman and get her to make you human again!

Teddy   No, Holly. I'm afraid that is impossible. A gypsy spell can never be reversed.

Holly   Never?!

Teddy   Do not be sad. We are together at last, a father and daughter, as it should be. Is that not the most important thing?

Holly   Yes, but –

Teddy   That is my girl! But we have one final problem to solve: The magic that has brought me to life lasts only for a day. If we do not find some way of keeping me alive, when midnight comes – I will be lost again – to the darkness; to the silence.

Holly   No. Because I know what we can do! I know how to save you!

Teddy   But – how?

Holly   The Magic Beard!

Teddy   Magic Beard? I have never heard of such a thing!

Holly   It was a strand of Santa's Magic Beard that brought you to life. So if one strand keeps you alive for one day – we just need lots more strands.

Teddy   Yes! Yes, that is right! We need more strands of the Magic Beard! But how will we get them?

Holly   Well, Santa's got to come back to get Bumblehole so – I suppose we'll just ask him for some.

Teddy   You think he will just – give them to us?

Holly   Of course he will, I mean –

The door opens and **Mum** *enters.*

Mum   Holly – what is all the – !

Surprised, **Teddy** *turns to see* **Mum**. **Mum** *sees* **Teddy**. *Simultaneously, they scream!*

Holly   It's all right, Mum – don't be scared!

Mum   It's moving! The bear is moving!

Holly   I know but let me explain –

Teddy   Holly – no –

Mum   It's talking! The bear is talking!

Holly   I know but he's not a bear, he's –

Teddy   Russian! She means to say that – I am Russian.

Mum   It's Russian! The bear is Russian!

She goes to the door.

Bernard – !

Holly   No but tell her – tell her who you are –

Teddy   Holly, no – she would not understand. It must be our secret.

Holly   But –

Teddy   Holly's mum, please – do not be alarmed. I am just a toy. Isn't that right, Holly?

Holly   Um – yes – that's right. He's just a toy.

Mum   But you've had him for years; and now – he can move, and talk, like he's alive!

Holly   Yes but it's just – computers.

Mum   Computers?

Holly   Yeah – Santa put, like – a microchip in him or something. And now he's a – sort of – robot. Santa brought him for me.

Mum   Oh – a robot, is he?

She touches **Teddy**.

Teddy   That tickles!

Mum   Well, I never. It's amazing what they can do these days.

Bernard *jumps into the room, kung-fu style.*

Bernard   What's going on! What's happening?! Is everybody all right?!

Mum   Everything's fine, Bernard. Look what Santa did with Holly's teddy.

Teddy *looks at* **Bernard**.

Teddy   Hello. Happy Christmas.

Bernard *yelps with fright and hides behind the chair.*

Bernard   It's come alive!

Mum   No, no, that's what I thought – but he's a robot. What else can he do?

Holly   Well, he can – dance. You can dance, can't you, Teddy?

Teddy   Uh – yes, yes – of course, uh –

He does a dance.

Mum   Isn't that clever?!

Bernard   I don't like it. It's creepy.

Holly   What do you know? You think the vacuum cleaner's creepy.

Bernard   It is! But not as creepy as this.

Mum   Talking of vacuum cleaners – why are there crisps all over the floor?!

Holly   Oh – sorry, I – dropped them.

Mum   Well, you can just pick them all up again. I spent all day tidying this room for Christmas, thank you very –

Suddenly, **Bumblehole** *stands up, groaning.* **Mum** *and* **Bernard** *shriek.*

Bumblehole   Oooh, my head!

Bernard   Good grief!

Mum   Who are you?!

Bumblehole   Um – I don't know . . . I don't remember . . .

Mum   Holly – who is this?

Holly   That's – Billy Gribbins!

Mum   Billy Gribbins?!

Bumblehole   Yes – I remember that name . . .

Mum   And who is Billy Gribbins?

Holly   He's a boy from school.

Mum   More to the point – what is he doing here at this time in the morning?! –

Holly   He's – an orphan.

Mum   What?

Holly   He's an orphan. His parents – were killed.

Bumblehole   No?! Were they?!

Holly   In a hurricane.

Bumblehole   In a hurricane?! Oh no – and I don't even remember them!

Pause.

Mum   Well, that's – terrible. But doesn't he have foster parents or something?

Holly   Yes –

Bumblehole*'s face lights up.*

Holly   But they died too. They fell off a boat.

Bumblehole *drops to his knees and shouts at the gods.*

Bumblehole   Nooooooooo!!

Holly   Now he just lives in a shed by the railway track and eats gravel.

Bernard   Oh well, he must stay.

Mum   Bernard –

Bernard   Come on, poopy. We can't throw a double orphan out on the street; not today, anyway. Let him stay for Christmas dinner.

Bumblehole   Christmas? That rings a bell. And 'bell' – that also rings a bell. Something to do with bells and Christmas. Oooh –

He starts to eat the crisps.

Bernard   Look, he's starving!

Mum   Goodness me – Holly – clean those up.

Holly   Yes, Mum.

Mum   I'm going back to bed.

Teddy   Goodnight, Holly's mum.

They leave.

Look at that cretinous elf! Eating crisps like a rat!

Holly   He must have lost his memory when I hit him with the frying pan!

Bumblehole   Oooh – a talking teddy!!

He tickles the bear.

Wooby wooby wooby!

Teddy   Get your hands off me!

Holly *steers* **Bumblehole** *out of the room.*

Holly   So what do we do now?

Teddy   Now we must wait for Santa to return.

Focus down on him:

And when he does, the Magic Beard will be mine!

He laughs maniacally. Behind him, the chorus appear, dressed as devils:

Song: Evil Bear

Ursus cave!
Santa adepto!
Patris cognoscere!
Aaaaah –
Santa!

End of Act One.

Act Two

Holly, **Mum**, **Gran** *and* **Bernard** *enter – they hand out presents;*
a choreographed representation of Christmas Day.

Song: Christmas Variation

Christmas Christmas Christmas
Christmas Christmas Christmas

Thank you that's exactly (yes exactly) what I wanted
Underpants and socks are always nice
Underpants and socks underpants and socks underpants
I really needed one of those
I think I needed one of these
Bubble-bath!

Is anybody hungry?
Now it's time to eat

Nibbles
Eat
Nibbles
Eat
Nibbles

I don't want to spoil my appetite
But I think I'll have one more mince pie

Time for dinner!

Bernard   Meat!

A chorus member enters, dressed as a turkey.

It's tender it's tender! This meat is tender!
It's lovely but it's far too much.
Another slice!
Another slice,
another slice another slice another
Full!

The turkey is stuffed.

Now it's time to watch TV

Isn't this exactly what they showed this time last year?
I don't know why we pay the licence fee

A slice of cake
A slice of cake
Another slice of cake
(I couldn't I shouldn't)
Another slice of Christmas cake!

Holly   Christmas is amazing!

That's what Holly Finnegan thinks! And I should know
because I'm Holly Finnegan! And this is my dad! And he
thinks Christmas is amazing too!

You might notice something about my dad. He's a teddy
bear. You might think that's funny or weird or something
but that just means that you're shallow. Because it's what's
on the inside of someone that counts.

So all we have to do now is get Santa –

Bernard   Get Santa?

Holly   Oh please, that is *so* first half! All we have to do is get
Santa to give us some of his Magic Beard so he can stay alive
for years and years. Santa's definitely coming back because
we've got his son here, Bumblehole. Well – except that he's
got amnesia and now he thinks he's Billy Gribbins, and
everyone else thinks he's Billy Gribbins too; which is quite
funny if you know Billy Gribbins, cos they're really nothing
alike – Billy Gribbins and him. What was I saying?

Oh yeah – so it was a brilliant day and the adults all gave
each other presents cos they don't get any from Santa so
they actually have to buy them – how rubbish is that? – and
then we had absolutely mountains of stuff to eat and we
watched some telly and now I feel a bit sick but in a good
way and – yeah –

It's been a brilliant day. And it's not over yet.

Teddy *is holding court, sitting in* **Bernard**'s *chair* – **Gran**, **Mum** *and* **Holly** *are delighted;* **Bernard** *not so much.*

Teddy   And so he says 'Why the long face?'!

Hysterical laughter.

Mum   Oh that is the funniest thing!

Gran   'Why the long-face?!'

Teddy   Yes! Because he is a horse! And he *always* has long face!

Mum   Bernard – is that not the funniest thing? This bear is hilarious!

Bernard   I don't see what's so funny about having a long face.

Gran   He's jealous, I think.

Mum   That's right, someone else is getting the attention.

Bernard   It's not that.

Gran   He's just a teddy bear, you know.

Teddy   That's right! I am just a little teddy bear.

Bernard   Hmm.

Gran   Though I must say – it's very realistic. I mean, I don't know much about robots but the algorithms involved must be incredibly complex.

Holly   Does anybody want another glass of whisky?

Gran   Are you trying to get us drunk?

Mum   I know. Anybody would think she was trying to get us to our beds.

Holly   No, I'm not. Why would I want you to go to bed? I'm just happy because I really love my Teddy.

Teddy   Thank you, Holly. I love you too.

Mum   Aww . . . he really is the sweetest thing, is he not?

Bumblehole *comes bouncing in.*

Bumblehole   I've got an idea – let's play that game again!

Mum   Does he never calm down?

Holly   I think it's all the sugar he's eaten.

Bumblehole   Come on – look –

He mimes fifteen words.

Gran   Fifteen words?!

Bumblehole   Yes and it's –

He mimes film and then book and then song, etc.

Mum   A film – a book – a song?

Teddy   It cannot be all of those things!

Bumblehole   Not yet, but it will be! The main character is a poor orphan called Billy – !

Gran   Yes but it has to be something that already exists, dear.

Bumblehole *crumbles.*

Bumblehole   Don't shout at me – please! I can't stand it when you shout at me!

Gran   I'm not, I'm just –

Bumblehole   Holly – have you got any more of those things?

Holly   What things?

Bumblehole   Those jelly sweet things –

Mum   I think he's had enough . . .

Bumblehole   No! Don't say that! I need more jelly sweets!

Holly   They're all gone.

Bumblehole   You're lying!

Gran   No, dear, you ate them all.

Mum   And all the other sweets too.

Bumblehole   Oh yes – I see it now. You're all against me because I'm an orphan!

Holly   No we're not . . .

Bumblehole   Where are you hiding the jelly sweets? Give them to me! I demand to have more jelly sweets!

Bernard   Now just steady on a second, young man –

Bumblehole *runs out.*

Mum   Oh just leave it, Bernard. He's over-tired that's his problem. I think it's time we all went to our beds.

Gran   Yes, that's Christmas over for another year.

Mum   And it'll be time for Billy to be going as well.

Holly   Don't worry – I'll make sure he leaves.

Mum   Right, well – by midnight. And then straight to bed with you, young lady.

Holly   I will, I promise.

Gran   Night, night, all.

Teddy   Goodnight, Holly's gran, Holly's mum!

Bernard *stares at him.*

Teddy   And goodnight to you – Bernard.

Bernard   No – goodnight to you.

Teddy   No – goodnight to you.

Bernard   No – to you.

Mum   Bernard, stop that.

Bernard   There's something not right about that bear, poopy.

Mum   Oh for goodness' sake. It's just a toy. And it's made Holly happier than I've ever seen her.

Bernard   I know. But there's something not right. I've got a nose for these things.

They leave. He bangs his nose against the door.

Teddy   That stupid dog. We must find a way to get rid of him.

Holly   I still don't know why we can't tell Mum who you are.

Bumblehole *enters.*

Bumblehole   I found one! Look – it was stuck to the doorstep!

He shows her something black and gelatinous.

A jelly sweet of some kind!

He eats it.

Holly   No – !

Bumblehole   Sorry – did you want a bit?

Holly   No, it's just – that wasn't a jelly sweet –

Bumblehole   What was it?

Holly   It was a slug!

Teddy   And you ate it, you fool!

Bumblehole   Eeeeeuuhhh! I'm going to be sick!

Holly   No, no – go to the bathroom – through there!

She ushers him out, laughing slightly.

Teddy   That elf is an imbecile!

Holly   He's quite funny though. Tell you what – let's play a game, just you and me!

Teddy   There will be time for games, Holly. But now we must be ready for Santa's return. Switch off the lights.

Holly   Why?

Teddy   Do as your father says, Holly.

She turns off the main lights.

And now we wait.

Holly   Can I put the telly on then?

Teddy   Yes, if you wish.

She turns on the TV.

Newsman   Well, there's just seven minutes of Christmas Day left and it seems to have been another success for Santa. Let's go over to our correspondent in the Arctic Circle. Hello, Jenny –

Pause – due to the time delay.

Jenny   Yes, hello, Brian. Well, as you can see, I'm standing outside the Magic Workshop and you can hardly tell that only a few hours earlier this was a hub of activity for the truly staggering task of delivering presents to over two billion children around the world. Let's just put that in context – that's approximately 50,000 presents per minute so it really is an impressive achievement.

Newsman   So is there any sign of Santa having returned? He must be looking forward to relaxing.

Pause.

Jenny   There's no sign of Santa yet but, frankly, we don't expect him back until about 1 a.m.

He'll have a few last things to do and then it'll take him a while to get here.

Newsman   But altogether a successful Christmas Day?

Paws.

Jenny   Altogether a successful Christmas, yes, Brian; with not even a massive Third World disaster to spoil the merriment.

He laughs.

Newsman   Well, we shouldn't –

She laughs, interrupting him. Paws. Simultaneously:

Newsman   – speak too soon –

Jenny   Hello, Brian?

Pause. Simultaneously.

Jenny   No we shouldn't.

Brian   I'm still here.

Holly *turns the TV off.*

Holly   At least we know he's still –

Teddy   Sssshhh! Listen –

Pause.

Holly   What?

Pause. A jingling sound.

Teddy   He's coming!

The jingling gets louder and louder – the light now through the roof.

Santa   Woah, there!

The sound of the sledge touching down.

Holly   Oh my God – it's actually Santa!

Teddy   Ssshh. Keep quiet.

Pause. From above:

Santa   Bumblehole?!

Pause.

Bumblehole, where are you, you stupid boy?! You were meant to be on the roof!

Pause.

Oh for goodness' sake!

Teddy   Holly – go to the light switch. When I say 'now' – turn it on!

They wait, staring up at the skylight.

Teddy   Where is he?

Holly   I don't know, I can't see him . . .

Santa *crawls in through the chimney.*

Holly   Maybe he's –

Santa   Bumblehole?

Teddy   Holly, he is there! Now! Now!

Holly *yelps and turns the light on.*

Holly   Santa!

Santa   Oh no!

He freezes in position.

Holly   Santa? What's wrong?!

Teddy   Yes, it has worked! He is trapped!

Holly   What do you mean?

Teddy   Santa cannot be seen by a child. Now he will be frozen like this until you go back to sleep!

Santa   Why is that bear talking?

Teddy   Hah – you are not such a big man now, are you, Santa? Now the boot is on the other paw!

Santa   What do you want with me, toy?

Holly   We just wanted to ask – for your help.

Santa   Hah! You trap me and then you want my help?!
Where's that idiot son of mine, Bumblehole?

Teddy   We have him!

Santa   So it's kidnap too, is it?

Holly   No, he's not kidnapped, he's fine. Well – he's eaten
too many sweets – and he thinks he's someone else, a bit –
but apart from that, he's fine. And you shouldn't be calling
him an idiot all the time.

Santa   Really? So who brought that teddy to life?

Holly   He's not a teddy, he's my dad!

Santa *laughs.*

Santa   Is he now?

Holly   Yes – a gypsy witch trapped him inside the
teddy bear.

Santa   A gypsy witch! That's a good one! I do like a bedtime
story, go on.

Holly   Well – we can't reverse the spell but – I just wanted
to ask if maybe we could have some of your beard so he can
stay alive and sort of be my dad.

Santa   You want 'some' of my beard?

Holly   Yeah.

Santa   How much exactly?

Holly   Well – if one strand equals one day – then we need –
a lot, maybe, like – a thousand or so –

Santa   A thousand.

Holly   I know it's a lot but I'd really appreciate it and I'm
sure you can grow them all back.

Santa   Well – let me think about it. All right, I've thought about it – NO!

Holly   No?

Santa   No!

Holly   Why not?

Santa   Because you're a selfish little girl! There's hundreds of children without dads. What makes you so special?

Holly   Nothing but –

Santa   Nothing, that's right.

Holly   But you're Santa! You're supposed to give me what I want. That's what Santa does!

Santa   Well that just shows that you're stupid as well as selfish.

Holly   How does it show that?

Santa   Because there are things children want and things children think they want. A good Santa knows the difference.

Holly   That doesn't make any sense.

Teddy   Holly – he will not give us the beard of his own free will. And time is running out – it is nearly midnight.

Holly   But what am I supposed to do?

Teddy   If he will not share his magic, he does not deserve to wear the beard! We must take it!

Holly   Take it?

Teddy   Take the beard, my daughter, and bring it to me.

Pause. She approaches **Santa**, *reaches out to the beard . . .*

Santa   Don't do it, Holly. Without the Magic Beard, no one can be Santa. There'll never be another Christmas, ever.

Holly   No Christmas ever again?

Teddy   Please, Holly – if you do not take the beard, I will die.

Holly   We can just take a bit of it –

Teddy   No, Holly – we will need it all.

Holly   All of it?

Teddy   If we want to spend our lives together, yes.

She goes back to **Santa**.

Santa   You see? It's what I said – selfish.

Holly   Stop saying that!

Teddy   Please, Holly – we are running out of time!

Pause.

Holly   I'm sorry, Santa. But I can't lose my dad again – I can't.

She takes the beard from **Santa**.

Teddy   That's it! You are a good girl, Holly! Now bring it to me!

She does.

Put it on me, that's it. Put the beard on me!

She attaches the beard to **Teddy**.

Yes! Now I control the beard! Me – a mere teddy bear – now in possession of the most powerful beard in creation! And now I will live for ever!

Santa – *now able to move – laughs.*

Holly   What's so funny?

Santa   You're even more of an idiot than Bumblehole.

Holly   Why?

Santa   What did he tell you? That the magic only lasts for one day?

Holly   Is that wrong?

Santa   No, it's right. The magic only lasts for one day. But that one day is Christmas Day. It doesn't matter how many strands you use – one, a hundred, a thousand! The magic ends at midnight tonight; which is about – one minute from now.

Teddy   I don't believe you! You are lying!

Santa   Really. Then try and move your arm.

Teddy *cannot.*

Teddy   Aaagh – oh no! I cannot move it!

Santa   The magic is fading. Soon you'll be just a toy again.

Teddy   No! But I have only just tasted life! Holly – you must help me!

Holly   But what can I do?!

Teddy *stands.*

Teddy   Take some hair from the beard!

Holly   But it won't work!

Teddy   We must try!

She pulls out some strands.

Now make the dust!

Holly   I'm trying!

She rubs it in her hands. **Teddy** *falls over.*

Teddy   My leg! My leg has gone numb! Holly, hurry –

Holly   I'm doing it!

She manages it.

All right, I've got some dust ! But how do you do the spell?!

Teddy   I don't know! There must be a magic word – Live!

She throws some dust over him.

Holly   Live!

Santa   Tick-tock, tick-tock.

Holly   It's not working!

Teddy   Another one –

Holly   Um – live – life!!

She throws dust. Then more.

Alive! Stay alive!! It's not working!

Teddy   I can't move my arms!

Holly   I need more dust!

She pulls some more beard out.

Bumblehole *bursts in.*

Bumblehole   Hey – all that vomiting's helped me remember – I'm not Billy Gribbins – I'm – Dad?!

Teddy   Holly, quickly!

Bumblehole   Where's the beard?!

Holly   I've got some!

Bumblehole   Some what? Holly – why is the beard wearing the bear?!

Holly   I'm trying to save him!

Bumblehole   No, Holly – you can't!

He tries to grab the beard.

Holly   Leave him alone!

Bumblehole   Give me the beard!

Teddy   Help me, Holly!

Santa   Any second now.

Bumblehole   You don't understand – He's lying – !

Holly   Tell me how to save him!!

Santa   Five –

Bumblehole   You can't – !

Santa   Four –

Teddy   Holly!

Santa   Three –

Holly   I'm telling you –

Santa   Two –

Holly   Back off –

Bumblehole   No – !

Santa   One –

Holly   Get BACK!

And the dust flies in the air and everything explodes in colour and sound and smoke. Finally, it clears. They are alone.

What happened? Where did everyone go?

Teddy   I don't know . . .

Again, the family enters, throwing wrapping paper around and popping poppers:

Song: Christmas (Short Reprise)

>   Christmas Christmas Christmas
>   Christmas Christmas Christmas

Gran *hugs* **Holly**.

Gran   Happy Christmas, Chicken Slippers!

Holly   Happy Christmas?

Gran   Oh come on, Holly, cheer up.

Bernard *enters.*

Bernard   Happy Christmas, everybody!

Gran   Happy Christmas, Bernard!

Holly   What are you talking about? It's not Christmas – we just had Christmas!

Gran   Wait until you get to my age. The years go by like minutes.

Holly   No – I mean we just had Christmas. Look – there's still food left, right there!

Bernard   Oh –

Gran   Oh Holly, what's all this? You've been eating the food?

Bernard   That's not on. That's not on at all.

Gran   What are we going to have for Christmas dinner?

Holly   You ate some as well! We all did!

Bernard   When was this?

Holly   Just a few hours ago, when –

She looks at her watch.

Oh. My. God.

Teddy   What is it ?

Holly   The time! It says nine thirty . . .

She looks up at the skylight.

In the morning!

Teddy   Holly – don't you see? We've gone back in time!

Holly   Yeah, that's right – the Magic Beard can alter time. So now it's Christmas Day again – and that's what he said: the magic only lasts until midnight – so as long as it's Christmas Day –

Teddy   As long as it is Christmas Day, I will stay alive. You have saved me, my dear Holly. You have saved me!

Victory dance. In the manner of an old computer game, all the characters perform repetitive gestures of triumph to a hard mechanical beat. Then stop.

Holly   Yeah, well – I am pretty smart, you know.

Mum *enters.*

Mum   Oh, we're all up, are we? Happy Christmas then.

Holly *hugs her.*

Holly   Happy Christmas, Mum!

Mum   Oh – smiling, is it? I'd forgotten what you look like when you're smiling.

Holly   I know, I'm sorry. I'll smile more. I'll smile all the time!

Mum   Oh that's nice – you put a beard on Teddy. Very Christmassy.

Holly   Yeah . . .

Mum   So is it time for the grown-ups' presents?

Bernard   Oh, right, yes –

Mum *stares at him.*

Mum   Bernard – ?

Bernard   What?

Mum   Why did you do that?

Bernard   Why did I do what?

Mum   Why did you open your present?

Bernard   I didn't.

Mum   You didn't?

Bernard   No.

Mum   So what's that you're wearing? That jumper?

Bernard   Oh um – well, that was just the jumper that was by the bed . . .

Mum   Bernard, don't lie to me –

Bernard   I'm not, poopy, I –

Mum   That's your Christmas present you're wearing. Do you think I don't know the Christmas present I bought you when I see it?

Gran   Yes, well, you can talk, Barbara . . .

Mum   What do you mean?

Gran   That friendship bracelet you're wearing – that's my present for you.

Bernard   But then – what's in these?

They open their presents.

Bernard *holds out a jumper – exactly the same as the one he's wearing.*

Bernard   Oh um – that's great, thank you. I needed one of these.

Mum   No you didn't. You've already got one exactly the same.

Bernard   Well – now I've got two.

He puts it on, on top of the one he's wearing.

See – twice as warm! I'm snug as a bug in a snug snug rug!

Gran *opens her present. It's a pair of fluffy slippers.*

Gran   Oh this is –

Bernard   Oh yes, that's those slippers you wanted.

They look down. She's wearing the same pair.

Oh – you've already got them . . .

Gran   That's funny. I don't remember buying them.

Mum   Now this is just downright odd!

Holly *and* **Teddy***:*

Holly   Uh-oh!

Teddy   Somehow the presents have been duplicated!

Holly   Oh dear. That's bad.

Teddy   Yes.

Holly   But it's also quite funny.

Teddy   It is! It's very funny! Look at Bernard – he will be a hot dog!

They laugh.

Bernard *picks some paper up off the floor, smells it.*

Bernard   This wrapping paper smells familiar.

Mum   What's going on?

She leaves.

Bernard   There's something fishy about all this. And it's not fish.

Gran   Holly – you're not playing some sort of joke are you?

Holly   No, Gran. I don't understand it.

She shares a laugh with **Teddy***. Suddenly – a scream.* **Mum** *enters.*

Mum   Bernard! There's a strange man in the bathroom!

Bernard   What?

Santa *enters.*

Santa   Any paper at all?

Mum   Who on earth are you?!

Santa   I'm Santa. Well – I used to be.

Bernard   There's no need to be sarcastic.

Mum   Did he say Santa?

Holly   No , he said – Santos!

Mum   Santos?

Holly   Yes, he's from – the kebab shop. On the corner.

Santa *laughs.*

Santa   Yes, that's right. I'm Santos from the kebab shop.
Why not?

Bernard   What's he doing in our toilet?

Santa   Do you really want to know?

Mum   Holly – what is going on?

Holly   Nothing – he just – all his family are in – wherever
kebabs come from and he was – lonely – so I thought maybe
he could – spend Christmas with us.

Mum   Well that's a nice thought, sweetheart, but we can't
be just taking in any old – person off the street. I mean,
where would it all end?

Gran   No but Holly's right – it is Christmas, after all. We
should set a good example.

Santa *and* **Gran***'s eyes meet. It is love at first sight. Harp strings – a
Zorba-esque Greek dance tune as they come together:*

Santa   And who might you be, young lady?

Gran   Well – I'm Holly's grandmother.

Santa   Surely not.

Gran   And funnily enough – my name's actually Donna.

Santa   Well – you certainly come with all the salad.

They move to kiss each other and **Holly** *shrieks and grabs* **Santa***,
pulling him away.*

Holly   What are you doing? Where's Bumblehole?

Santa   Ah well, that's time spells for you. You never know who's going to end up where.

Holly   Well you can't stay here –

Santa   Why not?

Holly   Well – because –

Santa   Listen – as far as the beard goes, you're welcome to it. I've delivered my last present. You made this mess, you can sort it out. I'm just going to put my feet up and enjoy Christmas Day. Each and every one of them.

Holly   What does that mean?

Santa   Well – if you want to keep that bear alive, you'll have to keep having Christmas Day, don't you? So I get the feeling we're in for quite a few more, don't you?

Holly's *eyes light up. She throws dust in the air.*

Holly   Go back!!

Another flash. A burst of sound and light, as before.

A very loud Christmas pop record is playing. **Holly** *is jumping around,* **Teddy** *dancing.* **Santa** *sits in the armchair, tapping his foot. Even* **Bernard** *– wearing several jumpers now and a stack of hats – ends up chasing his own tail, overcome by the merriment.*

Mum *comes in and turns the music off. Everyone protests.*

Mum   It's not even nine in the morning!

She turns on the TV. News flash:

Newsman   No one seems to know exactly how or why Christmas Day is happening over and over again. But whilst grown-up presents seem to regenerate everyday, children across the world have been waking up day after day to find their stockings empty. There's only one question on the lips of these disappointed youngsters: Where on earth is Santa?

Mum *turns the TV off.*

Mum   Well – Happy Christmas, everyone. Again.

All   Happy Christmas!

Mum *gives a present to* **Bernard**.

Mum   I'll bet you can't guess what it is.

He opens it. It's a jumper.

Bernard   Oh – a jumper – you shouldn't have bothered.

Mum   I didn't.

Bernard   Actually – would you mind if I didn't put this one on? I don't know why but I'm boiling hot!

Mum   Fine. Thanks for the earrings.

Bernard   Oh – no – my pleasure.

She throws them away.

Gran *enters, carrying a cake.*

Gran   Another cake's appeared so I presume it's still Christmas.

Santa *is trying to do a Rubik's Cube.*

Santa   I'll have a slice of that.

Teddy   Happy Christmas, Holly's gran.

Gran   Oh yes – you too.

Holly   Someone pull a cracker with me!

Mum   Not just now, darling.

Bernard   I'll pull –

Holly   Gran – pull a cracker!

Gran   D'you know – I don't actually think I have the strength.

Santa   Here, come here – pull my finger instead.

Holly   No! I know what that does!

Santa   All right, all right –

They pull a cracker.

Holly   I got it! I got it!

Santa   Pah! You always get the toy!

Gran *gives* **Santa** *a slice of cake.*

Gran   Here you go . . .

Santa   Cheers, Big Ears.

Gran   Here you go, Bernard.

She gives **Bernard** *a present.*

Bernard   Oh – goody –

Gran   I'm afraid it's just another hat.

Bernard   Ah well, no – marvellous – you can never have too many hats.

He tries to balance it on top of the other ones. **Santa** *helps.*

Gran   And for you, Barbara –

Barbara*'s arm is hanging with bracelets.*

Mum   No – let me give you yours –

She looks around. She picks up a mug, tries to wrap it.

Here you go.

Gran   Oh – not a hot water bottle then?

Mum   No. Not another hot water bottle. It's a mug.

Holly   Wow – that's a lovely present.

Teddy   It is. It's excellent.

Gran *just stares at it, close to tears.*

Holly   Don't you like it?

Gran   No, it's – the best present I've had in . . . eight or nine days!

She sits down, in tears.

Mum   What's wrong?

Bernard   Yes, what's wrong, Gran?

Teddy   Why is she upset?

Holly   Gran, don't be sad – it's Christmas . . .

Gran (*through tears*)   I know. I'm just a bit tired that's all. And – well –

Holly   Well what?

Gran   Well, what if it's Christmas for ever? I mean – I like it once a year but every day? I don't think I can take it. Not with the toilet broken.

Bernard   Is the toilet broken?

Mum (*nods*)   Fruitcake.

Santa *laughs, finding it all hilarious.*

Bernard   I say, hold on a minute. I don't think it's very nice you laughing at my mother-in-law being upset. Now, I never really understood Christmas. But it was a time that all the family were together and everyone was happy so I liked that. But everybody knows that this happening-every-day thing is dashed odd and I'm going to say it: I think it's got something to do with that bear.

Mum   Oh Bernard. . .

Bernard   I'm sorry. I know he means a lot to Holly but I don't think that's the same bear and for three reasons: It doesn't smell the same; it has a long white beard now, like a wizard; and it seems to be alive. And ever since it turned up, everything's been very strange indeed.

Santa *claps.*

Thank you.

Holly *attacks* **Bernard***, slapping his many-jumpered chest.*

Holly   That's not fair! You're just jealous, like Gran said. You're just jealous because I love him more than I'll ever love you because you're just a dog!!

Mum   Holly!

Bernard   Right. I've had enough of this –

He storms over to **Teddy** *and leans in at him – it's not clear what he's doing.*

Teddy   No – Holly!

Holly   What are you doing?!

She grabs **Bernard***'s tail and pulls him away from the bear.*

Bernard   What?

Teddy   He tried to bite me!

Mum   Bernard!

Bernard   No –

Teddy   He did! I saw his teeth! He was going to tear me apart!!

Holly   Mum! Make him go away! I hate him, I hate him!

Mum   Bernard –

Bernard   No but poopy –

Mum   I'm sorry, Bernard. I love you. But I can't have you upsetting Holly like that.

Pause. **Bernard** *looks hurt and confused.*

Bernard   Fine. I'll – I'll go for my walk!

Mum   Yes. You do that. And take your time!

Pause. **Bernard** *takes a bag and leaves.*

Teddy   You are an animal, Bernard! That's all you'll ever be! I know – I have seen you! And I know what you put in the plastic bags!

Mum *leaves by another door, upset.*

Gran   Oh, Barbara!

Gran *follows her.* **Teddy** *laughs darkly.*

Teddy   This is good, Holly. The dog is gone! At least for a while.

Pause. She shrugs.

What is wrong? This is what you wanted.

Holly   I don't want my mum to be upset. It's Christmas. People aren't supposed to be upset.

Santa   You see? This is what happens when amateurs start throwing magic around.

Holly   You're no help either. Well, I've had enough of today.

She pulls some strands from **Teddy**'s *beard and makes the dust.*

Teddy   Oww!

Holly   Go BACK!

She throws the dust up. Flash. Colour. Sound. News flash:

Newsman   Well, it's been twenty-two days of non-stop Christmas now and the country is slowly grinding to a halt. No trains are running, food supplies are dwindling and even the most famous person in Britain is feeling the strain. Here's an excerpt from yesterday's Queen's Speech:

The Queen appears. A long silence, then she blows a massive raspberry.

Newsman   That feeling is shared by many. Because whilst most people haven't been able to go to work – some others haven't had a single day off . . . since this all began and some of those people are feeling really, really awful.

He is passed a handkerchief.

Meanwhile – although there is still no sign of Santa, we are getting reports that at least some children are now beginning to get presents. Hello, Jenny – are you there?

Jenny *appears, absolutely freezing.*

Jenny   H-h-h-hello, B-b-b-brian.

Newsman   Happy Christmas to you.

Jenny   Yes – a h-h-h-happy C-C-C-Christmas t-to you t-t-too.

Someone puts a coat around her. She nods her thanks.

Well, I've been here outside the Magic Toyshop for twenty-two days now and –

Pause. She gathers herself.

Yes – it does seem that some presents have been delivered to some children now.

Only a few thousand but that's still quite an achievement given that nobody knows where Santa is. We're lucky to have here with us one of his representatives –

Bumblehole *appears.* **Holly** *and* **Santa** *are watching from the couch:*

Holly   Look – look who it is!

Santa   Good grief – it's Bumblehole!

Bumblehole   Am I on telly?

Jenny   Yes, you are.

Bumblehole   Hello, everyone – boys and girls – ho ho ho.

Jenny   Now you say your name is – ?

Bumblehole   Bumblehole. And I just want to say to all the boys and girls out there that we're trying our very best to get some kind of presents to you all. Unfortunately, we're having to do it without the use of any special magic so it's going to take a little bit more time than usual.

Jenny   But you've still managed to deliver over half a million presents –

Santa   That's not bad, considering.

Holly   That's brilliant!

Bumblehole   Yes, all the elves are working full time here and we've drafted in tooth fairies, Easter bunnies – Everybody's been pulling together to try and get those presents out there but we're still having to rely mainly on public transport, so –

Jenny   Bumblehole – do you have any idea why Christmas is repeating like this or – more importantly – any idea what might have happened to Santa?

Bumblehole   That's why I wanted to talk to you. I think there's a little girl out there who knows what's happening and I want to speak directly to her.

Holly – if you can hear this –

Holly   He's talking to me!

Bumblehole   Nobody loves Christmas more than me. But Christmas is supposed to be magical.

And nothing you have all the time can be magical. Holly – you have to take back the beard. You have to return it, no matter what it costs. Return the Magic –

The TV turns off. **Teddy** *has a remote control.*

Holly   Why did you turn it off?

Teddy   You should not listen to that lying elf.

Holly   Poor Bumblehole.

Teddy   Never mind him, Holly. It is getting late. We must turn time back.

Pause. She takes some strands of beard. She is about to throw it.

What are you waiting for?

Holly   Maybe this is wrong.

Teddy   How can it be wrong? Do you want to lose me again – your Real Dad, who loves you more than anyone else in the world?

Pause.

Holly   No, but –

Teddy   Then you must cast the spell! Please, Holly – do it now!

Pause. She throws the dust.

Holly   Go back!!

Flash. Colour. Sound.

Teddy *is singing:*

Teddy   Christmas, Christmas, Christmas!

Christmas, Christmas, Christmas! Santa is asleep on his back, his head in the chimney.

Mum *sits on the couch, looking despondent. She is peeling potatoes into a basin. Her hands are covered in plasters, her hair a mess.*

Teddy   Come on, everyone – sing a long!!

Stuffing, stuffing, stuffing turkeys! Hanging, hanging, hanging . . .

Nobody is singing.

What is wrong with you?! Sing!! Everybody – you must sing and be happy! It is great to be alive! Holly – put the television on!

Holly *turns on the TV. The newsman is half-naked and holding two whisky bottles. He sings repetitively:*

Newsman   Here is the news – here is the news – no news today – Christmas again – !

Holly *laughs.*

Teddy   He has gone insane!

Newsman   I hate Christmas! Here – I'll show you what I think of Christmas!

He climbs up so his backside can be seen.

This is what I think of Christmas!

And just as he's about to pull his pants down and moon, **Holly** *turns off the TV.*

Holly   Oh my God!

Gran *traipses in. She looks terrible and carries a bucket full of slops.*

Gran   Happy Christmas, everyone.

She blows on her party blower but it hardly extends.

Mum (*weakly*)   Happy Christmas.

Gran *sits by her on the couch.*

Gran   Time for presents, then. I don't have much to give you, really so . . .

She looks at her foot. It is sticking through her tights now. She tears something off her toe and passes it to **Mum**.

Mum   What's that?

Pause.

Gran   Toenail.

Holly   That's a horrid present! There must be something better than that.

Teddy   Yes, that's it, Holly. Everyone is being so miserable! Cheer them up.

Holly   What about this, look? An umbrella? Or this –

She takes a dog chew from the Christmas tree, offers it to **Mum**. **Mum** *takes the dog chew and stares at it wistfully.*

Holly   Come on, Mum. What would you like?

Mum   There's only one thing I'd like.

Holly   What's that? Anything you want –

Teddy   Yes, that's right – we'll get you anything you want –

Holly   What do you want?

Pause.

Mum   I want Bernard back.

Gran *hugs her.*

Gran   There, there.

Mum   He's been away for days now. Something must have happened to him. And the last thing I said to him – 'Take your time' I said. I'll never forgive myself if something's happened to him.

Pause.

I don't want any presents. I just want my Bernard back.

She squeaks the toy.

Holly   Stop being sad! You're spoiling everything! I had a rubbish Christmas every year and I didn't make it miserable for you! So now it's my turn! It's my turn to be happy!

Song: Everything I Want

> Now I've got exactly yes exactly what I wanted
> Maybe not exactly how I wanted it but basically.
>
> Everything a girl could want

I've got everything I want.

I've got my dad right there
Maybe he's a talking bear but pretty much
Everything I want
It's Christmas day every day for me
To give it up would be stupid, see

Everything I want

What do I care if someone else is sad?
They never cared when it was me that was feeling bad.

And if that makes me horrible I'm sorry
I've got everything a girl could want
I've got everything I want
Everything I want

Mum *and* **Gran** *have left by now.* **Holly** *is sad.*

Teddy   Holly?

Holly   Yes.

Teddy   It's nearly midnight. You must perform the spell now.

She takes a strand of beard. She makes dust from it and is about to throw it when she hesitates.

Holly – what is the matter?

Holly   I don't know. It's just – everyone seems so miserable and sad, and it's all because of us.

Teddy   How can they be sad? It's Christmas every day!

Holly   But it's like Bumblehole said – it's not special anymore.

Teddy   It's special for us! Who cares about anyone else?

Mum *enters.*

Holly   Mum!

Mum   What are you doing still up?

Holly   Um – well I was just –

Mum   Oh never mind. I don't suppose it makes any difference. It'll just be Christmas again tomorrow. Who cares when anyone goes to bed?

Pause.

Holly   No, wait – Mum – I have to tell you something –

Teddy   No, Holly – don't –

Holly   I'm going to tell her. She'll know what to do.

Mum   Know what to do about what?

Holly   Mum – don't get angry but – it's us. Me and Teddy – it's us that's making Christmas happen over and over again.

Mum   I'm too tired for jokes.

Holly   It's not a joke, Mum, it's true. Except that's not Teddy –

Teddy   Holly, no –

Holly   It's Dad.

Mum   It's what?

Holly   It's Dad. My Real Dad!

Mum   Holly – what are you talking about?

Holly   It was a gypsy witch that did a spell on him. She trapped him in a teddy bear's body and she left him on the doorstep that night, remember?

Mum   On the doorstep?

Holly   Yes, and he came alive but the magic that made him alive only lasts for Christmas Day so we've been using the Magic Beard to make it Christmas every day so he won't die!

Mum   Oh, Holly –

Holly   It's true, it's Dad! He's been here all along. Tell her!

Mum   Holly, just calm down. Listen to me. It's just a toy.

Holly   No – don't you recognise his voice?

Mum   Your dad wasn't a teddy bear.

Holly   I told you! He's trapped inside the teddy bear! It was a gypsy witch –

Mum   Cast a spell and left him on the doorstep, I know. Where are you getting these things from?

Holly   Tell her! Tell her what you told me!

Teddy   I am just a little teddy bear!

Holly   No, why are you saying that? – tell her the truth.

Teddy   Happy Christmas, everyone!

Mum   Holly, listen to me now. No gypsy witch left that bear on the doorstep.

Holly   She did!

Mum   She didn't.

Holly   How do you know?!

Mum   I just do.

Holly   But how though? You haven't even heard the story –

Mum   I don't need to hear any story.

Holly   Then how do you know?!

Mum   Because it was me!

Pause.

It was me that left Teddy on the doorstep. It was me that wrote the note.

Holly   You?

Mum   I'm sorry, darling. I know I shouldn't have. But I only did it to make you happy. So you'd think your dad had come to see you. But he didn't, Holly. He never came.

Pause. **Teddy** *starts to climb down from the chair.*

Holly   You lied to me.

Mum   Yes, but –

Holly   Not you. Teddy.

She grabs him by the scruff of the neck and sits him back on the chair.

Teddy   No – it is your mum who is lying. She never liked me. She wants to turn you against me.

Holly   Don't you call my mum a liar! You're the liar! Liar liar fur on fire!

Teddy   I am telling you the truth, Holly, I swear!

Holly   Liar! You're not my dad! I know you're not! Tell me the truth or I'll throw the dust away!

She holds out the handful of dust, ready to drop it.

Teddy   No, please – all right – I'll tell you the truth! Maybe I am not – your actual father. But I have been like a father to you, Holly, haven't I? When you have been crying I have been there. Please – the magic is fading!

Gran *enters.*

Gran   What's going on?

Mum   The bear's not a robot – it's alive!

Gran   Ah well – that makes a bit more sense.

Holly   You didn't look after me! You lied to me! And you lied about Bernard, didn't you? You made Bernard go away and that made my mum really sad!

Teddy   You wanted him to go away! You told me, all the time. I just did what you wanted!

Please – I can't move my legs.

Holly   Good! You're a bad, horrid bear and you don't care about anyone but yourself!

Teddy   You can talk! For years, all you have done is bash me about and drop me and make me dance to your stupid pop songs! I hate that sissy boy Bieber and I hate your imaginary tea parties! Now do as I say and turn back time!

Mum   Don't do it, Holly.

Teddy   Listen to me! I am the Santa now! I order you to turn back time! You must obey me! I have the Magic Beard!

Holly   Fine. Then do the spell yourself.

She lets the dust fall to the carpet.

Teddy   No! Holly! What have you done?!!

He tries to rub the beard.

Go back! Go back! Please, Holly – these useless paws – help me to make the dust!

Pause.

Teddy   Holly – what have you done? I just wanted us to be together. Can't we be together?

Holly   No. Not anymore.

Teddy   But, Holly, please – I've done things – no other teddy has done. Played charades – on the breakfast bar. Felt the coldness of a snowflake landing on my nose. All those moments – will be lost. Like tears . . . in fur.

Pause.

Time – for bed.

Pause. He is still. The magic is gone.

Holly *walks to him. She picks him up. He is just a teddy bear again. She takes the beard from him and hugs him.*

Holly   I'm sorry.

Mum hugs her.

Gran *looks at her watch.*

Gran   The date – it's moved on. It's not Christmas Day anymore. It's Boxing Day. It's Boxing Day at last!

Mum   You're a good girl, Holly Finnegan.

Holly   But what about you, Mum? It's my fault that Bernard went away.

The door opens.

Bernard   Who went away?

Mum   Bernard!! You're back!!

Bernard   What?

He turns in circles, trying to see his own back.

What's on my back?! Is there something on my back?!

Mum   No, I mean – where have you been?! I've been worried sick!

Bernard   There's no need to worry. I'd never leave you for long.

Holly   You were right about Teddy. He was very bad.

Gran   He was. I'm not surprised you tried to bite him.

Bernard   But I wasn't trying to bite him, that's the thing! I was getting the scent.

Mum   Getting the scent?

Bernard   Yes – you know – smelling him. I am part bloodhound, after all.

Gran   Why were you smelling him?

Bernard   Well, it occurred to me – if that bear was a present from Holly's Real Dad, it'd still smell of him. I thought if I could get the scent, then I could track him down.

Mum Ah well – that wouldn't work I'm afraid. Because it was me that bought Teddy for Holly. I only pretended he was a present from her dad. The only scent you'd have got was Holly's.

Bernard Really? Well, that's odd.

Gran Why?

Thomas Because it worked. He found me.

*From out of the shadows, steps **Holly**'s Real Dad. He is, quite obviously, a cat.*

Thomas I guess maybe we smell the same.

Mum Oh. My. God.

Thomas Hello there, Brenda.

Mum Barbara.

Thomas Barbara. You don't look a day older.

Mum You've got a nerve showing your face around here, Terry –

Thomas Thomas. Thomas Sparrowcatcher, at your service. You wouldn't have a glass of milk for me, would you?

Mum The only thing I've got for you is –

Gran Barbara –

*She nods towards **Holly**, who approaches her father.*

Thomas And you'd be Holly, I'm guessing.

Pause.

You not going to say anything to your old Dad? I've come a long way to see you.

Pause.

Holly You're a cat.

Thomas Somewhat. As are you.

Pause.

Holly   Why did you not stay with me? Is it because I'm ugly?

He kneels down to her.

Thomas   Oh no, no, darling – you're beautiful, you're – the most beautiful thing I ever saw.

Pause.

Holly   Why then?

Thomas   Well . . . I'm a cat you see. We're not so good at staying. And I didn't think that'd be much of a life for you. Out all night, under the stars, going from place to place.

Holly   Sounds exciting.

Thomas   No. It's a bit like having Christmas every day. You get tired of it. And that's what I came to tell you. Now, I won't lie to you – I'm not so keen on dogs. But Bernard here – he opened my eyes to how poor a dad I've been to you. And I came to make amends. I'm here to say I'll change for you, Holly Finnegan. I'll get myself a house and stop my philanderin' ways and I'll be a father to you, if that's what you want.

Pause.

I'm asking you to come live with me.

Pause.

Holly *looks at* **Mum**.

Mum   If that's what you want . . .

Thomas   Would it make you happy?

Holly   Yeah.

Mum *can't help crying.* **Bernard** *holds her.*

Holly   But I think it'd make you sad.

Thomas   Why do you think that?

Holly   Because you're a cat.

Thomas   And so are you.

Holly   Yeah, maybe.

She goes to **Bernard** *and* **Mum** *and hugs them.*

Holly   But I was brought up by a dog.

And she runs to hug **Bernard**.

Bernard   Oh, look – poopy –

Thomas   Poopy?

Bernard   Holly's hugging me! For the first time ever!

Mum   Don't tell me – you're chuffed?

Bernard   I am – I'm chuffed, chuffed, chuffed, chuffed, chuffed!

Holly   Chuffed, chuffed, chuffed!

Thomas   Fair enough. But I'm still going to get that house. And maybe you can visit me once in a while. Come over for Christmas even.

Holly   Can I?

Bernard   Well – Boxing Day perhaps.

Thomas   Yeah, well – we could just call it Christmas anyway.

Holly   That'd be amazing!

Thomas   Yeah, well – you know what they say –

Song: The Only Thing Better than One Dad Is Two

Thomas

The only thing better than one dad is two

Bernard

If your teddy goes bad you've got two dads to turn to

Holly
It might be even better with three
But that would be just plain greedy of me
Wouldn't it be?
The only thing better than one dad is two

Holly
I used to be sad but now I can see that it's true
Happiness is not about getting everything you want
It's not about worrying what you've not got
It's knowing how lucky you are to have what you have
One dad, two dads, three dads or no dad at all
If just one person loves you, you'll never feel small

Thomas
It could be a dog

Bernard
It could be an elf

Holly   He wasn't an elf!

Gran
It could be yourself –
And every day it'll feel just like Christmas, Christmas,
Christ –

Santa *enters suddenly, interrupting.*

Santa   Oh please, not another one!

Gran   No, no – we were just singing. Christmas is over
at last.

Santa   Thank Rudolph for that.

Holly   I've got something that belongs to you.

Santa   No! I don't want it. I told you, I'm retired.

Holly   Then you have to pass it on to the next Santa.

Santa   Who's that? You?

Holly   Me?

Santa   Why not?

Holly   Because you've got the perfect Santa right under your nose.

Santa   Have I? Who?

Sudddenly, through the skylight, **Bumblehole** *descends.*

Santa   Bumblehole!

Bernard   I thought he was Billy someone?

Bumblehole   Sorry, Dad – I tried to deliver all the presents but there were just too many of them!

Santa   Why, you complete and utter – Santa!

Bumblehole: Don't call me that, Dad, I'm not – what did you call me?

Santa   A complete and utter Santa! The Santa, in fact.

Bumblehole   Me?

Santa   Holly's right. You kept Christmas alive against all the odds. And I do now bestow upon you, as the last act of my Santahood, the Magic Beard itself.

He puts the beard on him.

I'm proud of you, son.

He hugs him.

Song: Bumblehole Chorus Reprise

Bumblehole! Ho-ho-ho, ho-hole!

The greatest Santa that there's ever been! Bumblehole! Ho-ho-ho, Three cheers for Bumblehole! The greatest Santa that there's ever been Bumblehole!

They watch him ascend through the skylight and fly off. The sound of a shout and a fall.

Gran   I thought you couldn't fall off a sledge?

Santa   It's not my problem anymore. I'm going to be living a normal life from now on.

Gran   Normal – is that what you want?

Santa   Yes. I'm thinking of going into catering – maybe on a cruise ship –

Gran   Well, I am a fully qualified magician's assistant . . .

Santa   Really? Then maybe we can combine the two . . .

Gran   Magic and kebabs?

Santa   See? We've got the name of the act right there!

Cheers from all.

Holly   Right, well, that's nice. Santa's tapped off with my gran, my teddy went evil and my Real Dad's a cat. Just another Christmas in the Finnegan household. And if you're thinking that's a bit weird, maybe you should take a look at your own family. Because I bet they're just as weird if not weirder. And you're probably weird too. And if everyone's weird, then weird's normal. And if you're actually normal – well, that's just weird. And that's what Holly Finnegan thinks.

Song: Finale

Holly
   And I should thank Bernard most of all

Chorus
   What should you thank him for?

Holly
   For making it so that my other dad and I could

They all look to **Bernard**. *A pause and then he understands:*

Bernard
   Meeeeeeet!

Chorus
Now we've got exactly yes exactly what we wanted
Turns out what we wanted's what we've always had
Except I'd like

Holly   A brand new bike!

Chorus
Except I'd like

Gran   A new computer!

Chorus
Except I want

Bernard   A pooper scooper!

Chorus
Except I need

Santa   A pair of speedos!

Mum   And while you're at it – I think I'll need some baby clothes!

They all stare at her pregnant stomach. From inside – a woof!

Holly   Oh. My. God.

Chorus
Another life! Another life!
Another slice of Christmas cake!

The End.

Narrative

Narrative was first performed at the Royal Court Theatre, London, on 5 April 2013 with the following cast and creative team:

Zawe	Zawe Ashton
Waitress/Imogen	Imogen Doel
Brian/Hitman 1	Brian Doherty
Chris/Chris as TV Exec/ Chris as Therapist	Christine Entwisle
Barney aka Noel/ Lawrence of Arabia/ Hitman 2	Barnaby Power
Olly	Oliver Rix
Sophie	Sophie Ross

Director Anthony Neilson
Designer Garance Marneur
Lighting Designer Chahine Yavroyan
Composer/Sound Designer Nick Powell

Characters

Olly
Waitress
Brian
Sophie
Barney
Zawe
Chris
Lawrence of Arabia

Notes

The text of *Narrative* is essentially a transcript of a live event, staged at a specific time, in a specific place and tailored to its participants. I have made no attempt to render it 'timeless' or 'universal'. As a result, it may require adaptation, depending on when and where you are staging it (especially if you live in a country without double-decker buses).

You will see that we have used various clips culled from the internet as connective tissue. I have indicated the content and titles of these clips and provided links, which may or may not remain active. If a link should disappear, try searching by the title. If no link can be found, attempt to find a substitute or cut entirely. It is up to you how closely you observe their content, or whether you use the clips at all.

You will also notice moments when we use the screen to flash up images. Unlike the clips, these images were not meant to support the narrative but to act as 'distractions' and/or commentary for the audience, I ended up using this technique less than I had originally intended; partly because I was worried it would tip the piece into an 'experimental' area, which was not my intention.

As time goes on, audiences may be more able to assimilate such distractions without getting unhelpfully stuck on their meaning. You should see this element as a 'free' area in which to distinguish your production and provide lateral/ parallel comment or subtext.

The same could be said of the video clips, with the caveat that you should think carefully about their purpose in the text as it stands – particularly those that reinforce the symbol of the bison, and those that set up the events of the Epilogue – and that you remain conceptually true to the spirit and themes of the play.

I am happy to enter into a dialogue about all of this and am contactable through my agent, unless I have died or something.

Prologue

Note: this voice-over occurs over a slide-show of the location described, only interrupted in the later stages by a subliminal frame – the content of which you may decide for yourself.

Narrator *(V/O)*   The earliest example of narrative art so far discovered dates back seventeen thousand years and can be found in the Lascaux caves of southwest France.

The central image of this painting – which may be the work of two to three artists – appears to depict a man with the face, or mask, of a bird in a violent struggle with a bison. The man has four fingers on each hand and an outsized penis. The bison is partly eviscerated, its entrails hanging in a loop from its body, and seems to have butted the man with its horns. The man appears to be falling backwards, either injured or dead.

Olly *is sitting in a café, texting.*

Narrator *(V/O)*   To the left of this central image, we see a rhinoceros. To its' right, we find what may be a staff of some kind, with a bird atop it. The significance of these elements to the narrative is unclear.

Also unclear is the purpose of the narrative. Is it fiction or reportage? Is it a warning or a charm? Who is the protagonist? Is it the man or the bison?

Assuming, however, that the story told is what it appears to be – man wounds bison; bison kills man – this cave painting may be not only the first ever narrative but also the first recorded representation of mortality. Indeed, it is only if we assume the man to have been wounded or killed that the narrative has linear momentum. His death provides us with an ending and allows us to extrapolate his life.

Without this consequence, the painting in the Lascaux cave would be only a picture of a struggle.

A **Waitress** *approaches* **Olly.**

Waitress   A guy said to give you this.

She hands him an envelope.

Olly   Who?

Waitress   He's – oh – I think he's gone now.

He looks at the envelope.

Olly   What did he look like?

Waitress   Just a guy. Can I get you anything else?
Another coffee?

Olly   No – thanks.

*She lingers too long, as if attracted to him. She blushes, then leaves.
With her gone, he opens the envelope and takes out a photograph.*

*(Note: the photograph, whenever looked at directly, is accompanied
by a noise or noises.)*

He's shocked by what he sees and stuffs it back into the envelope.

*He looks around the café, self-consciously, unsure if he's being
watched. He calls the waitress over.*

Olly   Excuse me – is this a joke?

Waitress   What do you mean?

In another area, **Brian** *and* **Sophie** *enter, having an argument.*

*(Note: two scenes now play. There can be overlap but allow the
audience to get the gist of each.)*

Brian   You know what you are? You know what you
fucking are?

Sophie   No, please tell me. Please tell me what I am –

Olly   This.

Brian   You're a quitter, that's what you are!

Waitress   I don't know. A guy just said to give it to you.

Brian   You're a fucking coward! People like you –

Sophie   People like me?

Olly   What guy, though? Where?

Brian   You never had to fight for anything your whole lives. You're born with a sense of entitlement, like happiness is a God-given right –

Olly   What did he look like?

Brian   And the minute you get a tiny sniff of anything less than perfect fucking bliss, that's it: you're off!

Waitress   I told you: Just a guy . . .

Sophie   What are you talking about, people like me?

Olly   Tall, short, fat, thin – ?

Brian   You – your whole fucking generation – !

Sophie   Oh right – so we should go back to the good old days, should we? Stay with each other 'cause we're worried what the neighbours say?

Waitress   He was just . . . normal-looking.

Brian   I'm saying love is hard – !

Sophie   Cos that really worked for our parents, didn't it?

Brian   Oh for fuck's sake – you're not your mother, ok? You're nothing like her.

Olly   Did he have a beard?

Brian   And I'm nothing like your fucking father, either!

Waitress   No, I don't think so.

Barney *enters, with a sock-puppet bison on his hand and addresses the audience directly.*

(Note: the other four actors improvise their scenes concurrently now – the lines that follow are only a guideline and can be used or not – they may take the scenes in whichever direction they wish. Do not attempt to delineate the scenes – the audience must choose which to follow – but allow **Barney** *to be heard until established.)*

Barney   Gas bills, electricity bills – they seem to be just rising all the time!

Sophie   You really don't get a fucking thing I'm saying, do you?

Olly   He had no distinguishing features whatsoever?

Barney   I'm worried that I'm not getting the best deal from my service providers. It's all so complicated!

Waitress   I didn't really look at him –

Brian   Yes, I get what you're saying – (what I'm saying is this is just the shit that goes on in your life and it never stops –)

Barney (*voicing puppet*)   No-um worry, Kemo Sabe! Leave it to um-bison!

Karaoke-style music intro begins.

Olly   You didn't look at him?

Barney (*as puppet*)   Every month I'll check online that you're getting the best deals possible from your providers! (*As self.*) Will you, bison?

Waitress   I did but I don't remember what he looked like.

Sophie   Fine, ok, but I can't just take your word for that –

Barney (*as puppet*)   And every time a better deal comes up, I'll change your accounts to the cheapest supplier!

Zawe *enters, microphone in hand, and sings a bad version of a song.*

(*Note: though you may choose your own song, in the original production, **Zawe** sang David Bowie's 'Where Are We Now?' which was appropriate both thematically and because, having just been released, there was much talk of it on social media. Note also that **Zawe** got the lyrics wrong, singing 'walking the dog' instead of 'walking the dead'.*)

*At one point, the screen displays an advert for the album,
emphasising that it's available 'in all formats'.*

*The music drowns out the other actors but they continue to improvise
their scenes. Again, these lines are only a guide. The chatter should
build to a cacophonous level.)*

Sophie   I need to find it out for myself, don't you get that?

Olly   You don't remember?

Waitress   Look there's a lot of stuff going on –

Barney *responds to an unseen director.*

Barney   Oh what, you want it more – ?

Waitress   The guy said to give this to you and I did –

Brian   Fine, ignore me, go ahead –

Barney   Oh right, ok – let me go back a bit –

Barney *retraces his steps.*

Brian   Waste your fucking life like I wasted mine –

Waitress   I didn't know who he was, I didn't know if he was
a friend of yours or what –

Olly   All right, calm down –

Barney (*as puppet*)   Every month I'll check online that
you're getting the best deals possible from your providers!

Sophie   You haven't wasted your life –

Barney (*as self*)   Will you, bison?

Brian   Forty-seven years old and fuck-all to show for it –

Waitress   I'm totally calm, I just don't get why you're taking
a tone with me –

Barney (*as puppet*)   And every time a better deal comes up,
I'll change your accounts to the cheapest supplier!

Olly   I'm not taking a tone with you –

Brian   Yes – I fucking have. And I just wasted *another*
fucking year of it –

Waitress   Yes you are.

Sophie   Is that what you think?

Barney (*as self*)   And I don't have to do anything?

Olly   I'm not, but you have to admit it's pretty strange –

Brian   Except it's you that's wasted it – It's you that's wasted my fucking time!

Barney (*as puppet*)   Not a thing! Just leave it to the bison!

Now, suddenly, all the actors abandon their scenes simultaneously and join in with the chorus of **Zawe**'s *song. The singing is rowdy rather than tuneful; the way a crowd sings.*

The song ends abruptly, perhaps even unresolved. Darkness.

In the darkness, a digitised female voice, glitchy, stuttering, steadily degrading.

Voice   What did you expect of life?

(Note: on the screen, the first YouTube clip plays. The clip depicts a group of tourists in a national park approaching a bison. The clip is called 'bison fury' and, at the time of writing, can be found here: www.youtube.com/watch?v=F7VghMbLiMA)

Voice   Why did you expect it? Who told you what to expect?

Still in darkness, the **Waitress** *drops a plate or cup, which smashes.*

Voice   What was expected of you? Who expected this of you? What did you expect of yourself? What do you expect of others? Of your friends, of your partners, of your children? Have they met those expectations? Was anything unexpected? Did you respond the way you expected?

Why do we expect?

The **Voice** *breaks down, repeating this last phrase, disintegrating.*

(Note: the video clip stops just before the bison, inevitably, charges the too-close tourists. It freezes and fades with the **Voice**.*)*

One

Olly *and* **Barney** *stare at the photograph, both amused and repelled.*

Barney   It's an arsehole! Jesus Christ, it's an arsehole! Isn't it?

Olly *shrugs.*

Barney   That's disgusting!

Olly   It's fucking gross, isn't it?

Barney   It really is. And you didn't see him?

Olly   No.

Barney   You don't have any idea who it was?

Olly   No.

Barney   That's unbelievable . . .

Pause.

Olly   So it wasn't you?

Barney   Me?

Olly   As a joke?

Barney   No – I mean, it's quite funny but no. I wouldn't even think of it.

Olly   I'm not angry about it –

Barney   No –

Olly   I'd be relieved if it was you, to be honest.

Barney   I'm sure you would but no – I mean, if I was going to play a joke like that, I'd have put it in your pocket or something maybe, for you to find – but this . . . how would I even have known where were?

Olly   I don't know. Unless you followed me.

Barney   Followed you? Seriously?

Olly   I know.

Barney   You think I've got nothing better to do than follow you around?

Olly   No – I know. I don't think it was you. I just don't know who'd do that.

Barney   Did anybody know you'd be at that café at that time?

Olly   I didn't know myself. I only went in because I was early for the audition.

Barney   And it wasn't some kind of set-up? There wasn't some . . . camera crew hidden somewhere?

Olly   I thought that but no – I didn't see anything. And wouldn't I have to sign a release form or something?

Barney   But why would anyone do that? Give a complete stranger a photo of an –

Chris *walks onto the stage, interrupting them.*

Chris   Sorry. Excuse me. Sorry.

They watch her take a central position on the stage and address the audience directly. She is nervous.

Chris   Hello um – this is a poem I wrote for my son, David. It's called just – it's called 'For David'.

She holds the note with trembling hands, gathers herself, then starts. She is not a performer.

David died a year ago
Such pain I hope you'll never know
My angel lived to seventeen
The most beautiful boy you've ever seen

Pause.

They told us he had overdosed
But we knew David was not morose
Something else was to blame
Finding out what became our aim.
We knew he'd been on medicine
To cure the acne on his skin
But to our shock and dismay
We found out it had been banned in the USA
Vyoclozamine, the drug is named
And we found out that it was famed
For causing suicidal feelings
Instead of its proper job of healing
Since my baby passed away

Pause.

I've dedicated every hour and day
To making sure this drug is banned
In every corner of the land
I'll never rest until I'm done
So please go to banvyoclozaminefordavid.com
And take a moment to sign your name
So no one else will feel this pain

Pause.

I never wanted to have this task

Pause.

Being a mum was all I asked
But with your help perhaps I could
In David's name –
Do something good.
Thank you for listening.

She exits, but stops and turns back to the audience.

Oh and if you look under your seats, you'll find a leaflet
which'll tell you some more about the campaign and the
website and stuff. Thank you.

(Note: the leaflets are there.)

Olly *and* **Barney** *watch her go. Pause.*

Barney   And whose arsehole is it anyway? Is it his?

Olly   I don't know.

Barney   Cos if it's his . . .

Olly   What?

Barney   Maybe it's an invitation.

Olly   An invitation?

Barney   Yeah, you know –

Olly   What – get a load of this?

Barney   Yeah, you know – have a bit of this.

Olly   Of this sweet candy?

Barney   Of this sweet, sweet candy.

Olly   Fuck that's horrible. But then why would he leave?

Barney   Cold feet.

Pause.

It's not nice, though, is it? I mean – I'm no expert on anuses but that one looks particularly . . . sticky.

Olly   It's definitely a man's though, right?

Barney   It's close-up, true. It's hard to tell.

Olly   Maybe it's his wife's.

Barney   What?

Olly   I don't know. Maybe he gets some kind of thrill out of giving people pictures of his wife's arsehole.

Barney   No, come on: It's got to be a joke. Maybe he was watching you from across the street or something.

Olly   Yeah but why me? There were lots of other people in there. Why did he single me out?

And he begins to sing:

> Am I an arsehole?
> I mean, I may be but I try my best to hide it.
> Is it obvious to everyone?
> Do people look at me and think:
> That guy's an arsehole?

Zawe *explodes into the room.*

Zawe   You're a fucking arsehole, you know that?! How dare you! How dare you fucking speak to me about my mother! What the fuck do you know about my mother or what she's been through?!

Olly   Nothing.

Zawe   My mother would do anything for me! My mother would fucking die for me! How dare you!

Olly   I didn't say anything about your mother –

Zawe   You should fucking wish anyone loved you as much as my mother loves me!

Olly   Fine. I'm sure that's true. I was just raising the possibility that maybe you're not quite as secure as you think you are –

Zawe   What the fuck do you know? You don't know a fucking thing about me!

Olly   No! That's exactly it! I don't. You don't know a person after just three months – you can't –

Zawe   Three and a half!

Olly   Fine – whatever – but you're right: I don't know you. That's my point.

Pause. **Zawe** *softens. She uses her hands to mimic cat's ears. She approaches him cutely, mewling.* **Olly** *sighs heavily. She butts her head against his leg.*

Zawe (*baby voice*)   You do, dough. Doo do know me.

Olly   Jesus Christ – !

Zawe   That's the thing about being soulmates. It's not about time. Something just connects. And I know – I understand: it's scary to think that this might be it; that we might never fall in love with anyone else again – but there's something much, much scarier –

Olly   Yes! Being trapped in a / relationship with you –

Zawe   There is no trap! / That's an illusion! You can walk away any time you want!

Olly   Which is what I'm trying to do – !

Zawe   No but don't you get it?! We're going to *die*, man! Do you get that? It's not miraculously not going to happen! You're not going to pass ninety, then a hundred, then two hundred, and someone says 'How come you're two hundred?' and you go, 'Oh I don't know, I just somehow didn't *die* for some reason' *No*! One day you'll wake up and that will be the *last* day you ever wake up! And that'll be it, you'll just be gone, nothing. You won't come back, not even as a zombie. Do you get that? Can you get your head around that?

Olly   So we're going to die: What does that have to do with anything?

Zawe   What does it *not* have to do with *everything*?! If you abandon this – if you walk out – one day I'll die and you won't even be there. You might not even read about it, if I don't get famous. You might not even know I've died. You don't think that's tragic?

He doesn't really.

Zawe   Oh. Ok. I see.

Olly   Oh come on – look – I like you and everything and I think it'll be very sad when you die. But you can't possibly feel this intensely about something after just three – three and a half months –

Zawe   No, you mean *you* can't. But you're not everybody, yeah? We're not all just people you've thought up in your head!

Olly   You don't love me, Zawe. You might feel like you do but it's not real.

Zawe   Don't tell me what's real! I'll decide what's real, all right? Is that all right with you?

Olly   It's an infatuation –

Zawe   Fuck you. I'm not infatuated with you, you piece of shit.

Olly   Ok. Ok.

She looks panicky all of a sudden.

Zawe   Oh God, just – tell me what's good about me.

Olly   What?

Zawe   I just can't hear any more about what's wrong with me. Tell me five things that are good about me.

Pause.

Olly   There's lots of good things about you. . .

Zawe   Then just tell me five. Please.

Olly   Well – you're pretty . . .

Zawe   Am I?

Olly   Yes, of course.

She blushes.

And you're . . . kind. You're generous.

Pause.

Sociable.

Zawe   Sociable?

Olly Yeah, I mean – I don't have to worry if I take you out that you won't – get along with people, or be shy. Aaaand . . .

Pause.

You're stylish. You dress well.

Zawe I try to.

Pause.

Zawe One more?

Olly That's five.

Zawe That's four. Pretty, kind, sociable, stylish . . .

Olly Generous.

Zawe That's the same as kind.

Olly No it isn't.

Zawe Pretty much.

Olly Fuck – fine, you're – a good – singer.

Zawe Do you think so?

Olly Yes. You're a very good singer. Ok?

Zawe So I'm pretty, I'm kind, I'm stylish and sociable and generous and (*sings*) I can sing!

Olly *nods.*

Zawe So why would you want to lose all that?! I mean, what do you *want* from a person?!

Olly Oh God, look – it's just not going to work out, ok? There's nothing wrong with you –

Zawe 'It's not you, it's me'?

Olly No – it's *not* me. Some things just don't work out. I'm sorry.

Zawe   Ok, fine. Fuck you. You die alone. You just go and blip out of existence with nobody there to give a shit. Go on.

Pause.

Olly   Ok, well . . .

He wanders towards the door.

Zawe   But not tonight. I'll be fine in the morning just – don't leave me here alone in this house, with all the memories –

Olly   What fucking memories?! Domino's Pizza? This is only the third time I've been here!

Pause.

You'll be ok.

Zawe   I won't. You don't understand: It'll be like a desert. Like a desert stretching out all around me, as far as I can see.

She looks bleak.

Stay until the sun comes up.

Olly   I can't.

Zawe   Please.

Olly   You'll be all right.

Zawe   I won't.

Olly   You will. Really.

Zawe   Fuck you.

Pause. He opens the door.

I want my jumper back!

Olly   What jumper?

Zawe   The jumper I bought you last week.

Pause.

Olly   Fine, I'll get the jumper.

Zawe   Tonight.

Olly   Not tonight . . .

Zawe   Tonight or I'll call the police.

Olly   And say what?

Zawe   That you stole it.

Olly   Well – good luck with that. I'll drop it off in the week.

Zawe   And the receipt.

She pronounces the 'p' in receipt. He holds his temper.

Olly   The what?

Zawe   The receipt.

She does it again. He counts to five.

Zawe   What?

Olly   It's *receipt*.

Zawe   What?

Olly   You don't pronounce the 'p'!

Zawe   That's how it's spelt.

Olly   I know how it's spelt! Have you never heard the word before?

Zawe   What word?

Olly   *Receipt*. Have you never heard anyone say it?!

Pause.

Zawe   Are you done?

Olly   Done what?

Zawe   Assassinating my character?

He leaves.

She sits there. The sound of a desert wind, gathering force. The desert sun begins to blaze.

Lawrence of Arabia *enters, in full Arab attire, sandy and exhausted. He kneels at the oasis and fills a canister with water, which he drinks needily.*

His thirst quenched, he sees **Zawe**. *She gives him a small wave and he half-waves back, as if he's seen her before somewhere.*

Lawrence *turns to address the audience.*

Lawrence   For his fortieth birthday, he decided to do something he had never done. He decided to jump from a plane. At precisely the right moment, he pulled on the ripcord, but his parachute failed to open. The emergency parachute also failed. As he fell towards the earth, he realised with certainty that he was about to die. 'Of course', he thought, quite calmly. 'Why did I expect any different? I have jumped from a plane.'

He exits.

(The next YouTube clip plays. It is called 'Is This What Grabriel's Horn Will Sound Like' [sic] and at the time of writing can be found here: www.youtube.com/watch?V=KjZRYgnibE0

The clip first shows text, read by a low American voice. This is the text:

'For the Lord himself will descend from Heaven with a shout, with the voice of an archangel, and with the trumpet of God. And the dead in Christ will rise first.

What will the trumpet of the Archangel sound like? Will it be a new sound? Or something all-too familiar, heard around the world?'

The clip then cuts to home footage of suburban houses, the sky heavy with clouds, and the unearthly, thunderous sound of a horn blaring, seemingly coming from the sky.)

Two

Brian *enters, talking on the phone:*

Brian   Solomon? It's Brian.

How's it going, my man?

I know, we've been playing phone-pong a bit, haven't we? Message tennis. No, I'm grand, I'm grand. I was just calling to say I've just read ep three –

Oh, it's terrific stuff. I tell you now, honestly, if the next three episodes are as good as the first three – I think we're talking about the best series yet.

Okay, so – there was just one thing I wanted to ask about: have you got the script to hand?

Grand, well it's bottom of 25 – end of that scene in the wine cellar.

Pause.

Got it? Ok – so I say 'Tell M'lud I'll be up in a minute'. Exactly.

Now then it says I cough, right? It says 'Hannegan coughs into his handkerchief'. Then it says 'He looks at the handkerchief' –

Beat.

Yeah. And I was just wondering what the thinking was with that?

Sophie *enters, also on the phone but in a different space.*

Sophie   No, I haven't: I don't really watch movies much anymore.

Brian   Why would they write that in, though? I mean – why end a scene on that?

Sophie   If I'm going to watch something, it's more likely a TV series, you know –

Brian   No but it's the beat. It says 'He looks at the handkerchief – Beat'. What's that about? What happens in the beat?

Sophie   Or like a box-set or something . . .

Brian   But what do I see in the handkerchief?

Sophie   Yeah cos it's like reading a really good book, you know? It's the same feeling I used to get from that.

Brian   Phlegm? What, so he's just got a cold? Because that doesn't seem like a very dramatic storyline. You know – given that the manor's just been hit by a Doodlebug . . .

Sophie   I don't really have the time for books . . .

Brian   But if it was phlegm, I'd just shrug – who cares about phlegm?

Sophie   I don't know, my mind just starts to wander . . .

Brian   There must be something in it. Something in the phlegm.

Sophie   I think I've got ADHD or something – seriously –

Brian   Sol – you're the producer: you don't know?

Chris *enters, also on the phone, also in a different space.*

Chris   Yes, I know he's very busy but he did say he'd meet with me before the next parliamentary session –

Brian   I'd like to know before the read-through, Sol: what does he see in the phlegm?

Sophie   Totally . . .

Brian   It's blood, Sol, isn't it? That's what he sees. Blood in the phlegm. Just tell me.

Pause.

Chris   But so did he definitely read the stuff I sent because he said he'd read it – ?

Brian   Come on, Sol – I've been in this game a long time. I know what it means.

Sophie   It's just – to see something all wrapped up in, like, a couple of hours – it just doesn't feel realistic anymore.

Brian   *Beat*. Beat is final face. He looks at the hankie – Final face. Final face isn't 'Oh I've got a cold'. Final face is terror. Final face is fear.

Chris   Yes but when it was the by-election and you wanted the votes, it was all about how accessible he was going to be, wasn't it?

Sophie   Oh yeah it's amazing. But you've got to stick with it –

Brian   Come on, Sol – just say it: I'm dying, aren't I? That's what that means – hankie, beat.

You're killing me off!

Sophie   The second season's better, the third season's fucking great.

Chris   I've been trying to get a meeting for over six months now – !

Brian   Well who decides? Who decides that? Is it you, the execs, who?

Sophie   And what's brilliant is they don't mind killing people off.

Chris   There's people – children – being prescribed a drug that makes them suicidal – what's a higher priority than that?

Brian   And do the fans not get a say? Because you shouldn't underestimate how popular I am. He is. Hannegan is. I mean – you should see my mailbox –

Sophie   I'm not going to spoil anything –

Brian   No, look – I can play it, fine, I'd relish it – but this isn't about me –

Chris   I know it's not your fault – I'm just tired of getting messed around –

Sophie   Yeah, well – stick with it, it gets better –

Brian   Now an *illness* – a long-term illness – that could actually be good. I could play that. I could grow from that . . .

Chris   Well, just tell him – I've got two hundred names on my petition already –

Sophie   Anyway – we shouldn't use up all our conversation –

Brian   That's all I ask, just – think it through, it's not too late.

Chris   Yeah but that's two hundred votes he stands to lose right there . . .

Sophie   Cool. What time do you finish?

Brian   All right, buddy. I'll see you at the read-through and we can –

Chris   Oh listen, don't worry, I'm not going to let it drop –

Brian   Exactly. Sorry to be –

Sophie   Ok – and I've got some interesting news –

Chris   You'll be sick of the sound of my voice, believe me.

Brian   All right, Sol, cheers now. Bye.

We hear a medley of goodbyes over theirs: 'Bye-bye, bye' / 'All right then' / 'Bye now' / 'See ya' / 'Ok goodbye', and so on. **Brian** *has hung up. Pause, and then he shouts angrily:*

Brian   Fucking Oxbridge twat! Posh, stuck-up fucking Oxbridge fucking cunt!

Beat. Suddenly paranoid, he puts the phone back to his ear.

Hello?

Imogen *enters, whistling. She stands at the bus stop, and raises her umbrella. She dips her shoe in a puddle and watches the water shimmer.*

Chris *lights a candle.*

Chris   They finished building that Tesco's. It doesn't look so bad as you thought. There's a few homeless people round the back but they seem nice enough. I give money to the one with the dog. I think most people do. I hope he buys dog food with it, not cider.

Pause.

Next time, I'll buy him an actual can of dog food; those ones with the ring-pull top.

Zawe *is having her palm read by* **Sophie**.

Imogen   It's funny what we care about and why.

(Note: on the screen, a photo of American singer Michael Bolton appears, incorrectly titled Michael Burton.)

Chris   Amanda – you remember Amanda – she gives money to Amnesty and I used to think that was really amazing, to care about people you'd never met who were so far away and nothing like you. But then she told me her dad used to lock her in the basement when she was little and it all made sense.

Imogen   Maybe we don't care for anyone else.

Maybe when we cry it's only ever for ourselves.

Pause.

Chris   Anyway . . .

She exits, leaving the candle flickering.

(The next YouTube clip plays. It is called 'Strange Sounds Heard Worldwide 2011/2012 – Corinthians 15:52'. At the time of writing, it can be found here: www.youtube.com/watch?v=EnyUcbSd4Kg

The clip begins with this text:

'Since 2011, the sounds have been heard worldwide . . .'

The clip is real footage taken in a snowy, presumably North American landscape. We can hear a strange and terrifying noise in the sky, to which the man's dog is reacting. We ended the clip after 61 seconds.)

Three

Zawe *enters briskly, with* **Barney** *in tow.*

Zawe   Ok, Noel, do you feel ready to do some improvising?

Barney   Sure, fine.

Zawe   You don't have a problem with that?

Barney   No, that's fine.

Zawe   Ok, so what we want you to imagine is this: You're dissatisfied.

Barney   Right . . .

Zawe   Can we see that?

Barney   Dissatisfied?

Zawe   Yeah, can we see you being dissatisfied?

Barney   Ok . . .

Pause.

Barney   What am I dissatisfied with?

Zawe   With life.

Barney   With life.

Zawe   With your whole life.

Barney   Ok, got you.

He thinks for a moment. He sighs heavily, shakes his head.

Zawe   Whenever you're ready.

Barney   No, this is it, I'm doing it now.

Pause.

Zawe   Ok but don't internalise. Tell the story. Tell us how dissatisfied you are.

He starts to pace, fretfully.

Ok good but more. You're anxious, depressed, disappointed. You're not where you should be in life; your career's going nowhere; you don't like where you live; you haven't found your soulmate; you don't like your body; you hate your thighs –

By now, he's loping back and forth like some kind of gargoyle.

Zawe   That's good. That's great. And now SUDDENLY – ! A tiny version of you jumps out of your body!

He continues pacing for a moment then stops.

Barney   Sorry, what? A tiny – ?

Zawe   A tiny version of you jumps out of your body.

Barney   A tiny version of me?

Zawe   Yes. A tiny version of you – exactly the same as you but, like, a metre high – jumps out of your body.

Barney   Ok . . .

Zawe   Can we see that?

Barney   Yeah, I'll just have to – go back a bit.

Zawe   Whenever you're ready.

He starts to pace again, building momentum.

Zawe   Ok, that's good – that's good – and – NOW!

He acts startled.

Zawe   Vocalise it.

Barney   Jesus Christ – !

Zawe   Not that.

Barney   No uh – Good grief!

Zawe   What's wrong with you?!

He stops.

Barney   Is this – ?

Zawe   This is the voice of the Tiny You.

Barney   Ok – sorry –

Zawe   What's wrong with you?!

Barney   I don't know, I'm just so – dissatisfied with my life.

Zawe   But you don't have to be!

Barney   Don't I?

Zawe   No, not if you use this – And Tiny You gives you a footmouse.

Barney   A what?

Zawe   A footmouse. That's the product.

He doesn't understand.

It's a mouse for a computer but you operate it with your foot.

Barney   Oh – ok . . .

Zawe   You don't have to be dissatisfied!

Barney   Don't I?

Zawe   Not if you use this!

He mimes getting the footmouse.

Barney   Wow – a footmouse!

He mimes operating it with his foot.

Zawe   And now everything that was bothering you just goes away.

Barney   This is great!

Zawe   This is the best thing ever!

Barney   This is brilliant!

Zawe   You feel free –

Barney   Wow!

Zawe   You feel free and full of joy!

Barney   Yay!

Zawe   Show us joy.

Barney   Wowee – this is amazing – !

Zawe   Say the product.

Barney   Footmouse!

Zawe   Dance with joy!

He does.

Zawe   Say the product.

Barney   Footmouse!

Zawe   Again.

Barney   Footmouse! Footmouse! Brilliant! Footmouse!

For what seems like an age, he hops around grinning, shouting 'footmouse'. Sad music bleeds in underneath. Then stops.

Zawe, *breathing heavily, gets up, unsteady.*

Zawe   Ok, thank you.

Barney   Ok.

She pushes past him.

Was that ok?

Zawe   Are you still with Marion – ?

Barney   No, actually I don't have –

She hurries out, as if to be sick. He is left confused.

What the fuck . . .?

Glumly, he reaches up to grab a strap and now he's on an underground train.

On the screen, we see footage of his audition as if on YouTube: dancing like an idiot, grinning, shouting the name of the product, played out in agonising slow-motion. The title of the clip is 'Footmouse Wanker' and it has been viewed nearly a million times.

*In a different space, we see **Zawe** enter, hyperventilating, having a panic attack. She slides out of view.*

Sophie *gets on the train. She takes out a mirror and applies lipstick.* **Barney** *watches her, longingly. She glances at him and he looks away.*

He puts earphones in and presses play on his audio device. We hear an audio drama, in American accents.

The next is all recorded:

Newsreader   Scenes of chaos today as the midtown branch of Unity City Bank was devastated by a huge explosion during the busy lunchtime period. We go now –

Static.

Barman   Hey, something's happening to the TV!

Magician   Attention, citizens of Unity! This is the Magician –

Bar   *The* Magician!

Magician   Today you have seen but a small demonstration of my power. I have the means to strike whenever and wherever I wish. If you wish to ever live in security again, my demands are simple: Bring Elastic Man to me, in chains, by sunrise tomorrow. If you do not comply, I will engulf this entire city in the flames of Hell itself!

Sophie *finishes her make-up.*

Newsreader   Well – you all saw that: It looks like evil genius the Magician is behind this mayhem and he'll only stop if we bring him Elastic Man.

Sophie *stands.*

News 2   That's right, Brooke, except there's one problem: No one's seen Elastic Man for two weeks now! Elastic Man – if you're out there – if you can hear this – Unity City needs you now more than ever!

Newsreader   Save us, Elastic Man – save us!

Sophie *gets off the train.*

She meets **Imogen** *and they hug.*

(Note: the actors can improvise around these lines for a more realistic feel.)

Imogen   So come on – what's the story?

Sophie   The story?

Imogen   The big news you said you had –

Sophie   Oh –

Imogen   Is it something good?

Sophie   I don't know: I think you'll think it is.

Imogen   So tell me!

Sophie   Can we at least get a drink first?

Imogen   No, I can't wait that long!

Chris *approaches them, clutching a clipboard.*

Chris   I'm sorry to bother you – have you got a minute?

Imogen   Uh –

Sophie   I'm sorry we're in –

Chris It's just this is my son, David. He passed on a year ago, from an overdose.

A mortified pause.

Sophie Oh, I'm sorry . . .

Imogen That's terrible . . .

Chris It was recorded as a suicide but he was a very happy boy, as you can see, so we never believed he'd have done that. It turns out he was on a medication for acne called Vyoclozamine –

Sophie I think I've heard of that . . .

Chris You might have. It's actually banned in the USA because it's been linked to several suicides there but it's still being prescribed here –

Sophie Really?

Chris Well, it's cheap, you see. So I'm gathering names for this petition to have it banned over here as well –

Sophie Yes, of course.

She takes the offered pen and signs.

Chris Thank you . . .

Imogen *signs next.*

Chris You girls out for the night?

Sophie Yeah, just catching up.

Chris That's nice.

Imogen *hands back the pen.*

Chris Thank you. And this is a leaflet, it gives you the address of the website and tells you a bit more about the drug and the progress we're making.

They take them.

Sophie   Good luck with it.

Chris   Bless you, thanks. Have a nice night.

She exits.

Sophie   That's fucking tragic . . .

Imogen   It's terrible. So anyhow –

They're in a bar – music playing.

Give me the gossip, what's going on?

Sophie   Well, just that – I'm single again.

Imogen   No! Seriously?

Sophie   Yup. We split up, finally.

Imogen   How do you feel about that?

Sophie   Good in some ways. Bad in others.

Imogen   Oh, Sophe, I'm sorry, that's a shame.

Sophie   A shame? I thought you were dead against it?

Imogen   Me?

Sophie   I thought you thought he was a sleaze.

Imogen   Why would I think that?

Sophie   I don't know: Because of the age difference.

Imogen   Did I say that?

Sophie   Yes! You said he was old enough to be my father.

Imogen   Well yeah, like – age wise. But he wasn't your father. That's the important bit.

Sophie   I can't believe you're saying this . . .

Imogen   You didn't listen to me, did you?

Sophie   You know – it was a factor, when I was weighing it up – I could hear your voice –

Imogen   God, I was just winding you up. Christ, my first boyfriend was twenty-five when I was fifteen.

Sophie   Seriously?

Imogen   Totally. Underage sex and everything. And I mean *everything*.

Sophie   You've never told me that. That actually is quite dodgy, isn't it? Being twenty-five and shagging a fifteen-year-old?

Imogen   Didn't seem that bad at the time. It's not like I was forced or anything.

Sophie   He could have gone to jail for that.

Imogen   Still could, I guess. Just as well we stayed friends!

They leave this venue and move to another one, with different music. On the way, they take out their phones and refer to them constantly from now on.

But, like, that wasn't my problem with your man. It just looked like it could have got pretty serious.

Sophie   It was, for a while.

Imogen   I was just thinking ahead. I mean, like – twenty years difference: If he croaked at seventy, you'd be on your own at fifty. And you don't want to be on the shelf at fifty.

Sophie   Fifty's not that old.

Imogen   It is if you're a woman. Can't have kids; tits have dropped, arse has dropped; neck does that vagina thing . . .

Sophie   What century are you living in? People are starting new lives at fifty . . .

Imogen   Still got the barren womb. Men want fertile women; always have, always will.

Sophie   You're actually quite old fashioned, aren't you? You sound like my grandmother.

They leave the venue and walk through the streets.

Imogen   So what went wrong? In your relationship?

Sophie   Nothing went wrong, exactly . . .

Imogen   Were you arguing?

Sophie   Not really. But we weren't having much fun either.

Imogen   You think you could do better.

They sit down by a water feature.

Sophie   I think I could do different.

Imogen   But you have to commit to someone eventually.

Sophie   No you don't . . .

Imogen   No but then it's just fucking – musical chairs.
Wherever you are when the music stops.

Sophie *opens her bag.*

Sophie   D'you want an apple?

Imogen   An apple?

Sophie   Yeah, you know – fruit? Do they have fruit where
you come from?

Imogen   Fine, yeah, let's get crazy. An apple.

Sophie *produces a knife from her bag.*

Sophie   D'you want it peeled?

Imogen   What the fuck is that?!

Sophie   It's a Swiss Army knife.

Imogen   You can't carry a knife around!

Sophie   Why not?

Imogen   I don't know – can't you get arrested for it?

Imogen *takes the knife from her.*

Sophie   Why? My dad gave me that when I was about twelve. It's more a tool than a knife.

Imogen   You're the tool.

She opens the knife, unfolds the various implements, fascinated.

Sophie   See, now you've confused me again. D'you think I made a mistake?

Imogen   About what?

Sophie   Ending it.

Imogen   I guess you just weren't happy. If you were, you would've stayed.

Sophie   Maybe I would've got happy again. That's what he said.

Imogen   There's someone out there that's right for you. You'll know when you know.

Sophie   That's bullshit, that's just rhetoric.

Imogen   Yeah, probably.

*She sticks the knife in **Sophie**'s neck. **Sophie** stares at her in surprise.*

Imogen   Oh my God – !

Sophie *staggers away, clutching her neck.*

Imogen   Oh my God, Sophie, I'm sorry, I don't know why I did that!

*Blood jets from **Sophie**'s neck in long arcs, spattering into the water. She drops to her knees, falls forward.*

She twitches violently then expires. Pause.

Imogen   Sophie . . .?

*The world shifts on its axis, visibly darkening. The other actors appear on the stage, watching **Imogen** reproachfully. **Olly** and/or*

Barney *drag* **Sophie**'*s body away.* **Chris** *stares at her before following them out.*

Brian *reads, and his voice is dislocated, unearthly.*

Brian   The little boy lifts the air rifle, takes aim and squeezes the trigger. The rifle pops and the bird falls from the tree. The little boy walks through the leaves to where it lies and watches it stop, like a watch stops.

Imogen, *beside herself with panic, runs away.*

Brian   There was nothing in his nine years to explain why he would shoot a bird. But here it lay, this thing that once flew.

Slowly, his voice returns to normal.

And suddenly, for the first time, the boy understands the direction of time; that it moves only forward; that he cannot turn it back. For some reason, this surprises him. In killing, he knows he cannot kill. In taking a life, he realises he is powerless.

He sways slightly, drunk and stoned. They both are.

What do you think?

Zawe   Wow.

Brian   Wow?

Zawe   It's just like – Mind? Blown.

Brian   Ok . . .

Zawe   You're a poet. Simples.

Brian   Except it's prose.

Zawe   Prose can be poetry, man. A song is poetry. A good meal is poetry.

Pause.

Zawe   A duck is poetry. A brick –

Brian   Yeah, I get what you're saying.

Zawe   It just speaks to me, you know? I just completely get where you're coming from.

Brian   I'm just sick of relying on other people's words, you know? I want to write my own words.

Zawe   Totally. I so get that. I want to write my own words. My mum would've loved that.

She would've loved you.

Brian   Why?

Zawe   Just – she would have: she was a poet too.

Brian   An actual poet?

Zawe   A fishmonger. But she used to sing. She used to make up songs and sing them to me.

Brian   Like what?

Zawe (*sings*)
   You are a princess, you are the best –
   everything you do is amazing –
   You will have the moon and stars and everything your
   heart desires –

Pause.

Brian   Nice.

Pause.

Zawe   But then she stopped.

Brian   Singing?

Zawe   Yeah. When her brother died.

Brian   Shit.

Zawe   She was brought up in an orphanage but then in her twenties, she went and found her real parents and she found out she had a brother and they got very close. But then I was maybe eleven, twelve? He got killed in a car crash.

Brian   Shit . . .

Zawe   Never sang again. Never even listened to music. Said it made her head go funny.

Pause.

Brian   Must have been difficult.

Zawe   For me? No – that was why she was so brilliant. She was just so determined I'd have the childhood she never had. Never hit me, never judged me, never stopped me doing anything – just gave me love and belief and confidence . . . yeah. And that's a precious gift, man. No matter what happens in life – I know – that I was loved. A lot of people don't ever know that.

Brian   No.

Zawe   Lot of people, they just jump from one relationship to the next. Because they're insecure. They're worried they'll lose themselves.

Brian   Tell me about it.

Zawe   You know what I mean?

Brian   I do. But it's the times as well: everyone's told they're entitled to nothing less than perfect happiness. Soon as that initial state of bliss wears off, they move on.

Zawe   Totally: that's so right.

Brian   Nobody wants depth anymore. The shallow, the insecure; that's what's prized.

Zawe   That's so true: nobody wants anything real.

Brian   They want to be lied to. Lies sell; the truth doesn't. I guess you know that, in your business. No offence.

Zawe   No, hey – totally: it's bullshit. I just work with the creative people; the actors, the directors. I don't come up with the campaigns or anything.

Brian   Look, we're just as bad. So-called artists: we all help sell the lie. It's worse in some ways. We know that adverts are lies but art – it's supposed to tell the truth. It's supposed to tell people the truth about themselves, so they won't feel so fucking . . . alone. But we sold out. And for what? For money, for fame. For fucking awards. The fucking BAFTAs, the Oliviers: they should give out white feathers at these things not fucking statues.

Zawe   Cool, totally. So would you turn one down if you got one?

Brian   Ah well – now that depends on a couple of things . . .

Cross-fade to:

Barney *sits in a bar, waiting.*

He hears a strange, throbbing noise. **Imogen** *enters, in a state of extreme distress, shaking, snotty, her make-up running.*

Also, she seems to have sprouted horns. Bison horns. He stares at her, unsure what is happening, as if the play has gone wrong somehow.

Imogen   Is it Noel?

Her voice echoes, strangely. She jumps at the sound of it.

Barney   I'm waiting for Sophie.

Imogen   Yes. Yes. I'm – Sophie. That's me – Sophie.

He speaks loudly, as if to backstage crew:

Barney   You don't LOOK like Sophie.

Imogen   I – Don't I?

Barney   You don't look like the PICTURE of Sophie on the WEBSITE.

Imogen   No. I've changed my hair.

Her voice echoes forcefully. She tests it:

I've changed my hair. (*Panicked.*) I've changed my hair!

Pause. He gets up and retreats towards the exit.

Imogen   So – then – can we have a drink then? Can we just have a drink and get on with it?!

Barney   Get on with WHAT?

Imogen   With the school. No! With the science. Shit! With the – *scenery*.

Barney   You're not SOPHIE though! This is meant to be with Sophie!

With a frustrated scream, she exits the stage. Lights go down on **Barney**, *still confused.*

Cross-fade back to **Brian** *and* **Zawe**.

Brian   The exact same sound?

Zawe   The exact same sound, man – all over the world. 2011. There's loads of clips online.

It's freaky as shit.

Brian   Yeah well – it wasn't the fucking rapture.

Zawe (*shrugs*)   Who knows?

Brian   Well, we all know. Because it wasn't. There weren't chariots in the sky and fucking Christians vanishing.

Zawe   Not this time . . .

Brian   Oh what – so it was like a drill? Like a fire drill?

Zawe   I'm just saying –

Brian   Are you religious?

Zawe   What?!

Brian   Fair enough if you are –

Zawe   No – fuck – religious? I'm like – the least religious person I know!

Brian   Until now.

Zawe Fuck religion, man! All of that stuff. The rapture –
it's fucking – American bullshit!

She passes him the joint, exhales.

I just sometimes think – what if we were wrong? What if we
were wrong and they were all right?

Brian Then we'd be fucked.

Zawe We'd be totally fucked.

Brian But they're not. They're insane.

Zawe No, I know, totally. Just sometimes you should ask.

Pause.

Brian You know what I like about you? You surprise me.

Zawe Is that good?

Brian It's good for me. Usually I can figure people out
pretty quickly.

Zawe Figure them out?

Brian Yeah, you know: make sense of them. But you –
you're a challenge.

Zawe I'm a very simple person.

Brian It's fine – a bit of mystery's good. It's attractive.

Zawe I don't want to be a mystery, though. That's not what
I want.

Brian What do you want?

Imogen *appears between them, breaking the mood. That strange,
throbbing noise again. They look awkward, as if she shouldn't be on
stage. She's trying to control her panic.*

Imogen Hey.

Pause.

Zawe Hi.

Imogen   What's happy? No. What's happened? Happening.

Zawe *raises her hand to point at* **Imogen***'s horns.*

Imogen   What?

She reaches up, only now discovering her horns.

Oh no, what the FUCK?! What the fucking fuck is THIS?!

Brian (*to* **Zawe**) I should probably call you a cab.

Imogen *runs to a mirror.*

Zawe   Oh. Right. Yeah. I guess it's . . . pretty late.

Imogen   I've got horned! D'you see that?

Zawe   Don't want to keep you up.

Imogen   I've got funky horns!

Brian   No, you're not keeping me up. I thought I was keeping you up.

Zawe   No – wow – I'm such a night owl.

Brian   Maybe we should move to the living room.

Zawe   Have you got music?

Brian   I have. I even have some gospel music.

They start to leave.

Imogen   When are you going?! You're supposed to stain on!

They are gone.

What if I don't?! What have I donut?! What have I *done*?

Olly *and* **Barney** *enter. They hesitate for a moment, seeing* **Imogen***, but continue with the scene:*

Barney   So come on – what's the big news?

Imogen *points at* **Olly**, *excited*.

Imogen   Youth! I know you!

Olly   Ok well – you know that audition I went to the other day?

Imogen   I was the waitress! In the cape! In the café. Remainder? Remorse. Remember? It was meat!

They ignore her. Pause. She runs off stage, taking the strange noise with her.

Barney   Oh yeah: the advert?

Olly   Yeah, well – thing is – it wasn't an advert. It was a film.

Barney   Oh, right. Why didn't you say?

Olly   I wanted to but I couldn't. They made me sign something saying I wouldn't talk about it. I'm not even supposed to tell you now but I just . . .

Barney   What, is it – a big film?

Olly   Yeah, well – big budget, yeah.

Barney   What, like Hollywood?

Olly *shrugs*.

Barney   Hollywood?!

Olly *can't help but smile*.

Barney   So come on – what is it?

Olly   It's stupid. It's a kids' film really. It'll probably be absolute shit and I'll never work again.

Barney   What is it?

Pause.

Olly   *Elastic Man*.

Pause. **Barney** *nods, just as something inside him dies*.

Olly I'm Elastic Man.

Pause.

Barney Is it a decent part?

Pause.

Olly Well – it's the lead, I suppose.

Barney It's a film of Elastic Man?

Olly It's a film of Elastic Man and I'm playing Elastic Man.

Barney What's it called?

Pause.

Olly *Elastic Man.*

Barney Brilliant.

Olly Yeah?

Barney Oh – yeah. I used to love Elastic Man. They're making a film of it?

Olly Yeah . . .

Barney Big budget?

Olly Massive. Fucking massive. Guess who's playing the villain?

Barney Who?

Olly Clooney.

Barney Clooney? Is he playing the Magician?

Olly I think so – I haven't seen the script yet –

Barney It must be the Magician. That's his arch enemy.

Olly You'd know better than me. I never really read comics.

Barney Wow. So who's playing Elastic Man?

Pause.

Olly   Me.

Barney   Uh-huh.

Olly   That's what I'm saying: I'm playing Elastic Man!

Pause.

Barney   Yay! Elastic Man! That's great! You're playing Elastic Man! This is brilliant! Yay!

He begins to dance around, like he did in the footmouse audition. It gets a little disturbing.

Wow! Wowee! Elastic Man! Elastic Man! Brilliant! Amazing! Elastic Man!

Eventually he tires and slumps into a seat, obviously devastated.

Olly   Are you all right?

Barney   I'm brilliant. That's great news . . .

Olly   Cos that was a bit . . .

Barney   No, no – that's terrific news. I'm happy for you, mate, I really am. Couldn't have happened to a nicer guy.

Olly   Thanks.

Pause.

Barney   So wow – that means . . . I know Elastic Man! Elastic Man is my mate. My best friend – Elastic Man! That's something isn't it?

Olly   It could be a disaster.

Barney   No, no way. It'll be huge.

Olly   People will go to see it, yeah. But I'm still going to be prancing about in a fucking skin-tight suit playing a guy whose body can stretch like elastic. I could end up looking like a total tit.

Barney   But a rich tit. A famous tit.

Olly   A famous tit . . .

He ponders this, whilst **Barney** *pours himself a stiff drink.*

Olly   But listen – Noel – I told you because – well, because you're my mate. But also because – I'm going to be away for a few months filming and . . .

Pause.

Well, you know we've been talking about moving on . . .

Pause.

Barney   Oh. The flat.

Olly   Kind of makes sense to do it now, don't you think?

Pause.

I mean, it films in July so I'll stay on until it's all done. So there's plenty time to find someone.

Barney   Nah. Another flatmate? Too old for that. I'll find a one-person place.

Olly   You'd be better staying here. You won't get anything decent on your budget.

Barney *drinks.*

Barney   On my budget.

Olly   I didn't mean it like that.

Barney   No, sure – but I'll just have to move, won't I? Out of London.

Olly   That won't do you any good . . .

Barney   Maybe it will. Maybe that's the best thing. Get this stupid acting idea out of my head. Maybe it'll save my life. 'Thanks, Elastic Man! How can I ever repay you?!'

Sophie *appears, on the screen, as if on a Skype call.*

Olly   Come on – don't be like that.

Imogen *hurries onto the stage – the sound again – and looks up at the screen.*

Imogen   Soapy?

Sophie *starts to talk but there's no sound.*

Imogen   Soapy, I can't heart you! Turn on your michael! Sophie, turn on your mic!

Barney (*to* **Olly**)   Has something changed?

Chris *enters, slowly, shedding her leaflets as she does, leaving a trail.*

Imogen   Sophie, can you hear me?!

Sophie *leans in and turns off the screen.*

Imogen   Sophie?

She turns to see **Chris**. *They stare at each other, desolate.*

Chris   He wasn't taking it.

Her voice echoes too, like **Imogen**'s.

Imogen   Taking what?

Chris   The drug. The acne drug. Vypo – vyspo – clora –

Pause.

David wasn't taking it. His flatmate found the boxes.

Pause.

He told me he'd been taking it.

Pause.

Imogen   Can you see me?

Chris   Yes.

Imogen   Does my voice sound weird to you?

Chris   A bit. What's wrong with you?

Imogen   I did something.

Chris   What?

Imogen   Something terrible. The worst thing you could ever do, ever.

Chris   Why?

Imogen   I don't know. I don't think there was any reason. Can you do something for no reason? Something bad?

Pause.

Chris   I hope so.

Pause.

That's me done then.

She puts on a pair of the bison horns.

What now?

Pause.

I suppose I go.

Pause. She starts to go, but then hesitates. She turns to **Imogen***.*

Chris   Which way should I – ?

Lights out.

Four

In the darkness, we hear the voice of the **Narrator***.*

Narrator *(V/O)*   The Democratic People's Republic of Korea, commonly known as North Korea, is a country in East Asia, in the southern half of the Korean peninsula.

On the screen, footage of Korean military propaganda plays: missiles paraded through the streets, huge armies marching, crude animations of attacks on America.

Its capital is Pyingyong but only a thousand people live there, with the majority of its four billion citizens living in rural areas devoted to noodle farming, its second biggest industry after arms production.

Zawe *bursts in, as if chased. She slams the door shut and presses against it, her breathing fast and shallow.*

Narrator *(V/O)*   North Korea is a single-party state under a united front led by the Korean Workers Party, or KPP. It is a totalitarian state with an elaborate cult of personality built around its leader, currently Kim Yung Guy, and the flow of information is so tightly controlled that most North Koreans remain unaware of their own mortality.

Zawe *drops to the floor and crawls to a place of safety.*

Narrator *(V/O)*   Women in North Korea must wear school uniforms until the age of fifty, despite the fact that they are not allowed to attend school. Punishments for contacting the outside world range from execution to the barbaric practice of turtling, which involves turtles.

Brian *enters, looking for her.*

Brian   Zawe? Zawe?

Narrator *(V/O)*   Genetically, North Koreans are closer to squid than human beings. One in five of its citizens serve in the armed forces. The national dish is boiled terrier. North Korea has declared itself a nuclear state, although some experts claim that their missiles are only drawings and therefore incapable of causing widespread destruction.

Brian *finds her cowering.*

Brian   Zawe, what the fuck are you doing?! What's wrong?!

Narrator *(V/O)*   Despite this, in 2012, UN Secretary-General Button Moon sanctioned sanctions against the country and relations with the West continue to deteriorate.

Brian   What's wrong, sweetheart? What's happened?

He helps her to sit. She's hyperventilating.

All right, just breathe. You're all right. Where's your bag? Have you got your bag?

She nods, taking a paper bag from her pocket. He helps her to put it to her mouth.

That's it, just breathe, nice and slowly –

The bag deflates and inflates as she does.

A television executive appears. It is quite obviously **Chris** *in disguise. She's placed paper bags over her horns to hide them.*

TV Exec   We think it's brilliant.

Brian *is still trying to manage* **Zawe**.

Brian   Oh – great –

TV Exec   Everyone's *very* excited.

Brian   Excellent.

TV Exec   Um – notes – we do have some notes –

Brian   Of course –

TV Exec   Now the – hitman character –

Brian   Yep . . .

TV Exec   We love him! He's a great character.

Brian   Oh – great, thank you –

TV Exec   In fact, we like him so much, we'd like two of him!

Brian   Two of him?

TV Exec   Yes. A pair of hitmen. People like two hitmen. They like the banter between them.

Brian   The banter?

TV Exec   Yeah. They like them quirky. Almost comedic.

Brian   Comedic?

TV Exec   Not that they're funny but you know – if they talk about – just normal stuff.

Brian   Normal stuff.

TV Exec   Yes, they talk about normal stuff but – they kill people in an unusual way.

Brian   Unusual?

TV Exec   Yes: not with a gun – with – something quirky.

Brian   Quirky.

TV Exec   Yes, like – a glue gun or – a blanket!

Brian   A blanket?

TV Exec   What do you think?

Brian   Honestly?

TV Exec   Oh yes, of course – be completely honest. That's all we want, is for you to be honest.

Brian   The 'hitman' in my script is an ex-member of the Ulster Volunteer Force. They go to people's doors and shoot them in the head. With a gun. Most of them aren't very bright and they're very fucking far from funny, let me tell you. So if you're asking me what I think, honestly: I think you're talking shit.

Pause.

TV Exec   You're right. I don't know what I'm talking about. I'm not qualified to be a television executive. I'm going to be a therapist instead. Rain.

Now we are in a therapist's. **Chris** *has put glasses on.*

Zawe   Wedding.

Therapist   Water.

Zawe   Reflection.

Therapist   Mirror.

Zawe   Smudge.

Therapist   Smudge?

Zawe   Mirror.

Therapist   No –

Zawe   Yes.

Therapist   No, stop –

Zawe   Bus.

Therapist   No, Zawe –

Zawe   No Zawe.

Therapist   Why did you say smudge?

Pause.

Zawe   Did I say smudge?

Therapist   I said mirror, you said smudge. Do you know why?

Zawe   Oh. My mum didn't like mirrors. She used to spray over them with furniture polish so they were all smudged and smeary.

Therapist   Why did she do that?

Zawe   She didn't like to look at herself. She said she didn't recognise the person looking back.

Therapist   So you grew up in a house without mirrors?

Zawe   I had my own mirror. Just a little one.

Therapist   You don't have a problem with them?

Zawe   Now? No.

Pause.

I don't like the full-length ones.

Therapist   Why not?

Zawe   I don't like how tall I am. I look like a tree. I feel like I walk like a tree would walk, if a tree walked.

Therapist   You feel like you take up too much space?

Zawe   I feel like if someone was going to start shooting, I'd be the first one they picked.

Sophie *appears on the screen.* **Imogen** *runs on again, addresses the screen.*

Imogen   Soaky wait! When are you? Sophie turkey mink on, plead!

Now **Sophie** *looks directly at her.*

Imogen   Sophie please – I'm soppy! You had to forget me, please! I'm scarce!

Sophie   They're coming for you. You *bitch*.

She turns the camera off.

Imogen   Wait, who? Who's coming?

Thriller-style music. **Barney** *and* **Brian** *enter, dressed as ultra-cool* **Hitmen** *wearing the obligatory shades.* **Brian** *as* **Hitman 1** *carries a glue gun.* **Barney** *as* **Hitman 2** *drags a blanket.*

Imogen *hides. The music stops.*

Brian *as* **Hitman 1** *sniffs the air. They've affected appropriate accents.*

Hitman 1   She's close. Not long now.

Hitman 2   What'll we do when we find her? Kill her?

Hitman 1 *holds up the glue gun.*

Hitman 1   Let's just say she'll come to a sticky end.

Hitman 2   Sex.

They move on, then **Hitman 1** *stops suddenly, turns on* **Hitman 2**.

Hitman 1   Wait a minute – what?

Hitman 2   What?

Hitman 1   What did you just say?

Hitman 2   Sex.

Hitman 1   Sex?

Hitman 2   Yeah, sex. As in genius. It's what people say if something's good. You know: I just got a new Ferrari. 'Sex'. As in – 'brilliant!'

Hitman 1   Do people say that?

Hitman 2   Yeah. Totally.

Hitman 1 *scrutinises him.* **Hitman 2** *shifts uncomfortably.*

Hitman 1   Did you make it up?

Hitman 2   What?

Hitman 1   Are you trying to start a word?

Pause.

Hitman 2   No . . .

Hitman 1   Are you trying to re-contextualise a word?

Hitman 2   What do you mean?

Hitman 1   You know what I mean: like 'wicked'; or 'sick'.

Pause.

Hitman 2   I've heard people say it.

Hitman 1   Have you? Look at me.

Pause.

Take off your glasses.

Hitman 2   Why?

Hitman 1   Take them *off.*

Hitman 2 *takes his glasses off and holds* **Hitman 1***'s gaze.*

Hitman 1   Have you heard anyone say that?

Long pause.

Hitman 2   No.

Hitman 1   No.

Pause. **Hitman 1** *shakes his head.*

No one would know. Even if it caught on – who would know?

Hitman 2   *I* would! *I'd* know.

Hitman 1 *puts the shades back on* **Hitman 2**.

Brian   Let's get this done.

They exit, to the thriller-style music.

Olly *enters, also wearing shades, and a puffy coat. He carries a rolled-up screenplay, which he places down.*

He looks around furtively, then takes a battered envelope from his pocket. From the envelope, he takes out the picture of the anus. He stares at it, chewing his lip nervously.

Zawe *enters. She looks glamorous but too thin, and despite wearing ludicrously high heels that accentuate her height, she bends down to compensate.*

Zawe   Well, well!

He jumps – stuffs the photograph into his pocket.

Olly   Zawe?

Zawe   Look at you, the big movie star!

Pause.

Olly   What are you – ?

Zawe   I'm here now.

Olly   You're directing?

Zawe   No – God, no: I'm doing the interview. They'll edit me out, don't worry. Replace me with the various presenters. But it's a step in the right direction.

Olly   To – ?

Zawe   To being seen.

Olly   Ok.

Zawe   Is that ok?

Olly   Bit of a surprise but ok. So how are you? You look good.

Zawe   I am good. I'm brilliant, actually. New career, new flat – new relationship.

Olly   Great.

Zawe   Oh, listen – for what it's worth? You were *so* right about us not being soulmates.

Olly   Well . . .

Zawe   I don't know what I was thinking! Just a crazy time, you know?

Olly   It happens.

Zawe   Bullet? Dodged.

Pause.

So how about you? You've done well.

Olly   Not yet.

Zawe   Hey – we're doing the PR so . . .

Olly   It's bound to do well.

Zawe   I'll know when *you* die, that's for sure. Ok – so just take a seat –

Reluctantly, he takes off his coat to reveal his ridiculous, skin-tight Elastic Man suit.

Hey . . .

Olly   Don't.

Zawe   *Very* stylish.

He sits on the stool. She touches her ear.

Ok, are we good?

Pause. Bizarrely, she adopts an American accent:

Ok – first question: Were you a fan of Elastic Man as a child?

Pause.

Olly   Are you going to do it like that?

Zawe (*normal accent*)   Like what?

Pause.

(*American.*) Were you a fan of Elastic Man as a child?

Pause.

Olly   Well – I was certainly aware of the comics and I saw a few of the cartoons; mostly because of my younger brother who was a big fan. I was probably more into Batman when I was a kid. But yeah, I certainly knew of the character, I mean –

Zawe   Wait a sec –

She touches her ear again, nods. In her normal accent:

Ok – so your producer says you shouldn't say that stuff about Batman. Just focus on Elastic Man. And be more positive generally. You're a big fan, you always were, yada yada –

Olly   Ok.

Zawe (*American*)   Were you a fan of Elastic Man as a child?

Olly   Yes, I mean – who wasn't? I read the comics and I saw the cartoons.

Faintly, we hear the sounds we associate with the anus.

I wouldn't say I was an obsessive fan but I certainly enjoyed what I read of them and, you know – he's such an iconic character so . . .

Zawe *giggles.*

Zawe   Exactly – and how will you approach the character?

Olly   Well, in the same way –

Zawe (*normal accent*)   Could you put the question in the answer?

Olly   Well – you approach a character like Elastic Man in the same way you approach a character like . . . Hamlet or Macbeth.

The anus sounds . . .

In some ways, it's actually harder than those parts because it's more outside your experience. I mean – we all know what it's like to be a stroppy teenager or a bit ambitious; but here's a man who suddenly has the power to stretch like elastic – he can stretch himself to the size of a football field; he can stretch his neck and look in a window ten storeys up, you know – what does that do to your body? What does that do to your mind? How does that kind of power change you? Those are really interesting questions, you know? It's meaty stuff.

Again, she giggles.

Zawe   Exactly – So is it intimidating to work with George Clooney?

Olly   George – Gorgeous George . . .

Anus sounds.

You do have to pinch yourself, you know – I'm wearing the costume and we're on this huge set and there's George Clooney playing the Magician – it's quite surreal. But George is such a professional – he knows you're going to be nervous and he knows how to put you at your ease – it helps that he's very funny and very generous with his time. There's no starry stuff. Pretty soon you're just relating to him as you would to any other actor. And he's doing something very interesting with the Magician so I think people are going to be surprised and very pleased.

Giggle.

Zawe   Exactly. So finally – can you say the famous catchphrase for us?

Olly   I knew you'd ask me that . . .

She nods. He squirms.

I actually said it for the first time the other day.

She nods.

Seriously, you want me to say it?

She does. Pause.

STRETCH IT!

He reddens.

Zawe (*normal accent*)   Really?

Olly   What?

Zawe (*normal*)   I don't know – do you want to do that again?

Olly   Not really, no.

Zawe   Your producer says to do it again but with more conviction.

He looks beyond her, to the unseen producer.

Olly   Shouldn't we save it for the film?

She touches her ear.

Zawe   He's asking if you should save it for the film?

Pause. She nods.

No, it'll sell tickets. So – (*American.*) Can you say the famous catchphrase for us?

Pause.

(*Normal.*) You can get up. Use the space.

He climbs down off the stool, paces.

On the screen now – for the first time – we see the anus, clear and close.

He sees it and turns away. The anus fades. With energy, he strikes a heroic pose and shouts:

Olly STRETCH IIIIIIIIIIIT!

Zawe Brilliant!

He can't speak for shame.

Ok, we're done.

He nods. She extends her hand, the accent dropped now.

Zawe It was *so* lovely to see you again. I hope it goes really well for you; lots of sequels – *Elastic Man Two*, *Three*, *Four*, *Five* –

He nods, aware his producer is watching.

Olly Hopefully . . .

Zawe See you on the big screen!

She exits.

(*On the screen, the next YouTube clip. It's called 'A 101-year-old woman grows horns, and now fears she's growing another one' and at the time of writing can be found here: www.youtube.com/ watch?v=mCMWRu_fl44*

It depicts a very old peasant woman from China with a long, horn-like growth protruding from her forehead. The clip was re-edited for time.)

Five

Brian *enters, raging, followed by* **Zawe**.

Brian   Jesus fucking Christ! With the actor? With this fucking – guy who's playing fucking – Plastic Man or whatever?!

Zawe   He's an ex-boyfriend –

Brian   Oh right – so that makes it ok does it?

Zawe   It doesn't make it ok but it's not as bad.

Brian   Oh right – so I can just fuck any of my ex-girlfriends can I? And you'd be ok with that?

Zawe   I wouldn't be ok with it –

Brian   No, you're fucking right you wouldn't!

Zawe   But it would be better than someone new.

Brian   How? How is that better? Cheating is fucking cheating!

Zawe   No it's just like – going back in time a bit.

Brian   Going back in time?

Zawe   We'd already had sex. So we just had it one more time than we'd had it before.

Brian   Are you seriously trying to use science fiction to justify this?

Pause.

Zawe   Look, I'm sorry, yeah? I know it was wrong. We were just – talking about old times – and I got too drunk. It didn't mean anything.

Brian   Oh, well, that's a comfort. It's great to know that you betrayed me for something meaningless. That makes it so much better!

Pause.

I mean, why even tell me about it? If it didn't mean anything –

Zawe   You wouldn't want to know?

Brian   No! Why would I want to know?

Zawe   I thought you'd want to know.

Brian   Don't fucking pretend it's about me! The time for thinking about me was just before your knickers came off! That was the time for consideration! No – You had a squalid little secret troubling your conscience but instead of just living with it, you decided to dump it into my fucking brain!

Zawe   You wouldn't tell me?

Brian   Oh no. No: you do *not* get to turn this round on me! I haven't done that. You've done it and now you've told me. And now it does mean something. Now it *has to* mean something.

Pause.

Do you want to be with this – fucking – Olly guy?

Zawe   No!

Brian   No?

Zawe   I told you –

Brian   Right. It was meaningless. So do you want to be with me?

Pause. A long pause. He crumbles.

Oh Jesus. Oh Jesus Christ, I'm an idiot.

Zawe   You're not.

Brian   I am. I am. Hollywood. Fucking Hollywood.

Zawe   Hollywood?

Brian   I thought this was it. You and me: I really thought this was that great fucking love thing they fill our heads with. But it's not, is it?

Pause.

Oh Christ, don't you ever learn? Don't you ever fucking learn?

Pause.

Zawe   I do love you.

He nods.

Brian   Prove it.

Zawe   Prove it?

Brian   Marry me.

Pause.

Zawe   Marry you?

Brian   Why not?

Pause.

Zawe   I can't.

Brian   Why not? If you love me?

Pause.

Zawe   It wouldn't be right.

Brian   Why not?

Zawe   I just told you I slept with someone –

Brian   Exactly. And by doing that, you've fucking smashed the trust we had. Do you understand that? You fucking – *girl*! You stupid fucking *girl*. Do you have any idea how hard it'll be to rebuild that?

Zawe   No, Brian, why don't you tell me? Why don't you tell me like you've told me everything else, from all your years of wisdom?

Brian   Hard. Long and tiresome and fucking *hard*.

Pause.

But I'll make you a deal, a one-time offer: marry me. Say it now and I'll just trust you. I'll use my emotional fucking etch-a-sketch and make like it never happened. Just commit, absolutely, here and now. Free pass.

Pause.

What do you say?

Pause.

Zawe   I do love you . . . I just –

Brian   Fuck you. Fuck you.

Pause.

What the FUCK do you know about love? Hmm? Oh no, wait a minute, I know: your mother loved you. That's why you're so secure, right? That's why you have panic attacks and hide under the bed all day. That's why you're in therapy: That's why you fucked fucking Plastic Man! Because you're so secure! Because your mother fucking loved you so fucking much!

Pause.

But what if she didn't, Zawe? What if she didn't love you?

Zawe *shakes her head.*

Brian   Come on – like you said: you've got to ask the question sometimes. What if you're *wrong*?

Pause.

Because tell me this – who did *she* learn it from? Your mother was brought up in an orphanage. You told me she was treated like shit. So where did she learn how to love? I'll tell you: from books. From the TV. From fucking Hollywood. She gave you stuff, she showered you with unqualified praise, she told you you'd inherit the fucking Earth and it was all fucking bullshit! A simulation; a cheap, superficial imitation of love by someone who didn't know the meaning of the word. And thirty years later, what's the result? You. You. A fucking – Easter Egg of a person.

Pause.

You don't know who you are, you don't know what you want, you don't know what you think – Life throws shit at you and you collapse and you know why? Because there's no core to you, no foundation, none of the things that real love – genuine, complex, awkward love – builds. Your mother loved you like a child loves a doll. She didn't know any other way. And you know what? Neither do you.

Pause. She nods. He's crossed a line and he knows it.

Zawe   And what about you? Were you loved?

Pause.

Brian   I don't know, Zawe.

Pause.

But I can sleep, you know? I can spend more than ten minutes in silence. I can look in a fucking mirror.

Pause. Lights down, in conventional style.

Sophie *appears on the screen.* **Imogen** *enters – that same unearthly sound.*

Imogen   Soppy – wait! Please – call you head me?

Sophie *looks at her.*

Imogen   Sophie, please – judge tall to me! Please!

*Pause. The image of **Sophie** speaks – her tone is fairy-tale dark.*

Sophie   Why should I?

Imogen   Because I'm sordid! I'm so funky sordid for who I did. I can't go off like this. I'm a total rectum, look at me!

Pause.

Sophie   Why did you do it?

Imogen   I don't know! The night was in my head and then I just did it. It was like my arm did it.

Sophie   Your arm?

Imogen   Like a mustard spasm.

Sophie   Oh come on . . . Obviously you hated me on some level.

Imogen   No, I loathed you! You're my best friend!

Sophie   Am I supposed to feel sorry for you? At least you're still in there. At least you're still a part of it.

Imogen   I know but look at me – I've got horns! I've got fucking horns now! And my voice sounds weird and my weirds are word and I don't fit anywhere –

Pause.

I know I don't dessert your hell but I'm scarred, Sophie! I'm so fucking scared. . .

Pause.

Sophie   They're going to need a reason. A reason why you did it.

Imogen   But what if there isn't one?

Sophie   Then they'll write you off. Is that what you want?

Imogen   No –

Sophie   Then give them a reason. One that makes sense to them.

Imogen   Like what though?

Pause.

Sophie   What about that boyfriend? The one who was twenty-five when you were fifteen.

Imogen   What about him?

Sophie   Well – technically . . . you were abused.

Pause.

Imogen   Yeah but that didn't –

Sophie   But maybe it *did*. Maybe you've been lying to yourself.

Imogen   What so – I stabbed you?

Sophie   You had a lot of anger. Years of suppressed anger and something triggered it.

Something like . . .

Pause.

The apple.

Imogen   The apple?

Sophie   Did that mean something to you, the apple?

Imogen *tries to think.*

Sophie   Did he *eat* apples?

Imogen   Yeah probably . . .

Sophie   Did he *like* apples?

Imogen   I think so.

Sophie   Do you remember him eating an apple?

Imogen   I guess so . . .

Pause.

But did he abuse me though?

Sophie   Did you ever do anything you didn't want to?

Pause.

Imogen   Sometimes I wasn't in the mood . . .

Sophie   But he did it anyway.

Imogen   Yeah. But I just went along with it.

Sophie   Of course you did. You were only fifteen. You didn't know any better.

Imogen   I guess . . .

Pause.

He did tell me to keep it a secret. He didn't want anyone to know he was my boy-band.

Sophie   So he knew. How it would look. That's good. What else?

Pause.

Imogen   He licked me in my school uniform. Liked me. To wear it.

Sophie   Good. You're remembering.

Pause.

Imogen   And sometimes he –

Sophie   Sometimes . . .

Imogen   Sometimes he'd make me choke on his cod, which made me crikey, not properly, but cos I was neatly sick! And then – and then he'd cumberbatch on my facade!

She's crying now.

Sophie   Good. The first step is acknowledgement. You need to acknowledge that you were abused.

She nods.

Say it.

Pause.

Imogen   But won't he get into trousers?!

Sophie   Fuck him! He should have thought about that at the time.

Pause.

Sophie   Do you want back in or not?!

Imogen   Yes.

Sophie   Then *say* it! Say it and it'll be true!

Pause. **Imogen** *turns to face the audience.*

Imogen   I was abused.

Pause.

I was abused as a child.

Suddenly – brightness. A mirrorball. Jaunty music. A party atmosphere.

(On the screen, a YouTube clip plays. It is called 'Kittens on Decks' and shows kittens trying to climb aboard a record player turntable. But any extremely cute animal video would suffice.)

The cast all enter, smiling and happy, and gather round **Imogen***, patting her, hugging her, and offering platitudes:*

You've been so brave.

If there's anything I can do.

We need more people like you.

You mustn't blame yourself.

People like you are the real heroes.

She accepts their embraces, happy but bewildered.

Imogen   I'm fine, really – I'll be fine.

And now they leave:

Just hang on in there.

If there's anything you need –

If you ever want to talk –

Just be kind to yourself, ok?

Imogen   I will. Thank you. Thanks for all your support.

The party's over and she's left on the stage with **Chris***, who still has her horns covered, and is still pretending to be someone else.*

Imogen *is ashamed.*

Imogen   Will you tell?

Chris   Tell what, dear?

Imogen   You know what.

Chris   I don't think I do . . .

Imogen   Yes you do.

Pause.

I know it's you. I saw you before.

Chris   I don't think so.

Imogen   I did! You were collecting names, for your son. But he didn't die like you thought he did. You had horns, like me.

Chris   I think I'd remember having horns, don't you?

Imogen   Did you ever find out why? Why he killed himself?

Chris *looks uncomfortable.* **Imogen** *is crying.*

Imogen   Do you think I'm evil?

Chris   I don't think anything.

Imogen   But you know what I've done –

Chris   I don't *know* – anything.

Imogen   Yes. You do.

Pause. Letting the facade drop, **Chris** *reveals her horns.*

Chris   I'll tell you what I know: I used to think *Deal or No Deal* was a load of superstitious shite! But now I watch it twice a day! And every – single – fucking – number has a meaning!

Pause. She regains her composure.

You're back in. That's all that matters.

Chris *pushes a few pages of script into* **Imogen***'s hand. A microphone is placed on stage.*

Zawe *storms in, raging.*

Zawe   You're a fucking arsehole, you know that?! How dare you! How dare you fucking speak to me about my mother! What the fuck do you know about my mother?!

Taken by surprise, **Imogen** *hurriedly searches for her lines on the page.*

Imogen   Oh fuck –

Zawe *joins her at the microphone.* **Imogen** *reads, as if recording a radio play:*

Imogen   Nothing! I just said –

Zawe   You're not the queen of suffering you know? We're all survivors.

Imogen   Um – You keep saying that! But what the fuck have you survived exactly?

Zawe   Ok, fine – you win: you win the suffering award. Here: here's your crown of thorns, Great Queen of Suffering! We're sorry that we burden you with our problems once in a while! We're sorry that this relationship can't always be about you!

*Over time, the scene becomes more real, the scripts less used, the stage
more taken.*

Imogen   I don't want it to be about me! I don't want to talk
about my shit – Jesus Christ: I'd give my left tit to never have
to talk or think about it ever again! You're the one that keeps
dragging it up and then the minute I start talking about it,
you start fucking nodding and telling me how you feel my
fucking pain!

Zawe   I do though.

Imogen   Why? Because your mother didn't love you?

Zawe   Yeah, well, we can't all have been abused and killed
our best friend and been to prison, yeah? That doesn't make
my pain less valid than yours, though, does it?

Imogen   No but that's not what I'm saying –

Zawe   No, you're saying I don't have any pain.

Imogen   Christ, no – you obviously have pain; you've
obviously got a fucking ton of pain. I just don't think it
comes from where you think it comes from.

Zawe   Right. Because you know better than trained
therapists.

Imogen   I just don't know where you get the idea that your
mother didn't love you. Jesus – I wish my mum had made
up songs about how amazing and fucking wonderful I was!
All I got was how I should marry the first man who showed
any fucking interest in me!

Zawe   But it was a lie, don't you get that? They were just
stupid songs and then they stopped! They just fucking
stopped and I had nothing!

Imogen   But you didn't have nothing though! Ok, she
stopped singing – she was obviously majorly depressed – but
she fed you, she looked after you, she supported you – what

the fuck else did you want from her? What do you think love is?

Zawe   I think that love . . . is what I feel for you.

Imogen   Is it though? See this is what I don't get – you say your mother didn't love you because she wasn't loved, right? So if you weren't loved – how can you say you love me?

Zawe   I don't know. I think maybe it's a miracle.

Imogen   A miracle?

Zawe   Like I was meant to meet you. So I could understand what love is.

Imogen   Woah – wait a second: where are we going with this miracle shit? Meant to meet me?

Zawe   That's what I feel.

Imogen   Meant by who, though?

Zawe   I don't know. By whatever means us to be together.

Imogen   Ok, listen – reality check – because we need to fucking address this, here and now: YOU are NOT a lesbian.

Zawe   What?! How can you say that? How the FUCK can you say that!

Imogen   Come on –

Zawe   What the fuck have we been doing this last month?! What was all that if I'm not a lesbian?!

Imogen   Letting me eat you out doesn't make you a lesbian, Zawe.

Zawe   I'm going to – do that to you, I told you! I'm just waiting till after I get my molars out!

Imogen   Come on –

Zawe   It's nothing personal, I just don't want to get an infection.

Imogen   Zawe – come on – I love you –

Zawe   And I love you –

Imogen   But seriously: there's no future in this.

Zawe   No – don't say that: there is a future. This is the future.

Imogen   This is?

Zawe   Not now, this is the past; but this bit coming up – is the future: See? There. That's the future. Just not anymore. Now it's this bit – see? The future. And we're still together.

Pause.

Imogen   Zawe – I'm so grateful to you for everything you've done for me. You've supported me and cared for me and that's how I know: that's how I know that you were loved. But you're looking for something, and this isn't it.

Pause.

Zawe   Fine. Just go then.

Imogen   Zawe.

Zawe   That's what you want isn't it? To leave. You leave, you're left; over and over and over until it all stops.

Pause.

And maybe that's ok. Maybe *that's* what's meant to be.

Pause.

Imogen   Look, we're both tired. Let's just – get some sleep and then –

Zawe   No. Just go.

Imogen   Go where?

Zawe   Go home.

Imogen   What, now? It's the middle of the night . . .

Zawe   So?

Imogen   So I know you're not good with nights.

Pause.

Imogen   This doesn't have to be a big scene. Let's just wait until the morning –

Zawe   No.

Unusually forceful.

Just go. I'll be fine.

Imogen   Will you?

Pause.

Imogen   Will you call me tomorrow then?

Zawe *shrugs.* **Imogen** *opens the door.*

Imogen   Zawe –

Zawe   I want those shoes back.

Imogen   The shoes you bought me? They won't even fit you . . .

Zawe   I'll take them back to the shop.

Imogen   Fine. But I don't have the receipt.

She pronounces the 'p'.

Zawe   It's all right: I kept it.

Imogen *leaves. The sound of the desert wind.*

Zawe *walks to the oasis and looks at herself, reflected there.*

Zawe (*sings*)
   You are a princess.
   You are the best.
   Everything you do is amazing . . .

And then she falls silent.

(The next YouTube clip plays. It's called 'Strange Sounds All Over the World, Jerusalem, Houston, New York, Belgium, etc.' and at the time of writing can be found here: www.youtube.com/watch?v=i7AXMmUrP2E

The section used runs from 0.10 to 1.00. The clip is real footage shot in New York by a young man hearing a loud, strange noise in the sky. He offers a profane commentary:

'I'm hearin' uh – I'm lookin' out my window right now – hearin' some strange fuckin' sounds out there. I've no idea what the hell they are – it's . . . rattling the earth around here, we're in Long Island, January 18th [2012] – and it's fuckin' loud. You hear that? You hear that shit?! 'Fuck is that shit? I've no idea, like – it's comin' straight out of the sky. What is that? This is for all you YouTube people – you hear that?'

Note: there are many such clips on YouTube covering the spate of noises heard in 2011/2012 and you may find more appropriate clips for your production, if you choose to include them at all.)

Lights up.

Barney *brings a cup of coffee to* **Olly**.

Olly   Aw, thanks . . .

Barney   It's good to have you back, man.

Olly   It's good to be back. Bit of normality.

Barney   Just for the weekend is it?

Olly   Back on Tuesday.

Barney   So – tell me all about it: How's it going? How's George?

Pause.

Olly   He's fine.

Barney   Is he a nice guy?

Olly   Yeah, he's a nice guy. But he's not a *normal* guy, you know what I mean?

Barney   Yeah, well – he doesn't have a normal life.

Olly   No, he doesn't. He's got Barack Obama's personal number. Like – that's one of his mates: the president of the United States.

Barney   Wow.

Olly   Yeah but it's just so different from what I'm used to. I mean, you might as well be mates with fucking – Hansel and Gretel, you know what I mean? It's just completely unreal.

Barney   Yeah but you're in there, mate. You've been selected by the big grabber thing of life.

The golden doors have opened.

Olly   I've got the feeling they might shut in my face.

Pause.

I've been invited round to Russell Crowe's house next weekend.

Barney   Wow. Why?

Olly   It's just what they do. They just invite you round because – you're new.

Barney   That's nice, I suppose. They're trying to make you welcome.

Olly   I guess. But it's not like kicking back with a few mates, you know? You're always on edge.

Barney *nods.* **Olly** *gets up.*

Olly   Just going for a piss.

He leaves. **Barney** *looks at* **Olly**'s *cup of coffee. A villainous look comes over him: checking the coast is clear first, he picks up the cup and lets a sliver of spit fall into the coffee. He puts the cup back.*

Olly *comes back*.

Barney   So tell me – give me all the gossip.

Olly   You know what? Could we just not talk about it for a while?

Barney   Ok –

Olly   I'll tell you all about it tomorrow. I'll take you out for a Chinese. I'll pay.

He sips from the coffee. **Barney** *watches*.

Barney   Brilliant.

Olly   I just want to be normal for a while.

Barney   Well – this is the place to do it.

Pause.

Olly   Honestly? I've been feeling quite weird recently.

Barney   Weird out?

Olly   Yeah. Bit paranoid.

Barney   About what?

Pause.

Olly   It's stupid.

Barney   What?

Pause.

Olly   You remember that picture?

Barney   What picture?

Olly   Remember: that picture of the arsehole?

Barney   Oh yeah.

Olly   It's been . . . preying on my mind.

Barney   Why?

Pause.

Olly   You know how we were wondering whose arsehole it was?

Barney   Yeah –

Olly   Well, I know this is stupid – but I was thinking – what if it's not some guy's, or his wife's –

Pause.

What if it's mine?

Barney   Yours?

Olly   What if it's a picture of my arsehole? What if there's a picture of my arsehole out there? What if when this movie comes out, someone puts it online and says, 'Look everybody: Olly Rix's arsehole!'

Pause.

Barney   But – how would they have got a picture of your arsehole?

Olly   I don't know. I know it doesn't make sense. I just had the thought. And now I can't seem to get it out of my head.

Barney   Yeah but it's completely ridiculous.

Olly   I know.

Barney   It's probably just anxiety. It's like when you think you've left the oven on.

Olly   Yeah. Except sometimes you *have* left the oven on.

Barney   Yeah well that's where the analogy breaks down.

Pause.

Look – you're under a lot of pressure. The mind does funny things.

Olly *nods, looking stressed.*

Olly   You're my friend, right?

Barney   Of course I am.

Olly   You're my best friend.

Barney   Yeah . . .

Pause.

Olly   Would you . . . look?

Pause.

Barney   At?

Pause.

At the picture?

Olly   Yeah.

Pause.

Barney   And then . . .

Pause.

Oh no . . .

Olly   It'd just ease my mind. If I knew, for sure.

Barney   No! Jesus – I'm not looking at your – !

Olly   Noel, please: I've got no one else to ask.

Barney   Ask Clooney! Ask Russell-fucking-Crowe!

Olly   I can't ask them to look at my arsehole!

Barney   So why are you asking me?! Why don't you do it?!

Olly   I've tried!

Barney   What and you couldn't see it?

Olly   Not properly. I couldn't be in the position I had to be in and hold the picture up for comparison.

Barney   Take a photo of it then!

Olly   Do you know how difficult it is to take a photo, one-handed, of your own arsehole?

Barney   No, I have to say I don't – !

Olly   I'm not asking you to rim it! Just take a look – !

Barney   Absolutely and utterly not.

Olly   It's just an arsehole –

Barney   No. No – it's not just an arsehole, it's a man's arsehole and it's your arsehole and those are pretty much the two things that – you know; it's the line I won't cross.

Pause.

Anyway – how would I know?

Olly   You might.

Barney   How?

Olly   There might be some distinguishing marks.

Barney   Like what? Have you got a mole or something? A birthmark?

Olly   No, I don't think so.

Pause.

But what about the spokes?

Barney   The *spokes*?! What the fuck are the *spokes*?!

Olly   The lines that come out from round it –

Barney   Jesus – what: count them?! Like the rings on a tree?!

Olly   No but they must be quite unique to each person. Like fingerprints.

Barney   Oh right – the spokes of your anus are like fingerprints?

Olly   They must be, mustn't they?

Imogen *enters with an envelope.*

Barney   I really don't know; I'm pretty sure they don't dust for them at crime scenes!

Imogen *gives* **Barney** *the envelope.*

Barney   What's this?

Imogen   I don't know. I was just told to give it to you.

Olly   We're not in a café, are we?

She exits. **Barney** *opens the envelope.*

Olly   That's strange: I'm sure that was the waitress from the café . . .

Barney *is staring at the letter.*

Olly   What is it? It's not another arsehole, is it?! Cos that'd be –

Barney   It says I've died.

Pause.

Olly   What?

Barney   It says I've died.

Olly   You've died?

Barney   Supposedly.

Olly   Of what?

Barney   It doesn't even say.

Pause.

This can't be right. Is this right?

Pause.

So what? That's it? We don't get to finish this story?

Pause.

Unbelievable! That's it! Done!

Olly   Shit. I can't believe that.

Barney   Can you believe that?!

Olly   No.

Pause.

Barney   Fine, I mean, if that's what's been decided! I just don't think it's fair on other people.

They're not going to see how it turns out!

Olly   That's shitty.

Barney   It is, isn't it?

He's getting tearful. **Olly** *gets up and goes to him.*

Barney   We were going for a Chinese.

He dissolves into tears. **Olly** *holds him in his arms until he's calmed.*

They separate and **Olly** *offers his hand.*

Olly   Well – it's been a pleasure.

Barney *takes it.*

Barney   It has. It really has.

Olly   We nearly got there.

Barney   Yeah. Nearly. That's me though isn't it? Nearly. Nearly got married. Nearly had kids.

Nearly got that part in *Call the Midwife*. Nearly, nearly, nearly.

He goes to leave but stops.

Hey, Olly?

Olly   Yeah?

Barney   I wish I could have been happier for you, mate. I just wasn't written that way.

As he exits, **Brian** *enters. They shake hands in passing.* **Brian** *sits down and addresses the audience.*

Brian   I've used the bus all my life; double-decker buses, now – not your single-deck jobbies. There's no nuance to those. There's an order to a double-decker bus.

You start your life downstairs, at the front of the bus, with your ma. You're either in a pram or in her arms; either way she wants you close to the doors. When you outgrow the pram, she moves you to the middle, but still downstairs. Eventually, you start making trips without her, and as you get bolder and more confident, you start moving to the back; but you're still downstairs.

Round about ten, twelve, you've got friends and you want to be part of the adult world; so you make the big move – upstairs. But you sit right at the front; so you can pretend you're driving. The more friends you make, the further back you move; you pretty much colonise the middle top deck until you hit puberty and then it's back of the bus, baby – all the fucking way! Drink, drugs, sex, music – it all happens at the back of the bus. And you stay there well into your twenties.

Then you turn thirty. You're properly an adult now. You don't want to sit with the assholes at the back but you're still young at heart, so you move back to the middle of the top deck. Now and then, you get together with your mates and you sit at the back just to show you've still got it; but left to your own devices, you start the incremental move forwards.

Past forty, something strange happens; just now and then, you sit in the very front seats; only now you're fucking glad you're not a bus driver.

Past sixty, the knees are starting to go, the stairs are unappealing and the people on the top deck are starting to scare and annoy and confuse you. Who needs it? So you move downstairs again, but at the back, where you can nurture that last scrap of defiance. But sure as shit stinks, you'll start that slow move forwards, just to get a little closer to those rearwards doors.

And then – then you're properly old. Christ, you're doing well to be getting the bus at all; why make life more difficult for yourself? What's the point?

And there you come to rest: downstairs, at the front, shortest possible distance from the exit; in the seats your long-dead ma made you give up for the old folks, all those years ago.

(The last YouTube clip plays, against music. It's called 'man attacked by angry bison' and at the time of writing it can be found here: www. youtube.com/watch?v=riCBGG_RiU0

The clip shows a man at a rodeo being caught on the horns of a bison and flung through the air. It plays out once in real time, then again in slow motion.)

Epilogue

In the darkness, a vast, frightening sound from the sky. Then silence.

Then again – the noise. A horn? So loud the building shakes.

One by one, the cast – even **Sophie** *– drift back onto the stage, wondering what the noise is. They murmur amongst themselves.*

Again the noise – terrifyingly loud. The cast look up towards the sky . . . Once more, we hear the digitised voice

Voice   What did you expect of life?

Why did you expect it? Who told you what to expect?

What was expected of you? Who expected this of you? What did you expect of yourself? What do you expect of others? Of your friends, of your partners, of your children? Have they met those expectations? Was anything unexpected? Did you respond the way you expected?

Why do we expect? Why do we expect? Why do we expect?

Whatever it is they see up there, they each take in their own way.

Fade to black.

Unreachable

This play is dedicated to the memory of our colleague Chahine Yavroyan, who lit virtually all my productions over the last fifteen years.

Most of us will forever be chasing the light. Chahine carried it with him. There are not words enough to thank you, my friend.

Unreachable was first performed at the Royal Court Theatre, London, on 2 July 2016 with the following cast and creative team:

Eva	Genevieve Barr
Anastasia	Amanda Drew
Natasha	Tamara Lawrance
Ivan	Jonjo O'Neill
Carl	Richard Pyros
Maxim	Matt Smith

Director Anthony Neilson
Set Designer Chloe Lamford
Costume Designer Fly Davis
Lighting Designer Chahine Yavroyan
Composer/Sound Designer Nick Powell
Video Designer Zsolt Balogh

Characters

Natasha
Maxim
Anastasia
Carl
Eva
Ivan

Notes

Aside from the Prologue, the entire play is set in and around the hotel where the film crew are staying. The design for most of the play was deliberately crude and based on the paraphernalia of film production: spaces were delineated largely by configurations of large reflector boards and flight cases. Much of the lighting was provided by standalone lamps.

This minimalist approach was intended to create as stark a contrast as possible with the play's final two minutes, where most of the budget was spent. I understand that some companies may not have the resources to achieve the same finale, so I have included an alternative ending after the main text. This ending was one I always considered viable: its effect is different – less visceral – but perhaps more poignant in its way. Companies producing the play are at liberty to use whichever version they prefer.

Prologue

Natasha *enters onto the stage and waits. She hears a voice over the speakers.*

Maxim (*O/S*)   Natasha, is it?

She nods.

Have you been told what this film is about?

She shakes her head.

It's set in the near future, after a virus has wiped out most of the population. There's no government; there's just factions fighting amongst themselves for what's left. The film is about how you and your baby survive in this world. Did you learn the speech?

She nods.

It was written specifically for this test. It's not part of the screenplay. At one point, your baby's father abandons you and you and your baby are kidnapped by a militia and taken to a compound. The speech describes what happens next. Do you have any questions?

Natasha   What's her name?

Pause.

Maxim (*O/S*)   There's no name specified. Are you happy to begin?

She nods.

All right: *Child of Ashes*, camera test: action.

She transforms. (Originally performed in a Southern American accent.)

Natasha   I could hear them, through the walls: their heavy boots thumping.

That was the worst thing: When you heard those boots and you knew they were coming for someone but you didn't know who; and how you was almost happy when it wasn't you.

Some would scream all the way through and some were quiet from the get-go but it always ended the same: just this 'pop!' sound; and sometimes 'pop' again, if they'd missed the first time. It was bad enough when it was a girl by herself but when she had a child with her – that was a whole other thing. There's a world of difference between how a person screams for themselves and how they scream for their children.

And then one day, my luck ran out; and those boots stopped at our door.

I didn't have much time: from hearing those boots stop to the key turning in the lock and the chain dropping and the door opening; as soon as he sees me, he'll know what I'm doing and he'll try to stop it. So I don't have the time to be gentle, my darling: I have to send you on your way, fast as I can and hope you'll forgive me when I get there; which won't be long, my angel; won't be long, my darling. Momma's going to be there soon. Momma will be right behind you.

And there's that key grinding in the lock; and little Jacob's looking up at me like there's nothing wrong; and there's that lock snapping and the chain pulling through; and he's so calm and trusting because why wouldn't he be? Momma's here, so he's safe. Momma always keeps him safe.

And there's that door scraping open – and I lift him up and now he's blinking like he's crying – and then I realise: those are *my* tears, splashing down on him, and that's *my* spit rolling from my lips onto his tiny hand and I pray to God to give me the strength to send my baby up to him –

– and the door is open now and there's a skinny one grinning, like his mouth is full of tombstones – and I pull my baby close to my breast and I close my arm 'round his head so it covers his eyes and then suddenly, God is in me and he takes my arm like I'm a doll and just *twists* it – like that – and it's like I'm not even there; and now I know, I just know, that my baby, my Jacob, he's not there either; and what I'm holding in my arms is just a doll now too, like me; and the skinny one comes at me and I hear laughing – wild, crazy laughing – and it's me – it's me laughing; and I can't stop, even with my head ringing from the first punch and my lip swelling from the second and it takes another two or three more until whatever you need to laugh gets so broken that I can't anymore.

When I come round, I'm lying in the big room and I can hear them devils arguing. And then one of them throws a punch at the skinny one and their boots all shuffle, like they do when men fight. And then one of the others bends down to me and all I can think is do it; do it now and let me get on my way. Momma's going to be there soon, my angel. Momma will be right behind you.

Then I feel something like water on my lips and this devil is propping me up; and it turns out that it's water and he's pouring it from a bottle into my mouth and he's asking if I'm all right and why did I do it and do what? I said and then I realise – I don't *know* this voice . . .

– and now my heart's beating like a drum and the more he tries to calm me down and tell me how I'm safe now, the harder it's beating; and then he gets me on my feet and he walks me outside, into the light. And when my eyes get adjusted, I see the treetops all around and that we're in the woods – we're in a clearing in the woods – and there, in front of me, is four, maybe five girls, all thin like me, with eyes like hollows – and now I can feel this scream coming up in me because one of them – one of the girls – she's holding a baby – she's – and there's another one with a boy stood beside her, maybe six years old – and I can feel that scream burning in my chest and choking at my neck – and they're staring at me with those hollow eyes – and now there's a man with a rifle and he's staring at me too and he's asking if it's true, did I really – ?

And they're all whispering – and the baby – did she really, is it true? – and I'm shaking and the trees – is it true, what you did, did she really? – and that scream's at my mouth – did you really *kill* – did you really *kill your* – ? and now I hear the scream like it's someone else doing it, someone else looking up at the sky and screaming –

She drops to her knees and screams:

WHY?! MERCIFUL GOD IN HEAVEN, WHY?! WHY WOULD YOU DO THIS TO ME? WHAT HAVE I DONE THAT YOU WOULD PUNISH ME LIKE THIS?! HAVEN'T I SUFFERED ENOUGH FOR YOU? OH JESUS GOD TELL ME PLEASE – WHAT DID I DO SO *WRONG*?!

Pause. The emotion slips off her like a coat. She looks up.

Hello?

Pause. **Maxim**'s *voice falters slightly, as if moved.*

Maxim (*O/S*)   Thank you, Natasha; that'll be all.

She stands, nodding.

Please leave the pages with reception.

She nods and starts to go; then stops.

Natasha   Sorry . . .

Pause.

Maxim (*O/S*)   Yes?

Natasha   Where can I take a piss?

Pause.

Maxim (*O/S*)   There's toilets on the next floor down.

She nods and leaves.

In the darkness, the sound of an orchestra tuning up . . .

Act One

Scene One

A hotel suite, somewhere in Eastern Europe.

Maxim, *the Director, enters – wearing a pair of headphones. He raises his hands, ready to conduct.*

Just as the orchestra seems ready to begin, the sound cuts out. We watch he conducting, silently, to whatever music he hears: only now, it is the light that ebbs and flows, in and out of darkness, at his command.

Unseen by him, **Anastasia**, *the producer, appears in the doorway and watches him for a while.*

Anastasia   Max . . .

He cannot hear her. She walks to him and taps his shoulder:

Maxim!

He jumps, startled. He takes his headphones off.

Maxim   Must you creep around like that, Anni? You know I've a murmur in my heart!

Anastasia   No. You *thought* you had a murmur in your heart; but the doctor corrected you.

Maxim   Doctors! What do they know? Who are they to tell me the condition of my heart?

Anastasia   Why have we stopped filming yet again?

Maxim   We haven't.

Anastasia   Really? Then why is the whole crew lounging around, at great expense, in the hotel bar?

Maxim   We haven't stopped *filming*, Anastasia, because *filming* would require *film*; and in two weeks not one *inch* of film has passed that lens.

Anastasia   Semantics, Maxim? Really?

Maxim   No – not semantics. I am speaking quite literally. I am saying that we must *start* filming.

She stares at him, trying to grasp this.

Child of Ashes must be shot on film.

Anastasia   Don't be ridiculous . . .

Maxim   I'm not being ridiculous. This is a film about real, raw humanity: it can't be reduced to ones and zeroes inside some computer. It was absurd to ever think otherwise.

Anastasia   But you *did* think otherwise.

Maxim   Yes. And that was a mistake.

Anastasia   Well, you must live with your mistakes, Maxim, like the rest of us. Now come on – get back to work: we're already days behind.

She claps, as if summoning a dog but he holds his ground.

Maxim   No.

Anastasia   No?

Maxim   I can't, Anni: you know how long I've waited to make this film: I can't compromise it now.

Anastasia   In what way is it compromised? The rushes look beautiful.

Maxim   It's not about pretty pictures! Any moron can make pretty pictures. It's about expressing something! It's about communicating a *feeling*!

Pause.

Anastasia   What is this about, Max? All this stopping and starting? It's not like you.

Pause. She tries a softer approach.

It's all right to be scared, you know. You just won the Palme d'Or. That's a lot to live up to.

Maxim   The Palme d'Or! It's meaningless! Why should I be grateful for the acclaim of corpses?!

Anastasia   Because we wouldn't be here without it: do you think we could have raised the thirty million otherwise?

Pause.

But it's a lot of pressure. Before now, our biggest set-piece was a fight between three living statues in a kebab shop. And now we've got horses and gun-fights and explosions . . . I'm *terrified* and I'm just the producer. But you're not alone, Max –

He sighs heavily, agitated.

I'm here for you, like I always am –

He squirms.

And so is Carl and all the cast and crew; more than a hundred talented, professional people who are all here because they believe in this film; because they believe in *you*, Max –

Maxim   Anni – I don't need a motivational speech from you; I need you to go to the investors and get me what I want!

Anastasia   Maxim – in case you don't remember – I just talked them into paying for another three weeks here because you were suddenly adamant we could only shoot at dusk and dawn. That wasn't a small thing, Max – they were like lobsters in a pot – and now you want me to tell them that everything we've shot is useless?

Maxim   It's a good job we've shot so little then, isn't it?

He smiles boyishly. She betrays slight amusement before shutting him down:

Anastasia   Don't bother, Maxim: you've never known what charms me about you and it's repulsive when you get it wrong.

Maxim   I don't have to charm you, Anastasia. I'm the director: you work for me.

Anastasia   Oh go to hell! I'm telling you that Jesus Christ himself could go in there and they wouldn't give him four rusty nails! So get the notion out of your head: we're not moving to film and that's final!

Carl   Anastasia – !

Both **Maxim** *and* **Anastasia** *jump, startled by* **Carl**'s *dramatic entrance.* **Carl** *is an anxious soul; constantly applying insect repellent.*

Carl   There you are. Have you heard what he's saying?! That we should move to film?!

Maxim   If it's *beyond* you, Carl –

Carl   It's not *beyond* me – !

Maxim   If you lack the necessary skills –

Carl   How dare you! I was shooting film before your mother taught you to crap in water!

Maxim *gives him a look.* **Carl** *realises what he's said.*

Maxim   Are you trying to be deliberately hurtful, Carl?

Carl   No you don't: don't try to make me the villain here: it's a figure of speech, that's all. Someone must have taught you to – was it nuns? Who runs an orphanage? Is it always just nuns?

Maxim *shoots a small smile at* **Anastasia**.

Carl   That's not the issue! I resisted shooting this on digital if you recall: it was you that said this new camera was revolutionary. So I agreed; and now everything – the lights, the lenses, the rigs I've brought – *everything* – has been chosen on the basis that we would *not* be shooting on film!

Maxim   And are you happy with the results?

Carl   Am I happy? Is a man happy to eat mutton rather than steak? He might prefer steak but steak is not on the menu. So he only asks; is the mutton good? And yes – the mutton is good. He is happy, by and large, with the quality of the mutton! And that, Maxim, is what makes him a man!

Maxim   Because he learns to like mutton? That makes him a dog, not a man. Are we dogs, Carl? Should we sniff each other's backsides when we meet?!

*He chases **Carl** around trying to sniff at his backside.*

Maxim   Come, Carl: Let me know you! Let me sniff at your arse for a whiff of your shit!

Carl   Get away from me!

Maxim   We are dogs, aren't we? This is how dogs know each other: by the stories in their shit!

Carl   Anastasia – get this madman from my arse!

Anastasia   Maxim – stop being childish!

Maxim *stops.*

Carl   You know what this is really about, don't you? It's this damned – mythical light of his!

Anastasia   What – ?

Maxim   It's not mythical –

Carl   Well, you can't explain it; and nobody's *seen* it – !

Maxim   Yet.

Anastasia   I thought you were happy with the light?

Carl   No – he's not! We've had every colour of sky on the spectrum; every kind of weather! We've had strong light, pale light – every conceivable kind of light except this light he's looking for – !

Anastasia   So why are we still only filming for four hours a day – ?

Maxim   That's still our best chance; when the sun is low. We've come close. We've nearly had it – it's just a matter of time –

Anastasia   Time? Maxim – do you know how much it costs for every minute we're here? Time isn't time here –

Maxim   Time is money – yes, I know. But even if we'd had the right light, we wouldn't have caught it – not with the camera we're using –

Carl   That's nonsense: the camera records what it sees –

Maxim   But it's about more than just *seeing*, Carl – !

Carl   So you keep saying! But bricks make only houses: it's people that make homes.

Maxim   *What?*

Anastasia   Carl – why don't you go back downstairs?

Carl   And say what? What should I say to my crew when they ask me? Some of them are young and know nothing of film. I will have to let them go, Anastasia. This is their livelihood and I will have to *fire* them!

Anastasia   Nobody will be fired. This is all academic: we'd have to shut down production for weeks; maybe months. It would cost literally millions. They won't give us money they've no chance of getting back.

Maxim   But they will get it back! I just won the Palme d'Or, for God's sake! Doesn't that mean anything anymore?

Anastasia   Not enough.

Maxim   Then LIE! That's what you do, isn't it? You tell greedy rich people you'll make them richer and then you take their money and spunk it on something that actually benefits the world! Isn't that what you do?! Or else what's the point of you?! What's the earthly use of you to *anyone*?!

Carl   Hey . . .

Maxim   Hey *what*?

Carl   You don't need to harangue her: she's just saying how it is.

Maxim   What does that even mean? 'She's just saying how it is'? That doesn't mean anything! Why are you standing there saying meaningless things and words like 'harangue'?!

Pause.

You should know something, Carl: I wanted the Brute for this film.

Anastasia   God in Heaven help us . . .

Carl *starts, reflexively, to scratch at himself.*

Maxim   I did. There's a part I wrote specifically for him. But I knew you wouldn't work with him –

Carl   Do you blame me?! He really *is* a madman!

Maxim   Nonetheless – even though he was perfect for the part, I gave him up. I chose you over the Brute. And this is the thanks I get: you're siding with the producer against me!

Carl   It's just Anni . . .

Maxim   It doesn't matter: if Da Vinci had had a producer, the Mona Lisa would have been painted on plywood! The medium is important, Carl. If anyone should understand that, it's you.

Carl   I understand it. I just don't think it will make the difference you think it will –

Maxim   I'm not asking you to agree with me, Carl: I'm asking you to support me!

Carl   How *can* I support you, Max? Can a husband support his syphilitic wife when every night he is back to the brothel?!

Pause. **Maxim** *looks to* **Anastasia**, *puzzled.*

Maxim   Do *you* know what he's saying?

Anastasia   Perhaps he feels . . . responsible?

Maxim   Responsible?

Carl   Well, clearly I am the problem here. My job description is lighting cameraman, after all: if you're not happy with the light, then that is down to me.

Maxim   You can't control the movements of the Sun, Carl . . .

Carl   No – but I can have some say in how it strikes the actors; and that seems to me the real issue here, however you dress it –

Maxim   It's not –

Carl   I've seen you watching the dailies, Max: you have the look of a man with no memory, repeatedly discovering the same turd in his wash-bowl.

Maxim *sighs.*

Carl   So if you are blaming the medium as a kindness to me, I appreciate it; but I would rather stand down now –

Maxim   Carl . . .

Carl   – than see everything we've done so far go to ruin!

Maxim   Oh stop playing the martyr! Do you really think I'd put up with your constant twaddle if I thought you weren't doing your usual exemplary job?

Pause.

But this light – it's not some generic sunset like they put on birthday cards to remind old people to die. This light is like a rare, exotic bird: it might only appear for a moment. And if we want to catch it, we must have the right net for the job.

Pause.

Carl   Sorry, I've lost track: am I the net in this analogy?

Maxim   No! The film is the net! Celluloid is the net we need to catch the bird.

Carl   And the bird is the light: Got you.

Maxim   Look, I know what I'm asking, I do. And I wish I could compromise; but it's just not in my nature. Either we shoot *Child of Ashes* on film . . .

Pause.

. . . or we don't shoot at all.

Pause.

Carl   You'd walk away?

Maxim   If I have to: yes.

Carl   You can't. They'd sue you. The financiers would sue you for every penny you have!

Maxim   Let them: I won't care what happens next. This is my line in the sand. This is the hill I will die on.

Pause.

Anastasia   You know, Max – I'm sorry you never knew your mother. But I knew mine. She worked like a mule and then she died. No obituaries; no retrospectives. There were precisely two people at her funeral: the local priest and some old woman she'd given a cat to, years before. Her one remaining daughter wasn't there. She was on set; with you.

She starts to leave.

Carl   Anni – wait: where are you going?

Anastasia   To pack my case. I suggest you do the same.

She exits.

Carl   Did you hear that?!

Maxim *remains sitting, smiling slightly.*

Carl   Why are you so calm about this?! This is the end of everything!

Maxim   Don't be fooled: she loves a fight.

Carl   Yes; but not one she can't win – !

Maxim   *Especially* the ones she can't win.

Pause.

Carl   All right, Max, I get it: you've known her longer than I have. But this is our third film together and I know how hard she's worked to get this film off the ground; how completely *devoted* to you she is – !

Pause.

I just think she deserves better. That's all.

Maxim   How do you know what she *deserves*? What does anyone *deserve*?

Carl *sighs, resigned.*

Natasha   Maxim?

Carl and **Maxim** *jump, startled.*

Natasha   You wanted to see me?

Maxim   Yes, Natasha, please – come in. Carl was just leaving.

Carl   Yes, that's right: I've got people to fire.

He exits, nodding to her as he leaves.

Natasha.

She watches him go.

Maxim   Please – sit down . . .

He pulls in a chair for her and she sits down. From above, several pairs of slightly soiled underpants fall to the ground.

Maxim   Excuse the mess in here, I'm just –

He hurriedly collects up the underpants.

Can I offer you something? Tea, perhaps?

Natasha   Have you anything stronger?

Maxim   Coffee?

Natasha   Have you any vodka?

Maxim   Oh, you mean – *stronger* stronger? Um – yes, of course – vodka –

He looks at his watch.

Natasha   Unless we're still filming later? I was told we wouldn't be.

Maxim   No, that's right, we're not. Just a technical hitch; nothing to worry about.

Natasha   What's happened?

Maxim   Oh it's just . . . Carl – you know: he's such a perfectionist, bless him. He's noticed some kind of – minuscule flaw in the lens. I told him nobody would notice but no, he's adamant: won't shoot another frame until we have a new one. And God knows how long that'll take. Could take days. What will you have with your vodka? Tonic? Soda water?

Natasha   We might not film for days?

Maxim   Yes, well – it's not just any old lens. It'll have to be flown in; from – Japan.

Natasha   Japan?

Maxim   It's very thin glass, you see. Very delicate. Only the Japanese have the right – sand. To make them with. Japanese sand. Have you been to Japan?

Natasha   No.

Maxim   The beaches are known for their – very fine sand.
Something to do with Hiroshima, I think. Here we are.
Vodka with lime. Try it with lime –

Natasha   Is that why he's firing people? Because of this lens
thing?

Maxim   Hmm?

Natasha   Carl: he just said he had to fire people.

Maxim   Oh – yes. This is the problem with perfectionism,
you see; it's admirable in itself but it can so easily tip over
into tyranny. Cheers.

She takes it, without thanks.

Natasha   Why did you want to see me?

Maxim   Why? Well – I just – wanted to tell you – how
pleased I am with what you're doing. I think it's –
remarkable. *You* – are –

She nods.

Not that I'm surprised: As soon as I saw your audition tape –
I just called the casting director there and then and I said,
'Anoushka? Cancel the auditions: burn all the other tapes:
I've found her.' And this might sound odd – but even after
I'd cast you, I must have watched that tape a hundred times.
I mean, I wrote that speech; but – when you played it – I
could suddenly see the whole emotional map of her, far
beyond the fragment I'd imagined. And whenever I lost my
way – I'd just watch that tape again: and every time, I'd find
some new turn or contour or secret path.

She shifts in her seat.

I'm making you uncomfortable . . .

Natasha   No, it's these leggings; they go right up my crack.

Pause.

Maxim   Anyway – I think you're – immaculate – in the part; and I think it's going to do great things for your career. So it's worth sticking with.

Natasha   How do you mean?

Maxim   Well, you know – if there was a short hiatus of a few days – or longer – I'm just saying that I hope you wouldn't – you know – *leave* or anything.

Natasha   The hotel?

Maxim   No: the film: *Child of Ashes*. And preferably not the hotel either – but mainly the film.

Natasha   How could I leave – ?

Maxim   No, well – that's good to hear –

Natasha   I'm under contract until August.

Pause.

Maxim   Yes, but – that's not the only reason, is it? I mean – it's important to you, isn't it?

Natasha   What?

Maxim   The film – the part – ?

Natasha   Oh. Yeah. It's a good part.

He nods. Pause.

But can I ask you something? You know this baby we're using in the scenes?

Maxim   It's actually three babies; but yes?

Natasha   Three babies?

Maxim   Yes: there are three different babies, all playing Jacob.

Pause.

Natasha   Right, well – anyway – I was just wondering if we always have to use a real one? Like maybe we could use a dummy one if it's not up close.

Pause. He nods.

Maxim   Why would you want that?

Natasha   Cos it keeps pissing itself and then I can't get the smell off me. It shits itself too but that's not so bad. The piss seems to get through to my costume; and even when I've changed, I keep smelling piss for ages after. It's fucking rank.

Pause.

Maxim   Well – I do think it looks better when it's real – but maybe for long shots . . .

Natasha   Or maybe like a computer effect or something?

He nods. Pause.

Maxim   No it's just strange; you always seem to have a good rapport with him. Them: the babies.

Natasha   She's supposed to, isn't she? Or it won't matter when she kills him.

Maxim   No, that's right. It's a testament to your acting, really; I'd just assumed you liked babies generally.

Natasha   What's to like? They cry, they suck tits, they shit themselves. That's about it.

Maxim   You could say the same of some actors I know.

He smiles at his own joke. She remains blank.

No but I'm intrigued: what is it that you're thinking about when you're holding one of those babies? A childhood pet? What are you drawing on?

Natasha   I'm not drawing on anything. She loves her baby. So when I'm being her, I do too.

Pause. She looks at her watch.

I should go. I said I'd meet Sebastian for lunch.

Maxim   Oh. All right.

She gets up. Pause.

Why?

Natasha   Why what?

Maxim   Why are you – going for lunch with Sebastian?

Natasha   He asked me to.

He nods. She starts to leave.

Maxim   Natasha –

She stops.

I think it might help if – outside of filming – you and Sebastian maintained a little – distance.

Natasha   How would that help?

Maxim   You know: with your characters . . .

Natasha   But we're meant to be in love . . .

Maxim   Well – not love exactly –

Natasha   But he's the father of my baby –

Maxim   Yes but he abandons you, remember? To save his own skin.

Natasha   But I don't know that yet . . .

Maxim   No but look – between us – Sebastian might be a bigger name than you for the moment, but he's not an artist. One look at those imbecilic clown shoes he wears should tell you that. He's more a clothes horse than an actor. And I just worry that his – lack of nuance – could make his ultimate betrayal of you seem like a cheap plot twist. So maybe we should downplay the whole 'love' angle, don't you think?

She shrugs.

Natasha   You're the director. But I should still go to lunch with him. People get pissed off when you don't turn up.

Maxim   Of course, just – stay at arm's length.

She nods.

Natasha   It's lucky we spoke. I was thinking of fucking him.

He blurts out a laugh which has little to do with humour. But she is quite serious.

He staggers a little and sits. She just watches him.

Maxim   It's all right: just a murmur of the heart . . .

Scene Two

As a general rule for scene changes, there is no blackout: it is represented instead by a noise. Scenery and costume is changed in plain sight. The actors leave or take their positions in full view. **Maxim** *takes whatever opportunity he has to look up at the sky through his viewfinder.*

When the noise stops, the scene begins.

Anastasia's *room.* **Anastasia** *is packing a case, energetic with anger.*

Carl *stands in the doorway, watching her.*

Carl   You're really leaving?

She jumps. Then goes back to packing.

You don't think it'll blow over; like that thing with the monkeys?

Anastasia   No. He means it.

Carl   I can't believe he could just walk away. How long have you been working on this?

Anastasia   Ten years. Since I read the first draft.

Carl   Ten years . . .

Anastasia   Don't underestimate Maxim's capacity for self-destruction.

Carl   But does he have to take us all with him?

Pause.

I told him how selfish he was being. Especially to you.

She zips the case shut.

Anastasia   What did he say?

Carl   He just assumes you'll do as he asks. He doesn't think of the position you're in. Or he does; but just doesn't care. He doesn't care how any of us –

She suddenly kisses him, hard, on the mouth. Pause. Then they separate; stare at each other.

Still – on the upside – that means we can tell him now, doesn't it? About us.

Anastasia   I don't want to talk about Maxim. Come on –

She hitches up her skirt and bends over, waiting.

Carl   Oh – right . . .

He hesitates, nervously. Pause.

Anastasia   Come on, quickly – I'm not asking for finesse. I just need to relax.

With false bravado, he enters her. (The two actors are entirely separate, facing out. **Carl** *humps a flight case, which substitutes for* **Anastasia**.*)*

Anastasia   Oh, ok – that's good –

Carl   Is that good?

Anastasia   That's good. Like that: slow and steady. Slow and steady.

Carl   Slow and steady –

They do it slow and steady.

Anastasia   Oh that's nice. The fog is clearing.

He tries desperately to keep his rhythm.

He's such an egomaniac . . .

Carl   I know. Just forget about him.

On the strokes:

Anastasia   Of course when you say *we* worked on it, it was basically *me* that kept *pushing* him back to it, *working* the screenplay with him; *forcing* it into some kind of *shape*. It was four hundred *pages* when he *showed* it to me –

He tries to stay in the zone.

Carl   It was *long* then – ?

Anastasia   Yes, it was long –

Carl   *How* long – ?

Anastasia   *Really* long – ! *So* long –

Carl   And thick – ?

Anastasia   Really thick – and *long* –

Carl   Thick and *long*. Thick and *long* – !!

Vigorous now –

Anastasia   And way too wordy. The structure was a mess. I mean there were moments of brilliance. But it was un-filmable as it was. It took five years to get it where it is now –

He does his best –

And all that time – even when I was producing his other films – I was out there, hawking it around to anyone who'd listen; so that if the moment ever came – bang! We'd be ready to –

He has slowed to a stop –

Carl . . .?

He fiddles with himself.

Carl   It's all right, I'm just – pulling the focus –

Pause.

Okay – slow and steady –

They start to build momentum again. But then she's off:

Anastasia   It's not just *his* anymore; that's what he doesn't get. I've invested just as much in it as he has. He doesn't have the right to just –

Carl   Anni, please – !

Anastasia   I know. You don't want to hear it.

Carl   I'm happy to hear it, just – it's one or the other –

Anastasia   All right: re-focus; re-focus.

He nods. Pause.

Maybe you should change the lens. Have you got anything wider?

Carl   You're not helping . . .

Anastasia   How about this?

Pause. She's doing something muscular.

Does that help?

Carl   Oooh . . . yes: that does help. How are you doing that?

Anastasia   I learned it from a Hare Krishna.

Momentum building again.

Carl   All right – take three –

Anastasia   Faster now. Let's wrap this up –

Faster, faster, until they reach climax. She bursts into a fit of helpless laughter.

He backs off, insecure. Finally, her laughter subsides.

Carl   I'm still amazed that you laugh when you climax . . .

Anastasia   They just seem to be connected.

Carl   It's just how you're wired, sure. No, it's great, I love it . . .

She takes out her phone and looks at it.

I mean, I guess you could find it disconcerting if you didn't know –

Anastasia   Carl, I'm sorry but I need to make a call; do you mind?

Carl   No, of course. When are you flying back?

Anastasia   Back here?

Carl   No – back home . . .

Anastasia   Oh – no – I'm not going home. I'm going to Milan.

Carl   Milan? Why?

Anastasia   Because I think I know someone who might give us the money.

Carl   The money – ?

Anastasia   So we can shoot on film.

Carl   Anni . . .

Anastasia   I know: he's an arrogant sod and I should leave him to hang. But I'm not going to let him cast me as another one of his 'abandoning women'.

She puts the phone to her ear. Pause.

Anyway – I like a fight.

*She winks at a deflated **Carl**.*

Anastasia (*in Italian*)   Dino, Dino! Anastasia: have you missed me, my love?

Scene Three

Maxim *sits with headphones on, listening to music.*

Anastasia *enters and sits across from him. He takes them off.*

Maxim   Anni – listen to this: there's a chord change on this track. It's close to the feeling of the light I'm after. Listen –

He puts the headphones on her and starts the music again. He contrives to listen through one side of them.

Here – this bit coming up – listen –

Pause.

There – do you hear it? That change? Now imagine that was light, not music – did you feel that?

She takes the headphones off.

Anastasia   It's nice.

Maxim   *Nice?* That's all you can say?

Anastasia   It doesn't matter if I feel it. As long as you do.

Maxim   But I want you to feel it, Anni: I want you to understand; why this is important to me.

Pause.

Anastasia   You know, my father used to paint. Landscapes mostly. It was just a hobby; he'd paint the fields around our house; but I thought they were wonderful. He'd try to get me to draw; give me some paper and pencils and put a bowl of apples in front of me. Deep-green apples from our apple trees. But I couldn't do it. They came out like just – blobs. I could see the fruit, the shape of it – it seemed like it should be easy – but when I put the pencil to paper it just . . .

Pause.

You do what you do, Maxim. And I do what I do.

Pause. She smiles.

And I did it, Maxim. I got the money. *Child of Ashes* will be shot on film.

Beat. He stares at her, almost tearful and then impulsively hugs her, with earnest relief.

Maxim   Anni. Thank you. Thank you.

She strokes his hair.

I know I'm a nuisance. I'm sorry.

She nods: it's ok.

But I'd be lost without you. You know that don't you?

Anastasia   Just make something beautiful.

Maxim   I will.

Anastasia   For both of us.

Maxim   For both of us.

Act Two

Scene One

The lobby of the same hotel, three weeks later.

The sound of thunder. **Carl** *enters, dragging a large suitcase. He sets it down.*

Carl   Well – here we are again.

Pause. He turns. Puzzled, he walks back to the main doors and opens them.

Maxim?!

He exits. Pause. **Carl** *and* **Maxim** *enter, struggling comically with a suitcase that seems ridiculously heavy for its size.*

Maxim   They've not hired any porters in our absence then?

Carl   You'd need King Kong to move this thing! What have you got in here?

Maxim   Everything!

Carl   Everything?

Breathless, they sit on it.

Maxim   Everything I own – is in this case.

Carl   Why?

Maxim   Because it's very likely – that I will die in this hotel – and I would like to have – my things around me – when I do –

Carl   And what is it – you think you will die of – exactly?

Maxim   Right now – the clear favourite – is a massive heart attack.

Pause.

Where's the receptionist? It's like the *Mary Celeste* in here!

Carl   It's off-season: most of the staff are on leave.

Maxim   There's no staff?

Carl   It was cheaper to just take the place over than to have us stay as guests.

Maxim   How do you know all this?

Carl   Well – Anastasia – told me . . .

Maxim   She didn't tell me. Why would she tell you and not me?

Carl *shrugs. Pause.*

Maxim   How am I going to get this thing up to my room if there's no porters?

Carl   At least there won't be any anxiety about the tip. Should I tip? How much should I tip? How often should I tip?

Maxim   That's fine if you don't have asthma –

Carl   Do you have asthma?

Maxim   Of course I do, Carl. Why would I say 'It's fine if you don't have asthma' if I didn't? Do you think I've developed some new-found concern for the general asthmatic community?

Carl   I've just never heard you mention it: how long have you had asthma?

Maxim   It's recent.

More thunder.

Good God, listen to that thunder: what's the forecast?

Carl   It'll dry up but we'll be fighting cloud cover. Of course, that wouldn't be a problem if we were still shooting digital . . .

Maxim   Maybe we should change back?

Carl *looks shocked.* **Maxim** *shoots him a smile.*

Carl   Not even in jest; seriously: Anastasia would spontaneously combust at the merest mention of it.

Maxim   Good riddance.

Carl *stares at him.*

Carl   'Good riddance'? You know, for someone so deprived, you may just be the most self-entitled person I've ever met. Anni just raised another six million for you and all you can do is complain?

Maxim   Carl: these new investors – whoever they are – have made it a condition that they have a 'representative' on set at all times. A *spy*, Carl! Some corporate apparatchik watching over my shoulder every minute and reporting back to his dark masters every night! And she agreed to it, Carl –

Carl   She had no choice –

Maxim   – without even consulting me! She signed away my creative liberty!

Carl   The only thing she's signed away, Max, is your ability to procrastinate with silly notions like strapping cameras to gibbons and chasing this elusive light of yours! Which is no bad thing, if you ask me.

Maxim   God, you're dull, Carl, do you know that? A foggy glass of a man; serving wine you can't taste!

Anastasia   You're here then –

Carl *and* **Maxim** *jump, startled. Anastasia enters with* **Eva**.

Anastasia   Welcome to the *Mary Celeste*!

Maxim   That's what I said . . .

Anastasia *embraces both of them.* **Eva** *watches these interactions closely.*

Maxim   And who is this charming young lady?

Anastasia   Maxim, Carl – this is Eva.

Eva *extends her hand and* **Maxim** *takes it.*

Maxim   Eva. What a melodious name . . .

Anastasia   Eva is here on behalf of our new financiers.

Maxim's *hand droops in hers.*

Eva   I liked your last film.

Maxim   What?

Eva   I like your screenplay too. It's very – different.

Maxim *looks at* **Anastasia**.

Maxim   Why is she speaking like that?

Eva   I'm deaf.

Maxim *stares at her.*

Eva   I was born deaf. But I can lip-read. Apart from that, I'm normal.

Maxim *begins to wheeze and gasp –*

Anastasia   Max . . .

Maxim   Inhaler – !

Carl   Where is it? Where's your inhaler?

Anastasia   Inhaler – ?

Carl   He has asthma –

Anastasia   He doesn't have *asthma* – !?

Carl   It's recent. Max, look at me – Where is your inhaler?

Anastasia   He doesn't have one –

Maxim   I don't have one –

Carl   What?

Maxim   Get me one! Get me an inhaler!

Anastasia *grabs him.*

Anastasia   Oh for God's sake – she doesn't have two heads!
She's deaf, that's all. Now stop being so unforgivably rude!

Eva   I've never had this reaction before . . .

Anastasia   I'm sorry, Eva –

Maxim *takes* **Anastasia** *aside, deliberately turning his back
on* **Eva***.*

Maxim   What is this? Is this some kind of tactic you've
cooked up with your new Shylocks? Do they think I'm going
to be any more amenable to being spied on because it's a
poor little deaf girl doing it? Because I won't be. They could
send a kitten in an iron lung and I'd still treat it with the
contempt it deserves!

Anastasia   Actually, Max, Eva is one of their junior
partners –

Eva   I don't want any special treatment.

Maxim *over-enunciates and shouts:*

Maxim   GOOD! BECAUSE YOU WON'T GET ANY!

Eva   You can just speak normally.

Maxim   WHAT?

Eva   Being loud doesn't help. Because I'm deaf.

Pause. He makes a pronounced placatory gesture.

Maxim   Fine!

She pushes his hands down. He brings them up again.

Eva   You don't need to use your hands –

Maxim   I LIKE USING – ! I like using my hands!

She shrugs.

I don't want you here, do you understand? I don't want it
and I didn't agree to it!

Eva   But you want our money?

Maxim   Yes; but that's not –

Eva   If it was your money and you gave it to me, would you want to know how I was spending it?

Maxim   That's different –

Eva   Why? Because you're an artist?

Pause.

Carl   I like her already . . .

Eva   I'm not here to interfere. As long as you don't waste our money, we won't have a problem.

Maxim   Define 'waste'.

Eva   I'll know it when I see it.

Pause.

Maxim   Just stay out of my way, do you understand? I don't want to *see* you; I don't want to *hear* you – ! Sorry – No, wait: that's not offensive. I'm not sorry. That's what I meant: neither of those things – !

Pause.

Fine! I'll take my own damned case!

He attempts to move his suitcase. Nobody helps. He can hardly move it.

Anastasia   You don't know what room you're in . . .

Maxim   I'll kick a door in! Not like there's anyone here to –

He strains at the case. Finally, he assaults it with a flurry of kicks, falls on his arse and then leaves.

I have asthma!

The others stand in awkward silence.

Eva   He's taller than I thought he'd be.

Anastasia   Don't take it personally. It's just his way of expressing anxiety.

Carl   Yes: loudly and without constraint.

Anastasia *shoots him a look.*

Eva   I'm used to men having tantrums. Shall we meet up later ?

Anastasia   That would be good.

Eva *leaves. Pause.*

Anastasia   Can you try not to openly undermine Maxim? We have to at least look like he has our confidence. And don't forget that she can lip-read –

Carl   Oh for God's sake – !

Anastasia   She doesn't work for us, Carl. We can't forget that.

Pause.

Carl   Am I just wasting my time, Anni?

Anastasia   On what?

Carl   Because it's always about what Maxim wants, what Maxim needs –

Anastasia   That's my job, Carl: I'm the producer.

Carl   And then what? Another film? And another; and another? When does the job of looking after Maxim ever end?

He stomps off. She sighs and then follows.

Scene Two

The hotel, a few days later.

The stage is absent of people. From off:

Anastasia (*O/S*)   Maxim?!

Pause.

Suddenly, **Maxim** *appears, scampers across the stage and then disappears again.*

Carl (*O/S*)   Maxim?!!

Pause. **Anastasia** *enters.*

Anastasia   Maxim?!!

Pause.

I know you're here: I can smell that sickening cologne!

Pause.

Maxim – get back on that set right now, do you hear me?!

Pause. **Carl** *enters.*

Carl   No sign of him?

Anastasia *jumps, startled. She shakes her head.*

Carl   I knew it was too good to be true. We were just about on schedule.

Natasha *enters, wearing her film costume.*

Natasha   What's going on?

Anastasia *and* **Carl** *both jump.*

Anastasia   Natasha – have you seen Maxim?

Natasha   Isn't he filming?

Carl   Not anymore.

Natasha   So where's Sebastian?

Anastasia   Sebastian?

Carl   He's still on set, isn't he?

Natasha   I just got this weird text from him . . .

Anastasia   Saying what?

Natasha   'Maxim is a knob. Can't take anymore.
Sorry – Sebastian.'

Anastasia   Oh God . . .

Natasha *stays staring at her phone.*

Carl   I'll see if he's in his room.

He exits. **Anastasia** *speaks into her walkie-talkie:*

Anastasia   Fyodor, have you got eyes on Sebastian?

The crackle of the walkie-talkie, then:

Fyodor (*V/O*)   Isn't he back with you?

Eva *enters.*

Anastasia   Not sure. Listen: if anyone sees him, don't let
him leave, all right? Keep him there 'til I can speak to him.

Fyodor (*V/O*)   Will do.

Eva   What's going on?

Everyone jumps.

Who's missing?

Natasha   Sebastian.

Eva   Sebastian?!

Anastasia   No – Maxim.

Eva   Maxim *and* Sebastian?

Natasha   Maxim's missing; Sebastian's leaving.

Eva   Leaving?!

Anastasia   We don't know that –

Eva   That can't happen: we can't lose Sebastian.

Anastasia   We won't. It's just a minor blow-up: happens all
the time.

Eva   Why did we stop filming?

Anastasia   I don't know yet. Eva – come downstairs. We'll get a better idea of what's going on. Natasha – if you see Maxim – ?

Natasha *doesn't look up from her phone.*

Natasha   I'll tell him to find you.

Anastasia and **Eva** *leave.* **Natasha** *continues texting. Pause.*

Then, an urgent whisper from somewhere:

Maxim (*O/S*)   Natasha!

Natasha *jumps. She turns, not knowing where it came from.*

Maxim (*O/S*)   Over here – !

She sees **Maxim,** *peering from his hiding space.*

Natasha   Maxim?

Maxim   Don't look at me! Keep staring ahead.

She obeys.

Natasha   Why are you hiding?

Maxim   I don't know, really. A lot of people are very annoyed with me; it seemed like the thing to do.

Natasha   Why are they annoyed?

Maxim   Because they're philistines: all that matters to them is how much film we shoot. They don't care that the light's not right; but what's a film about if it's not about the light? Tell me that!

Natasha   Is Sebastian leaving?

Maxim   Again with Sebastian: Why are you always so concerned with Sebastian?

Natasha   Because we've still got scenes to shoot.

Pause.

Maxim   Don't worry: he's just upset because I asked him if anyone in his family had Down's Syndrome. It was an innocent question: I was just trying to ascertain why he looks slightly like someone with Down's Syndrome.

Natasha   He does: I've noticed that.

Maxim   Exactly: I wasn't denigrating people with Down's Syndrome . . .

Natasha   You were just making an observation.

Maxim   Exactly. But then he tried to portray it as a moral issue and stormed off which made me look bad; whereas I would suggest that the fact he was so insulted clearly illustrates that he's the one with the prejudice, not me. I don't understand the world sometimes.

She nods, sympathetically.

Natasha – Can I ask you a favour? Can I hide in your room for a while. I just need some time to think.

Natasha   Ok.

Maxim   I knew I could rely on you. Is it safe to come out?

Natasha   Yes.

He comes out.

But if it smells in there, it's because I squirt.

Pause.

Maxim   Is that the end of the sentence?

Natasha   Yes.

Pause.

Maxim   Ok.

They exit.

Scene Three

The hotel bar. **Carl** *is talking to* **Eva**. *He is slightly the worse for drink.*

Carl   No, of course: to not know who your parents were; or what happened to them; to only be able to guess at exactly where you came from? It's unimaginable. And it excuses – or at least explains – a great many things. But my point is this: does it excuse everything? I mean, we all face adversity in our lives.

Pause.

Look at you, for example: you were born deaf, through no fault of your own; but you've clearly made something of yourself; and you seem to be a courteous and civilised person. You don't seem to exploit your situation. You don't whine about it. You just get on with things.

Eva   I had to.

Carl   Precisely: you weren't pampered. And that's a good thing, if you –

Anastasia *enters.*

Anastasia   Crisis averted.

Only **Carl** *jumps, spilling his drink.*

Anastasia   Sebastian is still on board. Just.

Eva   Have you found Maxim?

Anastasia   No, not yet. But he'll resurface: he's probably just shell-shocked by the pace we've had him working at.

Eva   It's completely unacceptable. We've lost nearly a day's filming.

Anastasia   Eva – with respect – you didn't help matters on set –

Eva   But the light was fine –

Anastasia   In your opinion –

Eva   You could see everyone. What else does he expect?

Anastasia   I'm just saying: it's best to leave Maxim to me. He has to be managed in a particular way.

Carl   Managed meaning pampered.

He nudges **Eva**.

Anastasia   I'll be in my room if you want me, Carl. Relaxing.

She starts to leave.

Carl   I'll bet I know where he is.

Eva   Maxim?

Carl *nods*.

Eva   Where?

Carl   All I'll say – is that he's very friendly with Natasha; if you get my meaning.

Anastasia   We saw Natasha: she didn't know where he was.

Carl   Fine. But you see things; through the camera. You see – all the tiny gestures and touches and – fleeting expressions that no one else catches. The camera never lies, Anni.

Anastasia   No. But the cameraman is occasionally a cunt.

She leaves.

Eva   I didn't catch that: what did she say?

Carl   I don't know why she protects him all the time. He doesn't appreciate her. Do you know – when we won the Palme d'Or – he didn't even let her speak? I wasn't even invited onto the podium.

Eva   Are they in a relationship?

Carl   No. Why do you say that?

Eva   You're sleeping with her. That's obvious. But she doesn't want him to know.

He stares at her, shocked.

I see things too.

Pause.

Tell me: if Maxim had to be replaced – would you stay on?

Pause.

Carl   How could he be replaced? I mean – that's not possible, is it?

Eva   But if it was? Would you stay on?

Pause.

Carl   Anni wouldn't: that much I'm sure of. Anyway – who could replace him at this point? It would take weeks to get a new director up to speed. We couldn't shut down production again. I mean, unless you had someone who was already . . .

Pause. Something dawns on him.

. . . up to speed . . .

Pause. He looks at her.

Eva   If you think of someone – let me know.

He nods slowly, in conspiracy.

Scene Four

Natasha's *room.*

Natasha   You can't just stay in my room for ever. You're the director.

Maxim   Am I though?

Natasha   Yes.

Maxim   No but am I?

Natasha   Yes. And we can't film without you. And if we don't film, I can't act. And I need to act, Maxim. It's the only thing I'm good at.

Maxim   But it's absurd, Natasha. I can't *direct* anyone! There are days I can hardly step outside my door!

Natasha   But you won some big award, didn't you? My agent says you did.

Maxim   Yes –

Natasha   So you must be good at it.

Maxim   I don't know, Natasha. I mean, the films I've made – I know I must have made them; it says so on the posters. But when I watch one by accident, I don't recognise the mind behind them. I don't connect with them intellectually; they don't move me emotionally. I feel like even if I did make films, they're not the films I'd make!

Pause.

Maybe I'm going mad. Maybe madness runs in my family. How would I know? I don't even know who my family was!

Natasha   Lucky you.

Maxim   Lucky?!

Natasha   Look, I don't know. I'm just an actress. Why are you even telling me all this?

Maxim   I don't know: I probably shouldn't. I just feel like you'd understand.

Natasha   What? That you can't remember making your own films? Why would I understand that?

Maxim   No – I think you understand frailty; loss; failure. You couldn't play this part so well if you didn't.

Natasha   You've got me all wrong: I'm not that deep
a person.

Maxim   I don't think you *judge* people: that's what I mean.

Natasha   Only because I don't care what they do.

Pause.

You still can't stay in here.

Maxim   I know: I just need a plan. That deaf fascist is
watching me like a hawk. I need to buy some time until the
light appears; or none of this will mean anything.

Natasha   What is this light you keep banging on about? The
light's just the light isn't is?

Maxim   No: this is a very particular light. I mean, I call it a
light but it's a feeling really. It's a feeling that's connected to
the light. Does that make sense?

Pause.

Natasha   People are happy when the sun's out. Like that?

Maxim   No but this is just a moment – seconds at most. The
light changes and you're hit by a powerful wave of emotion.

He addresses this outwards:

It's not one emotion – it's not just happiness or sadness; it's
as if every feeling you've ever had, however dissonant,
suddenly comes together in one harmonious chord. It's not
a memory; it's your whole life, from birth to death. It's as if
you can suddenly hear the tune of your life; but only a few
tantalising notes, carried on the wind; and you feel if you
could just get a hold of it, you could live in it – in that loop of
melody, blissfully, for ever; and just as you think you have it
– just as you think you could whistle it – the light fades; and
the tune escapes you: It slips away; like the details of a
dream.

Pause.

You don't ever get that feeling?

Natasha   Not really. I don't think about things that deeply.

Maxim   But it's not a thought. That's exactly what it's not. It's not some sterile intellectual pose to be picked apart by academics. It's beyond words; it refuses reduction; it can't be monopolised. It's the smell of the sound of the colour of the feeling of life! And I'm going to catch it, Natasha! Whatever it takes; whatever the cost.

A knock at the door.

Anastasia (*O/S*)   Natasha? It's Anastasia. Can I have a word?

Maxim *looks alarmed. He waves at* **Natasha** *– 'Don't answer'.*

Anastasia (*O/S*)   Natasha, are you in there?

Pause. They sit frozen.

Maxim?

Pause. **Anastasia** *finally leaves.*

They both let out sighs of relief. Half-whispering at first:

Natasha   That's fucked-up, man.

Maxim   I know – forgive me.

Natasha   Are you more important than her?

Maxim   What do you mean?

Natasha   Can she fire me if you don't want her to?

Maxim   No. Absolutely not. I have the final say on . . . casting . . .

His expression changes, as if realising something.

Natasha   I hope so. Cos if she ever found out –

He rises, excited by something.

Maxim   I have the final *say* on *casting*!

Natasha   Ok: get over yourself.

Maxim   But that's it, don't you see? That's the answer!

Natasha   The answer to what?

Maxim   I've been praying for a fire, a hurricane. Some unstoppable force of chaos that'll slow this production to a crawl. But he's been under my nose all the time! The Brute! I need the *Brute*.

Scene Five

Carl   No. No!

Maxim   Carl . . .

Carl   Not the Brute. No. Maxim – you *said* – you said you chose *me* –

Maxim   And I did, Carl – but now I need to choose him too –

Carl   No –

Maxim   For the good of the film –

Carl   No. Absolutely not.

Eva   You can't replace Sebastian –

Anastasia   It doesn't replace Sebastian. It's a different character.

Eva   Then what's the problem?

Carl   What's the *problem*?

He starts to roll up his sleeves.

Maxim   They've had some disagreements –

Carl   Disagreements?! Look! Look at this –

He shows his bare arm to **Eva**.

Carl   Just watch my arm. Say his name and watch my arm.

Eva   Ivan?

Carl   No – I've a friend called Ivan. The Brute. I'll say it – look – the Brute. The Brute. The Brute. Look – the Brute, the Brute, the Brute –

Anastasia   Carl, stop it –

Eva   You're getting a rash . . .

Carl   Yes – a rash: my skin raising in welts at the mention of his name! So no – you bring in the Brute and you lose the – Carl. Simple as that!

Maxim   Carl – be reasonable –

Carl   *Reasonable*?! Might I remind you, Max – that after his initial bonhomie – he always comes to despise you as well? The last time we worked with him, he hunted us both through the woods on horseback!

Maxim   That was actually quite witty, in hindsight –

Carl   He set traps, Maxim! If we'd stood on one it would have sheared off our legs at the shins!

Maxim   But we *didn't*, did we?

Carl   No: I'm not discussing this any further. If you want to hire him, fine – it's your funeral; literally – but you can find yourself another DOP.

He makes for the door.

Eva   Carl – wait – !

Carl   Eva – with respect – you don't know him –

Eva   But what if we built in safeguards? Contractual penalties; for bad behaviour.

He shakes his head, amused by her naivety.

Carl   A man with no head takes no comfort from hats.

Eva   What?

Pause.

Anastasia   Can I have a word with Carl? Alone?

Maxim *and* **Eva** *nod their agreement and leave. Pause.*

Carl   Unbelievable – !

Anastasia *kisses him aggressively. This time he pushes her back.*

Carl   Anni –

Anastasia   Come on – there's time –

She starts to unbuckle his belt but, again, he pulls away –

Carl   Anni – please tell me that you're not trying to fellate me into agreeing to this – !

Anastasia   Of course not –

Carl   I really hope not. Because that would be frankly wretched.

Anastasia   Do me then: I need to relax.

Carl   Anni, no – come on: have some chamomile tea if you want to relax.

She sighs.

I'm getting tired of being the comic relief around here. I have ambitions of my own, you know. It might surprise you but, in my life, I'm a leading man!

She smiles to stop from laughing.

Is that funny to you? Am I a joke to you?

Anastasia   No, Carl, it's just – the way you put things sometimes, look – you know I'm fond of you –

Carl   No: one is' fond' of uncles or walking boots or pets that smell. I don't want you to be 'fond' of me.

Anastasia   Then what do you – ?

Carl   I want you to see me, Anni! Not through me or past me – really, properly *see* me, standing here, in front of you! I've spent my whole life watching and now I want to be seen!

Anastasia   I do see you, Carl.

Carl   And do you see a future? For us?

Pause.

Anastasia   Maybe.

He nods.

I'm just being honest.

Carl   No, that's all right – 'maybe' is something. I can live with maybe.

Pause.

But I want you to tell Maxim –

Anastasia   Carl –

Carl   Why not? You say there's nothing between you – ?

Anastasia   Not like that, no.

Carl   Then why would he mind? We're his two best friends, Anni – he might even be *happy* for us! Have you considered that?

Anastasia   Happy? Maxim?

Carl   Well – perhaps not *happy* exactly. But he might well be indifferent.

Anastasia   Don't be naive. He'll be like a child with a bruise: it won't matter that it doesn't hurt; he'll scream the house down anyway.

Carl   We could all scream, Anni. I could scream – half the time I struggle not to. But is my suffering less valid for its silence?

Pause.

Anastasia   Fine. Then we'll tell him.

Pause.

Carl   We'll – ?

Anastasia   If it's causing you to suffer – we'll tell him.

Carl   As in – you and I?

Anastasia   Are you suggesting I should do it alone?

Carl   No I just –

Anastasia   But we need to choose our moment. We need to wait until he's overwhelmed, with no time to linger on it.

Carl   That makes sense . . .

Anastasia   What's our biggest set-piece?

Carl   Um –

Anastasia   The battle, right? The battle sequence.

Carl   Anni –

Anastasia   Why not? Hundreds of extras, horses, explosions – it's perfect!

Carl   It's also the last thing on the schedule. I know what you're doing.

Anastasia   What am I doing?

Carl   I know how this will go. We'll *all* be overwhelmed. And then it'll be, 'Well, we'll tell him when we wrap'; and then it'll be, 'We can't spoil the wrap party' –

Anastasia   You think I'm trying to trick you?

Carl   I didn't say that.

Anastasia   What else should I take from it?

Carl   I can't wait another month, Anni. The strain is too much.

Anastasia   So what's the alternative? What else will be sufficiently distracting within a time-frame acceptable to you?

Pause.

Carl   The dogs: the dog attack. We film that next week.

Anastasia   It's two dogs, Carl. You think two dogs trumps the battle scene? Really?

Pause.

Carl   All right, just –

Anastasia   No come on: clearly you don't trust me; so other than the battle scene, what? What's your alternative? The baptism? The candle-lit dinner with the Amish folk? What?

Carl   Anni, just let me –

Anastasia   Think, Carl? Let you think? Because that's what we don't want: we don't want him thinking. We want him with his hands full. So come on: other than the battle scene, what's your big idea? Or maybe you don't have any ideas. Maybe you just want to be obstructive. Maybe you're too comfortable playing the martyr.

Carl   The *martyr*?

Anastasia   I don't know, Carl. I mean you *say* you want to tell him; but now we come to it, maybe you're not so sure.

Carl   That's nonsense – !

Anastasia   Is it? Then I'll ask again: what's the alternative? If not the battle scene – if you can't wait that long – if you don't trust me to go through with it – then when? When do we tell him? What else will have his hands so full he won't think to throw a tantrum? You don't know do you? It's all just bluster! You don't have a single idea in that empty head of yours, do you?!

Carl   Well, if he's bringing on the Brute – I'd say that'll have his hands pretty full, wouldn't you?

Anastasia   Oh right! So you won't even be here? So I get to tell Maxim *and* deal with Ivan; whilst you sit at home with your feet up?!

Carl   What? No –

Anastasia   Well, you won't be here, will you? You said: it's you or the Brute. You're too delicate to deal with that. So basically you're off home and I'm left to do it all myself!

Carl   Look, fine – I'll deal with Ivan, if that's what it takes! As long as you know that the second he tries his luck with me, I'm going to bash his thick head in with a tripod!

Anastasia   Fine by me –

Carl   Is that fine by you?

Anastasia   That's fine by me: I'll join you!

Carl   Fine!

Anastasia   Fine: so bring him on then? Is that the plan?

Carl   That's the plan: bring on the Brute!

He exits defiantly. She registers a moment of relief then follows.

Scene Six

Maxim *struggles to push his case on to centre stage. He rests on it for a moment, then leaves it there.*

Pause. And then the case begins to move. Slowly, it opens . . .

A hand appears first, feeling at its edges; and then, like Nosferatu from his coffin, **Ivan** *– aka the Brute – emerges from the case.*

He takes a deep, triumphant breath and takes in his surroundings.

Now he sees the audience:

Ivan   There you are. I see you.

He looks out at them with mad-eyed contempt:

I see your faces, expectant. What do you want from me? Are you hoping I will brighten this dirge for you? That I will justify your decision to crawl out of your hovels to come see this excrement?!

Whores! Cuckolds! None of your faces surprise me! I have imagined them all! I have worn all your faces! I have used your eyes to witness the foulest depravities ever dreamt of by man! I have used your mouths to self-suck; and your tight throats to swallow my own, bitter semen! I have used your turned-up noses to smell the wine of gods and your grasping hands to throw that piss back in their faces!

Pause.

When I crawled from the rubble of Belgrade, my only friend was a mutt, his coat heavy with ash. He would come to me with his tearful eyes, whining and looking up to me as you look up to me now, begging for food and I would kick him away! I have no food, stupid mutt, do you not see?! I can hardly feed myself!! And yet he would return, pathetically, with his head hung low in subservience. I fed him my *snot*! And the stupid beast sucked it down gratefully and begged for more!

Pause.

I am ashamed of that.

Pause.

Years later, when I had fine clothes and the bourgeois scum were queuing at my door just to touch my hand, a twelve-year-old girl came begging to me in Dubrovnik. She offered to suck my manhood for a stale bread roll and I *let* her!

Pause. He stares at them defiantly.

Do you think you have the right to judge me?! In that moment, as she struggled to fit me in her mouth, I saw all the dignity of man! Do you think I should have denied her that? You who have known not a day's want in your fetid, verminous lives?!

Pause.

You cannot judge me. Even God cannot judge me.

Anastasia   Ivan –

Ivan *jumps, squealing un-manfully in fright.*

Anastasia   When did you get here?

He stares at her.

We sent a driver to pick you up. Did you not see him?

Ivan   I saw him. I decided to walk instead.

Anastasia   Walk? Ivan – it must be thirty miles – !

Ivan   I took my shoes off so I could feel every inch of my destiny; the grass, the gravel. I crushed flowers and insects as I walked. And with every step, my power grew.

Anastasia   You couldn't have walked here in two hours . . .

Pause.

Ivan   I hitched a lift some of the way. A kindly family stopped for me. Within minutes, I was making love to the wife and daughter; whilst the cuckold drove us, meekly sneaking glimpses of our passion in his mirror.

Anastasia   Well – you're here now.

He embraces her, softly.

Ivan   Anastasia: It's good to see you.

She pats his back.

Anastasia   It's – good to see you. Ivan.

Ivan   Where is Maxim?

Anastasia   He's in his suite.

Ivan   Take me to him.

Anastasia   I will. But I wanted to have a word first.

Ivan   I knew. I knew he would come crawling. He cannot keep from me.

Anastasia   Ivan – you need to understand something: we're already behind schedule –

Ivan   That stupid pig! Can he do nothing without me?!

Anastasia   Ivan – let's drop the charade, shall we? I've spoken to your agent –

Ivan   Agent?! Agent is too active a word for that maggot's husk!

Anastasia   Nonetheless – I spoke to him, and he confirmed what I already knew: that you've made yourself virtually unemployable in this industry.

Ivan   Industry! This is not an industry! Coal, steel, nuclear power: those are industries! This is a slaughterhouse! Where truth and beauty are butchered for mass consumption!

Anastasia   This is your contract, Ivan: you should take the time to read it –

He throws it to the ground.

Or don't; it's up to you. But it contains a list of incremental financial penalties for any delays we incur –

Outraged, he retrieves the contract and starts to read it.

– due to you being late or not knowing your lines or throwing tantrums or starting fights or doing anything, Ivan, other than what we've hired you to do; which is act.

Ivan   That worm! That crawling blob of phlegm! He agreed to this?!

Anastasia   It's not ungenerous, Ivan. If you behave yourself, you'll make more than enough to keep you in what we both know is the lifestyle you're accustomed to. If you don't . . .

On the contract, she points out a figure to him.

Pause. He softens and laughs.

Ivan   Anni . . .

He embraces her again.

Anni, Anni, Anni: well done. You have passed my test. I swear – if you had said anything less, I would have turned around and walked straight back out of that door.

Pause.

In fact, this mask I wear has long been an albatross around my neck; unlike the actual albatross I wear when protesting, which is deceptively light. Alas, the foetal vulgarians who now infest this – industry – seek only to exploit the icon and have no interest in the man. That is why I have turned my back on them; not the other way round. And if I thought you or dear Maxim were the same – it would have broken my heart. So – I thank you. This contract is a bond of trust, written in the blood of friends.

Anastasia   So we understand each other?

Ivan   We understand each –

Pause. He smells the air.

He is here! And he still wears the cologne I gave him!

Maxim *enters, tentatively.*

Maxim   Hello, Ivan.

Ivan *turns, dramatically, to see him.*

Pause. He opens his arms.

Ivan   Maxim: my friend, my brother; my captain: come to me.

Maxim   I don't want you to kiss me.

Ivan   Shame on you: should a man not kiss his brother?

Maxim   Not on the mouth, no.

Ivan   You are worried you will like it too much! Is that it, eh?

Maxim   No. I know very well that I won't. That's why I don't want you to do it.

Ivan *looks to* **Anastasia***, shaking his head.*

Ivan   A hug then. Give me that at least.

Maxim   A hug is acceptable.

They hug. Pause.

Ivan   Maxim, Maxim: I thought you had abandoned me.

Maxim   I couldn't if I wanted to.

Pause. **Ivan** *tries to kiss him but* **Maxim** *manages to hold his face back until he can break free.*

Carl *enters, seeing this.*

Carl   Oh good God. He's real. He's here and he's real. What have I agreed to?

Ivan *and* **Maxim** *separate.*

Maxim   Ivan, look: it's Carl.

Ivan   Carl – my friend –

He walks towards him. **Carl** *backs off, arms raised defensively.*

Carl   Keep away from me! I'm serious!

Maxim   Ivan – Carl's a little wary of you after the last time and all the other times. You need to reassure him you'll behave yourself.

Ivan *stops. He hangs his head.*

Ivan   I need no spur but my shame: my shame to see how a good man cowers from me.

Carl   I'm not cowering: I'm just prepared.

Ivan   What would you have me do, Carl? How will I earn your forgiveness? I have treated you wretchedly and I can offer no excuse except to say that it wasn't me that did those things! I was possessed by a demon! A demon of my own making, fuelled by drinks and drugs and self-loathing. But that demon has been vanquished, Carl. I swear it on the lives of my children that I know about! And now my redemption is in your hands. What will it take for you to forgive me? Here – strike me! Strike me as hard as you like! Here –

He presents his belly.

Strike me with all your – !

Carl *punches him in the stomach. Immediately,* **Ivan** *grabs* **Carl** *by the throat, throttling him with a look of intense seriousness.* **Anastasia** *and* **Maxim** *manage to pull* **Ivan** *away.*

Carl   Do you see?! Do you see?! Does that demon seem vanquished to you?!

Anastasia   Oh for God's sake – !

Ivan   It's all right! Let me be! Let me be!

Carl   One chance – I said: he had one chance and that was it! That was his chance! He touches me again and I'll kill him! Do you understand?! I'll kill you!

He storms out.

Maxim   Anastasia – go after him!

Anastasia   And say what?

Maxim   I don't know: calm him down –

Pause.

Anastasia   This is exactly what that contract is supposed to prevent. And that's your first penalty, Ivan. Bravo! Ten minutes into you arriving!

She exits, furious. Pause.

Maxim   Why did you do that?

Ivan   He punched me! You saw it!

Maxim   But you told him to!

Pause.

Ivan   Yes, yes: I know. But when someone hits me, I hit them back. I've no control of it.

Pause. **Maxim** *starts to laugh.* **Ivan** *laughs too. And then they're both laughing hysterically, like children.* **Ivan** *puts his arm around* **Maxim** *and* **Maxim** *doesn't resist.*

The laughter subsides.

Maxim   So – shall we make another masterpiece?

Ivan   We shall, my friend. We shall!

They exit.

Interval.

Act Three

Scene One

Natasha's *room.*

Natasha (*in a Southern American accent*)   WHY?! MERCIFUL GOD IN HEAVEN, WHY?! WHY WOULD YOU DO THIS TO ME? WHAT HAVE I DONE SO WRONG THAT YOU WOULD PUNISH ME LIKE THIS?! HAVEN'T I SUFFERED ENOUGH FOR YOU? OH JESUS GOD TELL ME PLEASE! WHAT DID I DO SO WRONG?!

Pause. **Maxim** *dabs at his eyes with cotton wool.*

Maxim   Thank you. That was wonderful, as always.

Pause.

How did it feel to you?

Natasha   It felt good.

Maxim   Is that how it should feel? Should it feel good?

Natasha   *Should* it?

Maxim   It's just that usually when I have actors play harrowing scenes, they seem a bit shaken afterwards and I have to be pretend to be sensitive to what they've gone through.

Natasha   That's bullshit. It always feels good. But I'm getting bored doing this speech all the time.

Maxim   You said you needed to act . . .

Natasha   I do. But when do we get back to filming? Haven't you got this light yet?

Maxim   Not yet. But as soon as they get Ivan down from the roof, we'll do another of your scenes, I promise.

Pause.

In the meantime, why don't you try the speech again? But perhaps this time . . . try it in your own accent; just
this once.

Natasha   What's the point of that?

Maxim   I just think it might help you – to connect her pain with yours.

Natasha   With my what?

Maxim   With your pain.

Natasha   What pain? I'm not in any pain.

Maxim   We're all carrying pain.

Natasha   I'm not.

Maxim   Natasha – I just don't believe you can give a performance like that and not be drawing on some kind of pain. It's impossible.

Natasha   There's a bird in the Amazon that can make the sound of a chainsaw.

Maxim   Ah but the question is: could a chainsaw make the sound of a bird?

Natasha   If you stuck a fucking speaker on it.

Maxim   You're not just a mimic, Natasha: your pain might not be hers –

Natasha   For fuck's sake – !

Maxim   But it must have a source – !

Natasha   Yes! The screenplay! That you wrote! And if you'd written her happy, I'd play her happy! But if I told you I was just pretending to be happy – you'd accept that! You wouldn't go poking at me for the source of my happiness, would you?

Maxim   I might.

Natasha   No you fucking wouldn't! Because for some reason you want to believe I'm in pain! That's the fucking question: why do you need me to be in fucking pain?!

Maxim   You're getting very upset for someone so cold . . .

Pause.

Natasha   I'm sorry: am I sucking on a lollypop?

Maxim   What?

Natasha   Am I sucking on a lollipop?

Pause.

Maxim   No . . .

Natasha   No. I'm not. You know why? Because I'm not a fucking CHILD. So I'm not 'upset'. I'm just fucked-off with emotional cripples telling me what I should be feeling. I'm an actress: that's what I am. You want me to feel something? Fucking PAY me!

Pause.

Maxim   Well – technically, I am paying you.

Natasha   Fine. What do you want me to feel?

Pause.

Maxim   Regret.

Pause. She crumples.

Natasha   Look – Maxim – this is getting too heavy. I'm sorry, ok? You're right: I am carrying pain, like you, like everyone; and I have built up a wall to keep people out and it usually works. But then someone like you comes along and cares enough to ask and I just – lash out. Which pushes them away too. But you're not the enemy, I know that: my only enemy is myself. It's my shit, not yours. You understand that, don't you?

Pause. He nods. He's fallen for it. Until she says, sarcastically –

Don't *judge* me, Maxim.

Pause. He smiles, caught; claps slowly.

Maxim   Oh bravo, very good. All right – Fear.

Pause.

Natasha   Oh God. I've messed up, haven't I?

Pause.

Stupid stupid stupid Natasha – !

Pause.

And now you're going to fire me! My first film and you're going to fire me! Which means my agent will probably drop me as well. Oh God – my whole career – everything I dreamed of – just ruined; just like that! What am I going to say to people? What am I going to say to my mum? After all the sacrifices she made to put me through –

Maxim   Love.

Pause. She stares at him; all kinds of things in the silence.

Did you hear me? I said: *Love*.

Pause.

Natasha   Let me know when you want to start filming.

She leaves the room.

Scene Two

The compound set, a few days later.

Natasha *is virtually thrown, in costume, into the space.* **Ivan** *follows, dressed in military-survivalist gear. Following them both are* **Maxim** *and* **Carl**, *crouched so they can take the viewpoint of a camera.*

Ivan *stands over* **Natasha**.

Natasha   Why are you doing this?

Ivan   Why? Why?

He laughs. He crouches down to her.

There is no such word anymore. There is no 'why'. There is only what is and what has always been. 'Why'! This is my answer to the question 'why?'.

He produces a gun and presses it to her face.

Because I *am*.

Carl *suddenly realises:*

Carl   Hold on – that's not a prop!

He backs off.

That's not a prop gun: Maxim – that's a real gun!

Ivan   Stop your squealing, pig!

Now **Natasha** *pulls away too.*

Natasha   What the fuck – ?

Maxim   Ivan – is that a real gun?

Ivan   Here we go: now we will hear the chorus of insects!

Natasha   Is that loaded?

Maxim   Show me the gun, Ivan –

Ivan   Here – !

He stands and points the gun at **Maxim***, who ducks.*

Ivan   You want to see the gun?

He turns to point it at **Carl***, who also takes cover.*

Ivan   Here is the gun!

Natasha   Put that down, you arsehole!

Carl   Someone call the police!

Maxim   Ivan –

Ivan *lowers the gun.*

Ivan   All right, you pansies; stop messing your pants!

Carl   Maxim – take that thing away from him!

Maxim   Ivan –

Ivan   What's all the fuss? It's not loaded –

Carl   It doesn't matter! You don't bring a real gun on set!

Maxim   He's right, Ivan. We have prop guns you can use –

Carl   I'm not running around with some toy, like an idiot child! Do you think this putrid trash we're making should be any more infantile than it already is?!

Natasha   Fuck you – !

Ivan *pushes at the walls of the set.*

Ivan   It's true! Look at this – fake, flimsy fakery! It's fooling no one! This whole thing is a cartoon! A lurid, worm-ridden, revenge fantasy written by a child in piss-drenched pants!

Natasha   Maxim wrote it –

Ivan   Exactly! He is a disease! He is the virus in this film, killing everything it touches! And he should be stamped out, like any disease!

Natasha   What the fuck is wrong with you?

Ivan   There's nothing wrong with me! There's something right with me! But I know what's wrong with you! I know exactly what you need, negress!

Natasha   *What* did you call me?!

Ivan   What? You want to pretend we are the same?! Are you so ashamed that you wish for a world where we are all tanned hermaphrodites speaking Esperanto?! Is that the world you want?!

Natasha   Fuck you – Nazi prick!!

Ivan   How dare you?! I am no Nazi! I kill Nazis!

Maxim   All right, let's take a break, shall we?

Ivan   You don't tell me when to break! I tell you when to break!

Natasha   Fuck this – !

She leaves.

Maxim   Ivan – did you eat pastries this morning?

Ivan   I will eat what I like! I will lick chocolate from a pig's anus if it pleases me!

Maxim   Would that please you?

Enraged, **Ivan** *gets nose to nose with* **Maxim** *and stays there.* **Maxim** *holds his ground.*

Eva *enters whilst this is going on and stands by* **Carl***.*

Eva   What are they doing? Is this real?

Carl   That *gun* is real.

Eva   The gun?

Carl   He's brought a real gun on set.

Eva   Hey – !

She goes over to them. She taps **Ivan** *on the back.*

Ivan   Get away from me, fishwife!

She taps him again.

Eva   Turn around!

He turns to her, furious.

Ivan   What do you want?!

She puts her hand out.

Eva   Give me the gun.

He slaps down her hand. Instinctively, she slaps his face.

Ivan *staggers back. Both* **Carl** *and* **Maxim** *wince.*

Eva   Do you think it's acceptable to hit women? Is that why they call you the Brute?

Carl *and* **Maxim** *wince again.* **Ivan** *reddens like a volcano and then:*

Ivan   Who calls me that?! Show me the craven scum that call me that! Was it this one – this cretin?!

He points at **Carl**. *Then at* **Maxim**.

Ivan   Or this one – this cathedral to mediocrity?! Tell me! Which one filled your empty blonde head with their playground taunts?!

Eva   Everybody calls you that.

Pause. He stares at her. She stares back. He breaks it.

Ivan   How dare they . . .?

Pause.

I feel all the suffering of the world, every minute, every second – and because I howl with anger, they call me Brute?! I seek out the oldest, ugliest streetwalkers so they might taste desire once more – and they call me Brute? I sit all day outside the local school and weep for the tenderness of youth – and they call me Brute?!

An explosion:

I HAVE WALKED A THOUSAND MILES TO SAVE A FLY!

I HAVE DELIBERATELY LOST A CHESS TOURNAMENT TO A FEEBLE-MINDED CHILD! TWICE!

AFTER MY ONE-MAN SHOW IN THE AMPHITHEATRE IN VERONA, THE AUDIENCE APPLAUDED ME FOR

SEVEN HOURS WITHOUT CEASE AND I STOOD
THERE THROUGH IT ALL IN MY *UNTERHOSE*!

Pause.

AND THEY CALL ME – *BRUTE*?!

Pause. **Eva** *claps, sardonic but amused.*

Ivan *turns and stares at her. He looks ready to blow again . . .*

Instead, he hands her the gun, bows to her and leaves – in an unusually dignified fashion.

Eva   What do I do with this?

Carl *quickly takes the gun from her and they leave.*

When they are gone, **Maxim** *nearly jumps for joy.* **Natasha** *enters behind him.*

Natasha   Maxim . . .?

Maxim   Oh – Natasha –

Natasha   What the fuck was that?

Maxim   That was Ivan. I did tell you –

Natasha   You said he'd cause trouble; not stick a gun in my face.

Maxim   Oh don't worry about that. He's essentially a coward; and a terrible shot to boot.

Natasha   That's a comfort.

Maxim   But it's going to work, Natasha. He's going to bring this whole thing to a grinding halt.

Natasha   And that'll get you this light of yours?

Maxim   Natasha – you make me sad. It's not 'my' light. I'm not the one up there on that screen. This light is the frame in which your beauty will live for all eternity. This light is for you. For us.

Pause. She is moved by this, in her way.

Natasha   I just need to act.

Maxim   And you will. I promise you will.

Scene Three

Communal area, outside. **Eva** *is reading, wearing sunglasses.*

Carl *enters. He sits beside her, acting furtive.*

Carl   Eva.

Eva   Carl.

Pause.

Carl   I don't want anyone to hear what I'm about to say so I'm just going to mouth it. Will you understand?

Eva   Did you just mouth that?

Carl   No. Well – I did – but with sound. But the next things I say will be without sound, ok?

Eva   Ok.

Carl (*mouths*)   If Maxim was to be replaced –

Eva   If Maxim was to be replaced . . .?

Carl   You're not going to mouth your reply then? Because that sort of defeats the purpose.

Eva   Can you lip-read?

Pause.

Carl   No. That's a good point. All right –

He holds up his finger to indicate more.

(*Mouths.*) I would be willing to step in as director.

Eva   You would be willing to step in as director?

Carl   Ssshhh!!

He nods.

(*Mouths.*) If that will save the film – yes.

Eva   All right, Carl. If it comes to that, I'll keep you in mind.

He bows, clasping his hands.

She nods. Furtively, he goes. She shakes her head and goes back to reading.

*As **Carl** is leaving, **Ivan** appears, carrying a plate of food. **Carl** veers out of his way and exits.*

*Cautiously, **Ivan** approaches the table.*

Ivan   May I sit here?

*Pause. **Eva** nods. He sits down. Pause. She looks at his plate.*

Eva   No vegetables?

Pause.

Ivan   No. My father had an allotment. I could hear them scream as he ripped them from the ground.

Eva   No you couldn't.

Pause.

Ivan   No.

Eva   If you ate more vegetables and less meat, maybe you wouldn't be so angry all the time.

Pause.

Ivan   My father did have an allotment. I wanted to help him but he wouldn't let me. It was his private space where he could be away from his family. He spent most of his time there.

Pause.

He said he called it an 'allotment' because it 'meant a lot'
to him.

She smiles.

Meant a lot. A lot meant.

He laughs and so does she. Pause.

Ivan   I used to hold in my anger. But a therapist told me –
that if you hold your anger in –

Eva   It becomes depression . . .

Ivan   Yes. So he worked with me to start letting it out.

Eva   Was he a good therapist?

Ivan   Yes, he was very good; until I threw him down a flight
of stairs. He wouldn't see me after that.

Pause.

Eva   I don't know if you're joking or not.

Ivan   No. Neither do I anymore.

Pause.

They call me the Brute because of the light.

Eva   The light?

Ivan   There is a film light called a Brute. And one time, on
a film set, I smashed one with my head. Feel –

Gently, he guides her finger to his head.

Can you feel it?

Eva   It's deep. Was there a lot of blood?

Ivan   Yes. So they call me the Brute; but I think it would be
better to call me the Moth.

Eva   Because they go to the light?

Ivan   And smash their heads against it.

Eva   But moths are small, delicate things. Nobody would say that of you.

Pause. He feigns offence. Then he looks around: he retrieves two round reflector boards and disappears behind a screen.

Now in silhouette, he uses the boards as wings and flaps them. He then runs at the screen, his shadow growing larger, banging it with his head. He does this a few times, to her amusement.

Finally, he emerges, a little bashful.

Ivan   Did you like that?

Eva   I did. It made me laugh. People don't try to make me laugh.

Ivan   Then they are missing something beautiful; like a sunrise.

Eva   Thank you. That means a lot to me.

The Brute smiles.

Scene Four

The compound set.

Carl *is wearing protective headgear of some kind and adjusting lights.* **Maxim** *and* **Natasha** – *carrying a fake baby by its arm – enter.*

Maxim   Good morning, Carl: you look absurd.

Carl   Yes, well – there is many a well-dressed corpse.

Natasha   What?

Carl   Maxim, can you tell Ivan just to walk this through for now? We might get further if he saves his histrionics for the take.

Maxim   Why don't you ask him? It might justify that ridiculous helmet.

Carl   If I were the director, I would. It might justify my ridiculous salary.

Maxim   Very cocky these days, aren't we, Carl? What's gotten into you, I wonder?

Ivan *enters, looking surprisingly breezy.*

Ivan   Good morning, good morning! And how are we all this morning?

Pause. **Maxim** *looks at him with suspicion.*

Maxim   I'm fine, Ivan.

Ivan   Carl. Natasha.

He nods to them and they nod back.

And what delightful scene will we be playing today?

Pause.

Maxim   Well, I thought we could – take another stab at – the interrogation scene?

Ivan   Of course –

Maxim   If you don't mind.

Ivan   Not at all. Where would you like me to begin?

Pause.

Maxim   Ivan – are you all right?

Ivan   Yes, Maxim. Thank you for asking. In fact, I am better than all right.

Eva *enters.*

Maxim   Uh – oh.

Ivan   What?

He nods in **Eva**'s *direction.*

Maxim   The fascist.

Ivan   What?

Eva   He said 'the fascist'.

Maxim (*aside*)   Damn! The lip-reading!

Ivan *turns to see* **Eva**.

Ivan   How could he call my sweet munchkin a fascist?

He goes to her and kisses her. **Natasha** *and* **Carl** *are astonished.* **Maxim**'s *jaw literally drops.*

Maxim   What – is this – ?

Ivan   What is what, my friend?

Maxim   This – you – with the munchkin and the – what is that? All this with the – ?

Ivan   Maxim, I am proud to announce that Eva and I are now having sex with each other.

Eva   Ivan –

Ivan   No – I will say it, my sweet: I will sing it from the rooftops! The Brute is dead! Long live the Moth!

Maxim   The Moth? What is he talking about?

Carl   He says the Brute is dead . . .?

Maxim   What do you mean the Brute is dead? You're the Brute –

Ivan   No. The Brute was but a ludicrously broad character I played in order to conceal my true sensitivities. But I will play it not a day longer. Like a moth, I have seen the light and that light is Eva; and I have flown to her.

Maxim   Really. Well she must be quite the fuck to have inspired such an epiphany. What – do deaf girls do it sideways or something?

Eva   That's enough –

Ivan   It's all right, my sweet. He is just trying to bait me. He still believes that greatness comes only from conflict.

He goes to **Maxim**.

Ivan   And Maxim, I will admit that when I came here, it was my plan to kill you, then Carl, then probably myself.

Carl   Me?!

Ivan   But there is a better way: if you will only open your heart to love, you too can escape the prison of your fear. Take my hand, Maxim, and we can both fly free –

Maxim *pulls his hand away.*

Maxim   Except you're not free, Ivan; I've got a contract to prove it. And I didn't hire a Moth! I hired a Brute –

Ivan   Of course. And I am a professional. I will play the part as you want it; but only when the camera rolls; not a second more or less.

Maxim *can barely contain his anger. He turns on* **Eva**.

Maxim   This was you. You did this.

Eva   Did what?

Ivan   Leave her be, Maxim. She did nothing but show me kindness.

Maxim   Don't be an idiot, Ivan! She's using you, don't you see that? This is just a ploy to keep us on schedule and when we're done, she'll be done with you: at best you'll be a dinner party anecdote for her bean-counting crones in the City. Why else would a girl like this take up with the likes of you? It's a good job she's deaf or she wouldn't even – !

Ivan *grabs* **Maxim** *by the throat.*

Ivan   I said leave her BE!

Natasha   All right, I'm out.

She leaves. **Maxim** *is smiling despite the chokehold.*

Maxim   Or what, Ivan? You'll kill me? And then Carl?

Carl   Can we stop talking about killing me perhaps?

Maxim   It's all right, Carl. The Brute is dead. Isn't that right, Ivan?

Eva   Ivan, don't.

She puts her hand on his arm.

You're a better man than he'll ever be.

Pause. **Ivan** *releases his grip.*

Eva   Go back to the room. I'll be all right.

Ivan *nods. He kisses her and leaves.*

Maxim   Carl – get Anastasia. Bring her to me.

Carl   She's still in Berlin . . .

Maxim   I know – I mean on the phone. Tell her to come back.

Carl   I'm not your secretary.

Eva   Look, Maxim – I didn't know he'd announce our – involvement. I don't want to cause any –

Maxim   Don't bother. I'm not needy like Ivan and I don't buy your 'magical deaf girl' act. I just wonder if your corporate bosses will see fucking the actors as part of your remit?

Eva   Is there a law against it?

Carl   If there was, you'd not be alone in the dock.

Maxim   Don't side with her! It's not about the *law* – it's unethical! And I'll make Anni make sure you pay for it! Now get off my set!

Eva   We have to start filming –

Maxim   We'll start filming when I say we'll start filming. And if you want to have me fired, all I can say is good luck finding a replacement!

Pause. She nods, casting a quick glance at **Carl**.

Eva   Have it your way.

Maxim   I will!

She exits.

Carl   Maxim – you know I've always been truthful with you –

But **Maxim** *drops to his knees, hyperventilating.*

Maxim   Inhaler! Inhaler!

Scene Five

Maxim's *room. He's lying down, groaning feverishly. The scene is lit by candles, like some Russian tragedy.*

Maxim   Natasha! The light! The light, Natasha!

Natasha *enters, carrying hot towels and water.*

Natasha (*in Russian accent*)   Yes, Maxim, I hear you.

Maxim   The light – !

Natasha   What, my husband? What about the light?

Maxim   It's slipping away, I can feel it! I'm losing the light!

She dabs his brow.

Natasha   There, there: try to rest.

Maxim   I can smell oranges. Why can I smell oranges?! Isn't that a sign of a brain tumour?!

Natasha   No –

Maxim   But I can smell them! Why can I smell oranges?!

Back to her normal accent:

Natasha   Because I ate a fucking orange, is that all right?!
Or am I supposed to do without food as well?!

Maxim   Don't break character –

Natasha   This is too weird for me, Maxim.

Maxim   Too weird – ?

Natasha   I don't know what I'm doing here –

Maxim   I just asked for sympathy. You were the one that
needed a scenario. I'd say that was weird, wouldn't you?
That you need to be someone else to express sympathy?

Natasha   I can't help it. I'm just not good with those things.

Maxim   What? Basic human feelings?

Natasha   Sympathy. I got tested for it when I was a kid and
I got a really low score.

Maxim   A sympathy test? What does that involve?

Natasha   It's just lots of questions.

Maxim   Wait – do you mean an *empathy* test?

Natasha   Empathy? Oh – yeah, maybe – same thing, isn't it?

Maxim   Not really, Natasha, no: you failed an empathy test?

Natasha   It's not my fault. It's like – I go to the room in my
mind – where the feelings are kept . . .

Maxim   But you can't open the door?

Natasha   There isn't a door. Like it's been papered over;
and there's no way in.

Pause.

Isn't it like that for you?

Maxim   Me? No – I wish! For me there's a hundred doors,
all banging in the wind!

Natasha   But did you ever do the tests?

Maxim   Empathy tests? No. There isn't an empathy chart big enough. That's my problem: I feel everything too deeply. It's exhausting.

Pause.

Natasha   They said it might be because of my –

Maxim   Oh God, Natasha! What am I to do?! Ever since Ivan fell for that deaf strumpet, he's been meek as a lamb! Another day of this and we'll be right back on schedule: that means we'll be done before winter; and that's our best chance of catching the light –

Natasha   Winter?

Maxim   The sun should be lower in the sky. I remember now: every time I've seen that light it was lower in the sky, less vertical. It's a matter of angles, densities, particulates –

Natasha   But Sebastian's got another job in winter.

Maxim   Sebastian! He'll be done by then; and if he's not, I'll just write him out. This film is about you, not Sebastian. Let him go back to selling watches and coffee machines. About all he's good for.

Natasha   Maybe we should just move on though. Get the light the next time.

Maxim   But what if there isn't a next time? People like me, we die young. We're not meant to grow old. We burn bright and live half as long. And it will be so sad when I die, Natasha. Such a tragic waste. Why can't people understand that now, when I'm alive?! Nobody cares about you dying when you're alive because we're all dying, we're all just equally dying, until some narcissist leaps ahead of the pack! And then they say, 'Oh how awful that they've died; we didn't realise how much we'd miss them'. And then a day later they're laughing at videos of people getting hit in the groin by footballs; like nothing's changed at all. Like you were never even there.

Pause.

It's a cruel world, Natasha. And we're alone. We're completely alone.

Pause.

Compassion?

She speaks softly, as if it were a comforting prayer:

Natasha   Why? Merciful God in Heaven, why?

He smiles and joins in, weakly, like a child.

Why would you do this to me? What have I done so wrong that you would punish me like this? Haven't I suffered enough for you? Oh Jesus God, tell me please: What did I do so – ?

Anastasia *enters.*

Anastasia   Good God, Maxim.

They jump.

I go away for a few days and it's like a scene from the Crimean War!

She turns on the light.

Natasha – ?

Maxim   It's all right, Anni: she's tending to me.

Anastasia   Is she now? And is this a real illness or a romantic one?

Maxim   It's real. A migraine or something: my brain feels like a sponge someone's dropped in a urinal.

Anastasia   Well, thank you, Natasha: I'll take it from here.

As **Natasha** *leaves,* **Maxim** *reaches for her.*

Maxim   Natasha –

He takes her hand.

Thank you. You're a good friend.

Natasha   Friend?

Maxim   Yes.

Natasha   We're friends?

Maxim   Yes. Of course we are.

Pause. She leaves.

Anastasia   She seemed surprised: that you're friends.

Maxim   She did, didn't she?

Anastasia   Maybe she thought you were more than that?

Maxim   I don't know what she thinks. I'm beginning to suspect she might be a sociopath.

Anastasia   Just your type.

Maxim   Hardly. Though I'll admit it's strangely relaxing; to have no effect on a person.

Anastasia   I'm not sure we ever know the effect we have.

Maxim   I haven't slept with her, if that's what you mean. That would be unethical.

Anastasia   It's never bothered you before.

Maxim   That's unfair. I've sometimes mistaken a creative attraction for a romantic one; but I've always been sincere.

Anastasia   Unlike Eva?

Maxim *grunts sulkily.*

Maxim   Did you speak to her?

Anastasia   Not yet; but I met Ivan in the foyer.

Maxim   Was he being 'pleasant'?

Anastasia   He was actually. Almost like a normal person.

Maxim   Chilling, isn't it?

Anastasia   It doesn't seem to be affecting his performance . . .

Maxim   He's going through the motions – but look at his eyes; they're glassy, like a stuffed animal.

Anastasia   I suppose it's better than him running around with a pistol.

Maxim   You heard about that.

Anastasia   And I had his luggage thoroughly checked on arrival too. I wonder how he managed to get hold of it?

Maxim   He's always been resourceful.

She nods, knowingly; not unamused.

Anastasia   Bit of a fork in your plans, isn't it? Ivan in love.

Maxim   I'm happy he's in love –

Anastasia   Maxim . . .

Maxim   I am. But she's using him, Anni. And I fear if we don't intervene –

Anastasia   Maxim, please: do you think I don't know you? I know you better than you know yourself. Which is why I'm going to tell you the truth.

Pause. He looks at her.

This light you're chasing is a phantom –

Maxim   No, Anni – you're wrong –

Anastasia   I don't doubt that it's real to you. And I can't tell you what it represents. I'm just a producer. But I know that chasing it will be your ruin. And I won't let that happen, Maxim. I won't let you destroy yourself.

Pause.

Maxim   You're good, Anni. You're very good. But I know you too. And you don't get to disguise your self-interest as concern for me; or pass off your utter lack of belief in me as loyalty. Well, fine: I don't need you, Anni. You're convenient; but I don't need you to get what I want. I've never needed anyone. I am the Child of Ashes. And the light is real. You'll see: I'll show you.

Scene Six

Anastasia *enters briskly, talking into her phone.*

Anastasia   No – Sergei – don't take him in the van. These roads are bumpy as hell. If he's got a spinal injury or –

Pause. **Eva** *enters, looking worried.*

Anastasia   Exactly. And he's sedated. So just wait for the airlift. It won't be much longer. If it's not here in ten minutes, call me back. Ok.

Eva   What's happened? Is it Ivan?

Anastasia   No – it's Sebastian. It seems he was on a horse and – it bolted for some reason. He got thrown off over some wall –

Eva   Is he all right?

Anastasia   I'm not sure. They said he couldn't move; but I don't know if that's because he was concussed or unconscious or – I don't know – something worse. They said the horse was going top speed so –

Eva   But why did it bolt? Were there guns?

Anastasia   There shouldn't have been. Hold on –

She answers her phone.

Is it there? Ok, good. Has Veronika called his agent?

Carl *enters, looking disturbed.*

Eva   Are you all right, Carl?

Carl   Yes, I'm all right – I wasn't on the horse –

Anastasia   Tell her to tell them that we'll make travel arrangements –

Eva   Did you see it?

Anastasia   Find out when they're getting in and meet them at the airport –

Carl   I didn't see him get thrown –

Anastasia   Ok. Keep me informed.

Eva   But did you see it bolt?

Carl   Yes. I saw that.

Eva   This is bad.

Anastasia (*to* **Carl**)   Where's Maxim? Has he gone to the hospital?

Ivan *enters and* **Eva** *goes to him.*

Carl (*to* **Anastasia**)   I don't know. Can I have a word with you?

Eva *hugs* **Ivan**.

Eva   Are you all right?

Ivan   Yes, munchkin, I am fine. But the boy – I don't know. I've been thrown by horses but not at such a speed.

Eva (*to* **Anastasia**)   Maybe we should go to the hospital?

Carl   Anni –

Anastasia   Could you do that?

Ivan   Yes, of course; if it would be helpful –

Anastasia   It really would –

Carl   Anni, I need to –

Anastasia   Speak to Vassily: do you know Vassily?

Eva   The – first – assistant director? Is that right?

Ivan   *Wunderbar!* You see: she is one of us now!

Anastasia   Vassily will get you a driver.

Eva   Go and get your headache pills first.

Ivan   Yes. Good idea.

Maxim *enters, passing them.*

Ivan   Maxim – ?

Maxim   Fuck you, Ivan.

With a shrug to **Eva***,* **Ivan** *exits.*

Maxim   That's it, little Moth: fly away!

Eva *shakes her head and follows* **Ivan** *off.*

Carl   Anni, I need to *talk* to you – !

He grabs her arm –

Anastasia   Oww! Carl, what's wrong with you?!

She pulls away from him.

Maxim   Well that was an eventful morning.

Anastasia   Maxim – what the hell happened?

Maxim   What do you mean?

Anastasia   With Sebastian!?

Maxim   Oh – Sebastian. Well, he fell off a horse. Didn't you hear?

Anastasia   Yes, Maxim, I heard. But how could that happen?

Maxim   No idea. Maybe the horse took against him. That bony backside of his.

Anastasia *is appalled by his lack of concern.*

Anastasia   Max –

Maxim   He'll be fine. A few broken bones.

Carl   There was blood streaming from his head!

Maxim   Those things always look worse than they are. He'll be back in a week or two, right as rain. In the meantime, I thought we could get some pick-ups. There'll be a good low sun in an hour or two.

Anastasia   Look at you: happy as a sandboy. This suits you down to the ground, doesn't it?

Maxim   What do you mean?

Anastasia   You think this means we can spend all day waiting on this light of yours but it doesn't: we've got plenty of other scenes to shoot.

Maxim   Carl – are you all right? You look constipated.

Carl   No – just concerned.

Maxim   About what?

Carl   About your lack of concern.

Maxim   He'll be fine, Carl. The insurance will get him the best doctors around.

Carl   And if he's not?

Maxim   Then my concern won't matter one way or the other. Now get the crew back on the hill: the one overlooking the valley. Take the eighteen mill; and the sixteen for safety. Anni, get Natasha up there, will you?

He leaves, whistling.

Anastasia   What did you want to say to me?

Carl   You just saw it. Sebastian's been injured and all he cares about is his precious light!

Anastasia   Well, we know he doesn't care for him. Should he pretend to now, for appearance's sake?

Carl   Stop defending him, Anni: It's a matter of basic decency. Do you know, when he heard what happened, he laughed, Anni. He *laughed*! I mean, how do we even know – ?

Pause.

Anastasia   Know what?

Pause.

Know what, Carl?

Carl   How do we know – that he didn't do it himself?

Anastasia   Did you see something?

Carl   No –

Anastasia   Was he near the horse when it bolted?

Carl   Well, I'm not sure but look – the point is – though it pains me to say it – I am no longer confident of Maxim's ability to steer this ship to port. I believe it's time for –

Anastasia   Oh shut up, Carl, you – idiot!

She storms off. He shouts after her:

Carl   And when are we going to tell him about us?!

Eva *enters, behind* **Carl**.

Eva   Carl? We're leaving for the hospital now.

Carl   Eva – I need to talk to you.

She nods. He looks furtively over his shoulder at **Anastasia**.

Carl   I'm going to mouth the words to you again.

He takes her by the shoulders and stares intently at her. Begins to mouth:

You remember what we talked about?

She nods. He looks again to see where **Anastasia** *is. He starts mouthing again, with his face turned away from* **Eva**'s.

Carl   The time to act is now. I am ready –

Frustrated, **Eva** *puts her hands on his face and turns him so he's facing her properly.*

At this moment, **Ivan** *enters. He sees them in this seemingly intimate pose:* **Eva**'s hands on **Carl**'s face, staring into each other's eyes.

Carl   I am ready to take the reins –

Ivan   Eva?

Startled, **Carl** *quickly backs away from her.* **Ivan** *approaches them.*

Ivan   Carl? What is this?

Carl   Nothing: we were just – talking.

Ivan   It seemed a little more than that . . .?

Eva   It wasn't.

Ivan *nods, still dubious.*

Carl   I should go: we're moving to the hill again. Trying for that damned light of his.

Carl *nods goodbye and, scratching nervously at himself, all but runs away.*

Eva   The car is waiting for us.

Ivan   Eva – what is going on?

Eva   Nothing –

Ivan   Because this is not the first time I've seen you this way.

Eva   No, really – I'll tell you about it later.

Anastasia (*on phone*)   All right thank you.

She returns.

(*On phone.*) Please just keep me informed.

She hangs up the phone.

That was the hospital.

Eva   We're just leaving for there now.

Ivan   Is there any word of Sebastian?

Pause.

Anastasia   They're saying he's unconscious. They're not sure he'll come out of it.

A mixture of puzzlement and horror.

Act Four

Scene One

Eva *and* **Ivan**.

Ivan Do you want me to be sorry? For being what I am? For raping and killing women and children?! I am not sorry because God is not sorry! I am a man! I am the avatar of God!

She consults the screenplay.

Eva Perfect.

Ivan My last scene.

Eva I know. It will be strange to be back home.

Ivan Usually I am desperate to leave a film set; and they are desperate to see me go. But I have found a happiness here – a happiness I thought was beyond me –

She nods, smiling.

And I cannot let that go. I will not.

He gets down on one knee. She looks shocked. He takes a ring from his own finger.

Eva – due to the remoteness of our location –

Eva No – Ivan –

Ivan It's all right –

Eva No – Ivan – get up; stand up –

She stands him up.

What are you doing?

Pause.

Ivan I want you to be with me.

She shakes her head. Pause.

Eva Ivan – I can't do that.

Ivan Why not?

Eva Why not? Because I have a life – back home.
Another life.

Pause.

I've loved being here. I've loved my time with you. It's been
like a dream in so many ways. But it's time to wake up now.

Pause.

Ivan But – why?

Eva Because we're totally different, Ivan. You know this, in
your heart. We're from totally different worlds.

Ivan Then stay here, in this world. With me.

Pause.

Eva I don't want to.

Ivan Why not?

Eva Because this world is *cruel*, Ivan. Where everyone is
damaged and lies and uses each other. They're monsters; all
of them. Do you not see that?

Ivan But was I not a monster too when you met me?

Eva Yes. You were.

Ivan But you see? I changed.

Eva Love will do that; for a while. But the monster would
return, Ivan. Or it would find a new home in me.

Ivan Maybe it is living there already.

Eva Maybe. Which is all the more reason to go.

Pause.

Ivan   So Maxim was right about you.

Eva   Maxim: he's the worst monster of all. Everything he touches dies. Do you know he told my company? About us? Hoping to get me fired. Luckily my father is the CEO. And he never gave a damn what I did; as long as I was out of his sight.

Pause.

Let's not part on bad terms. We can talk more tonight.

She turns to go.

Ivan   Wait – !

Pause. She turns to him.

I could live in your world. With you.

Eva   You would hate my world.

Ivan   No. I would like any world with you in it.

Pause.

Eva   But I don't want you in that world. That's the truth.

Pause.

Ivan   So your world is cruel too.

He remains standing as the set for the next scene forms around him.

Scene Two

Anastasia *enters and addresses* **Ivan**.

Anastasia   Ivan, please – you've one more scene to film. You've hardly incurred any penalties on your contract.

Carl *enters now.*

Carl   That's right: I never thought I'd say this but you've actually been a pleasure to work with this time.

Maxim *enters.*

Maxim   Leave him alone: can't you see he's heartbroken? He thought it was a great *romance*; when it was just a little holiday fling.

Anastasia   Stop trying to stir things up, Maxim –

Carl   That's right. That's what he's doing.

Anastasia   Ivan, listen – I'm sorry about Eva –

Ivan   Do not speak her name, succubus! You are not worthy to speak those syllables with your lizard's tongue! Look –

He takes out a small plastic bag and thrusts it at each of them in turn:

– you see this? A few precious hairs clipped from my beloved's pubis as she slept! That is all I have left of her! And not one of you is worth even a single golden strand!

Maxim   That's disgusting.

Ivan   Disgusting?! I will tell you what's disgusting! This acrid vomit you call a film is disgusting!! A cheap, gaudy carnival of faeces! Roll up, roll up! See the turds of all shapes and sizes atop their painted horses! Bobbing up and down for your delectation, whilst you watch them with chattering mouths, like cats at a window!

Anastasia   All right, listen – I'll revoke the penalties; I'll wipe the slate clean –

Ivan   You think I will be swayed with money! What use is money to me when I must walk the Earth alone?!

Carl   Ah well – it might not seem important now: but a wise man plans for a flood even when struck by – lightning . . .

Ivan *stares at him, trembling with anger.* **Carl** *squirms awkwardly.*

Maxim   If Ivan doesn't want to do the scene, we can't force him. Maybe he should take a few days off –

Anastasia   No! We're nearly there! This damnable film is nearly done and we can all go home!! Ivan – please: one last scene.

Pause.

Ivan   All right – I will film your wretched scene; if only because it is the last thing Maxim wants.

Maxim   Do as you wish.

Ivan   I will film it on one condition: this one –

He points at **Carl**.

Must mount my faeces.

Pause.

Maxim   Must – ?

Ivan   You heard me: I will drop my pantaloons and excrete. This one will then copulate with my stool until climax. Then – and only then – will I perform your wretched scene.

Carl   Well, that's not going to happen so –

Anastasia   No, Ivan – that's ridiculous. What do you want? Do you want a share of profits?

Ivan   I have made my terms clear.

Carl   Fine. So we re-shoot his scenes, recast; I don't care. If you want me, I'll be in my room.

He starts to go.

Maxim   Carl, wait –

Carl   Why, Maxim? I don't intend to have sex with his faeces and that's an end to it. It's the most ridiculous thing I've ever heard. How would one even go about it? The logistics alone are absurd.

Maxim   Don't worry, Carl –

Carl   I'm not worried. If anything, I'm amused. Or I would be; if it weren't for the fact that this is clearly some kind of twisted fantasy he's already had about me.

Anastasia   Ivan – what are you trying to achieve?

Ivan   Nothing. It is you that have a film to make. If you wish to spend millions more re-shooting my scenes, so be it. If not – he must seed my dung, like the pig-snake he is.

Maxim   Nobody's seeding anyone's dung. Come up with something else.

Ivan   Why are you protecting him? He knows even less of loyalty than you! His is the gurning face of all betrayers. Do you know he has been plotting against you?!

Carl   What? That's nonsense!

Ivan   It's true! Eva told me all about it! He wanted her to fire you and then to take your place as director!

Pause. **Maxim** *turns to* **Carl**, *intrigued.*

Carl   That's not true! She came to me –

Anastasia   Eva?

Carl   She said: *if* you were to be replaced – would I – as someone who was familiar with the project – be willing to step in? It was a purely hypothetical question!

Maxim   But you said yes?

Pause.

Carl   Hypothetically –

Anastasia   And who would produce? Eva?

Carl   It was just – talk, Anni.

Pause.

Anyway – is that so wrong? *If* you had been replaced – if that couldn't have been be avoided – wouldn't you *prefer* it was me that took over? I mean – aren't I a part of this team? I mean – we won the Palme d'Or together, didn't we? We all did that.

Maxim   You think you could take over from me, Carl? The film I've worked on for ten years?

Pause.

Carl   Actually, yes. Why not? Would I make the same film? No. Would I make a better film? Unknown. But do I have the skills necessary to direct a film? Yes. I believe I do!

Anastasia   And what about me? You'd have been happy with her as producer?

Carl   No of course not! I love you, Anni – you . . .

Pause.

Maxim   Sorry, what?

Anastasia *drops her head.*

Carl   We're together, Max. Anni and I. We've been together since we started here. I wanted to tell you.

Ivan   You see? A snake!

Maxim (*to* **Anastasia**)   Is this true?

Anastasia   This isn't the time, Max –

Maxim   It *is* true. You and *Carl*?

Anastasia   It's not serious.

Carl   Anni – what?

Maxim   I'll say! It's about the most absurd thing I've ever heard! You and Carl?

He laughs.

Carl   You see? You see how much he cares, Anni?

Maxim   If I'd have known you were so bored –

Anastasia   Max, please – we can discuss this later. Can we just film this scene and be done with it? Can we find a way to get this done?

Pause.

Maxim   All right –

Pause.

What if he wets himself?

Pause.

What if Carl wets himself; like a little boy; right here, in front of you? Would that be enough for you?

Carl   What – ?

Anastasia   Maxim – don't do this –

Maxim   Ivan? Would you play the scene? If Carl wets himself?

Carl   Don't make suggestions for me – !?

Pause.

Ivan   I would accept that. If he pees himself, like a frightened child; yes: I will film your scene.

Carl   My answer hasn't changed. I don't intend to humiliate myself for him; not for any reason.

Maxim   Humiliation is part of being an artist, Carl.

Carl   You do it then.

Ivan   Not him. You. Traitor.

Maxim   Yes, you. *Traitor*.

Pause.

Carl   You're wasting your time. Anni – make them understand . . .

He looks at her. She stares back at him, fraught.

Maxim   Yes, Anni – please: make us understand.

Pause.

Anastasia   It's not that bad, Carl . . .

Carl   Not that bad . . .?

Maxim   Compared to the other option.

Carl   Anni . . . ?

Anastasia   You'll be wet for a few minutes until you change. It's only degrading if you let it be.

Pause.

Carl   I can't believe you're saying this.

Anastasia   Carl for God's sake! I just want to get this done! I just want to get out of this hotel and go home! Don't you want that?! Don't you want to go home?!

Carl   You're sick. All of you. You're all –

Suddenly – blackout. The noise of film snapping and spooling out of the projector.

Subtitles read: 'SCENE MISSING'.

Silence for a time.

Lights up: **Carl** *is gone.*

Maxim *and* **Anastasia** *sit in shameful silence. A pool of urine on the stage between them.*

Eventually:

Anastasia   Someone should clean that up.

She leaves.

Scene Three

Natasha *enters. She sees* **Maxim**, *still staring at the puddle of piss.*

Natasha   What happened here? Someone spill something?

Pause. She starts to tap her shoe in the puddle, oblivious.

So I heard we should be done by tomorrow. Does that mean you got your light?

Pause.

Maxim   There is no light, Natasha. Or if there is, it's not coming. And if it did, we couldn't catch it. Some things aren't meant to be caught.

Pause.

Some things must stay out of reach.

Natasha   Right. *Now* you fucking tell me . . .

Maxim   I don't get you . . .?

Natasha   Well. After all that with Sebastian.

Pause.

Maxim   All what with Sebastian?

Natasha   You know – the accident. With the horse?

Pause. She shrugs, pleased with herself.

Maxim   You did that? You made the horse – bolt?

Natasha   Yeah. Stuck a spike in it and off it went; with him on the back. I know he was only out for a week or two but . . . better than nothing, right?

Maxim   Better than *nothing*? Natasha – he was comatose for days. He could have been paralysed. He could have died, for God's sake!

Natasha   Yeah but he didn't did he?

Maxim *can't believe what he's hearing.*

Maxim   Why, Natasha? In God's name, why?

She shrugs.

Natasha   Because we're friends. Friends give each other things. Don't they?

Maxim   And you think that's what I wanted? For you to nearly kill someone?!

Natasha   No but – for your light and stuff.

Maxim   Oh Jesus Christ – what is wrong with you?! It's a film, Natasha! We're making a film! Nobody's supposed to get hurt! Nobody's supposed to die for it! What is wrong with you? Are you some kind of *monster*?

Natasha   All right, look: I was trying to help. I thought you'd be pleased but you're not.

Maxim   *Pleased* – ?!

Natasha   I get it. I did something bad. Move on.

Pause.

Why don't I do the speech again? Would you like that?

He backs away from her.

Maxim   Leave me alone –

Natasha   Just tell me what you want. What emotion you want. Just direct me.

Maxim   Go away – please –

Natasha   I think I can do love now. I've been working on it. Do you want to see? Do you want to see love?

Maxim   I said go AWAY!

He pushes her back violently but slips in the piss and falls. Disgusted, he scrabbles to his feet and runs away.

Natasha   Maxim – !

Pause.

Jesus. So fucking dramatic.

Scene Four

The compound set.

Ivan *is pacing, in character.* **Natasha**, **Anastasia** *and* **Maxim** *waiting.*

Ivan   In God's name, when are we filming this sewage?! I can't bear to keep these words in my head a second longer!

Natasha   Shut the fuck up.

Anastasia *approaches* **Maxim**.

Anastasia   This isn't right: Carl shouldn't have to film this.

Maxim   He said he wanted to.

Anastasia   I don't care, Max. I don't want him to.

Maxim   Anni –

Anastasia   No – it's not right. It's not right.

Carl *enters. He looks deranged.*

He raises the gun and points it at **Ivan**.

Carl   Brute!

Ivan *looks alarmed.*

Ivan   No!

Carl   BANG!!

Everybody jumps. They check themselves. No damage.

Did you wet yourself? Like a frightened child?!! Did you, Brute? Did you?!

He begins to laugh hysterically.

Natasha   What the fuck is wrong with you?!

Carl   They're blanks – it's all right –

Pause. **Maxim** *laughs with relief.*

Maxim   Very good, Carl –

Ivan   No . . .

Maxim   Can't say we didn't –

Ivan   No!

Maxim   – deserve it –

Ivan *takes the gun from* **Carl***.*

Ivan   They were not blanks!

Pause.

I wanted it real.

At the back, **Anastasia** *drops to her knees, holding her chest. Blood blossoms there. They watch her sway for a moment. She looks up to the sky, as if seeing something and says:*

Anastasia   Apples . . .

Then falls forward, dead.

Carl   ANNI!

Carl *rushes to her.* **Maxim** *stands stunned.* **Ivan** *points at him.*

Ivan   Eva was right: you are a disease, Maxim. Not the Child of Ashes. The ashes themselves.

He storms out.

Scene Five

Anastasia'*s body is wheeled away.*

Natasha *takes* **Carl** *out, her arm around him as he sobs.*

The entire stage is cleared.

Maxim *sits downstage on the bare floor. Finally, he is alone.*

Maxim   Well – here we are again. You know what to do, Maxim. You've done it before.

Outside, the wind picks up, blowing leaves in through the hotel doors . . .

Music starts to rise . . .

He is oblivious at first, until he notices a change in the light –

Slowly, he stands up and turns to see. The sound and music build.

He watches in wonder as an image forms in front of him: a forest of cherry blossom trees, their branches meeting to form a canopy above him, dappling the light from the golden sun that rises behind them –

It's here – Anni, it's here – !

He runs in amongst the trees as the sun begins to move, in an arc above him, and he's swallowed by the light –

Maxim   The light, Anni, look – somebody – I told you! I told you! The light!

Blossom swirls around him – the trees seem to stretch for ever ahead of him until they're swallowed by the light –

And then – the music still rising – a face appears, seemingly forming from the branches of the trees, almost an illusion; indistinct except for the mouth, the lips full and turning from blossom pink to cherry red –

*And **Maxim** reaches up to the lips and as soon as he does they fade away and he drops to his knees as the music builds and builds to its height –*

And then drops suddenly to just an expectant shimmer as the light settles and becomes sepulchral, wavering between light and dark –

*And the face has gone and the blossom has stopped falling and **Maxim** kneels there amongst it; and then a fox appears, sniffing tentatively towards him and he reaches out to it but before it can reach him the lights fade to darkness and everything is gone.*

This has all happened in seconds.

End.

Scene Five (Alternative Version)

Anastasia's *body is wheeled away.*

Natasha *takes* **Carl** *out, her arm around him as he sobs.*

The entire stage is cleared.

Maxim *sits downstage on the bare floor. Finally, he is alone.*

Maxim   Well – here we are again. You know what to do, Maxim. You've done it before.

After a moment, he straightens, as if seeing something.

He gets to his feet, excitement building.

It's here – Anni, it's here – !

He begins to run about the stage, waving his arms, delirious with joy.

Cameras! Someone bring the cameras! Carl! Anni – it's here! I told you!

He closes his eyes, bathing in the blissful light.

The light, Anni, look – I told you – the light!

And he stands there, triumphant, his arms up to the sky.

But we can see and hear nothing.

End.

The Prudes

The Prudes was first performed at the Royal Court Theatre, London, on 18 April 2018 with the following cast and creative team:

Him   Jonjo O'Neill
Her   Sophie Russell

Director Anthony Neilson
Designer Fly Davis
Lighting Designer Chahine Yavroyan
Sound Designer Nick Powell

Characters

Him
Her

Notes

Lines or phrases in square brackets indicate references which may be specific to the UK, or to the time of writing, which can be omitted in future/non-UK productions or altered to suit the time or location of productions.

The set consists of two high chairs, separated by a chair bearing flowers and wine glasses. Until the last quarter of the play, all scenes of intimacy are played from these chairs, with no direct physical contact. The flooring was memory foam, suggesting a giant mattress. The entire auditorium was tented, fluffy and exceedingly pink.

The net curtain twitches as the couple take peeks at the audience. Eventually, they step out. They take their seats – separated by a table, on which sit two glasses of wine – in front of the audience.

Him   Hello –

Her   Hi . . .

Pause.

Him   Bit nervous as you can imagine . . .

Pause.

Umm – I'm James. James Prude.

Her   No you're not! He's not –

Him   No, I'm not. We're not 'the Prudes'. That would be cheesy.

Her   We're not 'the' anything . . .

Him   No –

Her   We're not married.

Him   No. Marriage is an irrelevant relic of the male patriarchy.

Her   Unless you're gay . . .

Him   Yes. In which case, it's fine.

Pause.

Her   I'm Jessica, by the way. Jess.

Him   And I *am* James. Friends call me Jimmy. [Sort of discouraged that since the whole Savile thing but . . . hard to turn the ship around.]

Pause.

Her   We live together. Six years come July.

Her   I've got to say though – thinking about it – I kind of resent the implication that we're prudes. I'm not a prude.

Her   I'm a little bit prudish.

Him   You're not.

She smiles: You're telling me what I am?

Him   You know what I'm saying – we're not uncomfortable with sex, generally. We've had a pretty adventurous sex life; until recently. Sex toys; role-play . . .

Her   Yes, ok: Don't need the gory details.

Him   I'm just saying: we've not stuck to the beaten path. Not *crazy* –

Her   No –

Him   Not, like – dogging and stuff.

Her   No. No dogging.

Him   No –

Her   We don't have a car, for one thing.

Him   Well – you don't need a car to go dogging.

Her   Sounds like you know.

Him   I do know. Doesn't mean I've done it. Doesn't mean I *want* to do it.

Her   See, I'm a bit prudish about that: having sex in a car whilst men in rainwear peer in and – flail at themselves. And what are the dogs doing all that time? Just running around, unsupervised?

She shakes her head.

Him   But that's not prudish. You don't want to go dogging – *we* don't want to go dogging – but we don't mind if other people do it, do we? We don't object morally –

Her   Morally? No.

Him   Exactly. I mean, I don't like the idea of golden showers – it defeats the whole purpose, in my opinion – but a sizeable minority clearly do. More power to them, I say.

Her   Live and let die.

Him   So it's not that we're prudes. It's just that we haven't . . .

Pause.

Her   Had sex.

Him   Yes. We haven't – *had sex* – in –

Her   Fourteen months and four days.

Pause.

I keep a diary.

Him   She keeps a diary.

Her   Since I was thirteen.

Him   But to be clear: this isn't an age thing.

Her   No.

Him   I mean, I'm only thirty-eight and Jess is only –

She honks a horn.

And that's young these days. So it's not a mid-life crisis thing, is it?

Her   Well – it's a crisis –

Him   Of sorts –

Her   In that you can't go on not having sex; otherwise what's the point?

Him   Well – companionship . . .

Her   That's why you get a dog.

Pause. He looks hurt.

What ?

Him   Like to think I've a *bit* more to offer –

Her   You know what I mean: if you don't have children, there's nothing you get from a relationship that you can't get elsewhere; except the sex.

Him   You can get sex elsewhere.

Her   Meaningless sex, maybe.

Him   See, I don't get that: maybe I'm exceptional but I've never had meaningless sex. It's always been meaningful for me.

Her   You never had a one-night stand?

Him   I didn't say that –

Her   Cos I know *that's* not true.

Him   But it was always meaningful; even if it just meant I shouldn't drink so much. The point is: if it doesn't matter where you get the companionship, why is the sex any different?

Her   But it's the whole package, isn't it? The sex makes the companionship special and then that makes the sex special.

Him   So just have sex with your friends then.

Her   But then you're in a relationship. Aren't you?

Pause.

Him   How did we get on to this?

Her   Umm – dogging . . . children . . . crisis!

Him   But not a *mid-life* crisis –

Her   No. You've not started wearing skinny jeans and riding a Segway.

Him   No. And you're not having hot flushes and worrying that your life is a hollow charade.

Her   Nope. No flushes.

Pause.

Him   What else is it not?

Her   Umm –

Him   Oh: it's not a seven-year itch.

Her   Couldn't be really.

Him   No –

Her   Been together nine.

Him   The point is: it's not boredom. We're not bored with each other, are we?

Her   No . . .

Pause.

I mean, we're not like *teenagers* –

Him   No – 'course not –

Her   We don't pine for each other after a day apart –

Him   No – !

Solo lights on her:

Her   Roger was my first school crush. Roger Manley; swear to God. I'd find ways to drop his name in conversation; and just saying it was like [Fizz Wizz] in my heart . One day in the playground, he reached out and touched my tunic, just briefly, to remove a stray hair; and to this day, I swear, it might be the most powerfully erotic moment of my life.

Pause.

Sadly, Roger became the subject of sustained and widespread ridicule when he shat himself on a trip to [Blenheim Palace]; so I was forced to sever all ties.

Lights on both:

But no – we're not *bored* with each other. We're still – attracted to each other, I think . . .?

She looks at him. He realises.

Him   Yes!

She makes a buzzer noise [à la Just a Minute *(a radio game show)].*

Her   Hesitation!

Him   No, honestly, that's not –

Pause.

And just for the record – if you're thinking it's *her* fault – you're wrong.

Her   Why would they think it's my fault?

Him   Well that's the cliché, isn't it? The guy always wants sex but the woman doesn't cos she's – got a headache or something. But I'm saying right now, upfront, that's not what this is. If anyone dropped the ball on our sex life, it's me. I'm holding my hands up to that. Do *not* blame the woman. Ok?

She nods. Pause.

You agree with that?

Her   Well –

Him   You think it was me that dropped the ball?

Her   You just said –

Him   I know what I said; but it takes two to drop a ball.

She looks puzzled: Does it?

Because let's be fair: something happened, didn't it? Something that made us both drop the ball; for a bit.

She sighs.

I'm not blaming you. I'm just saying that, tracing it back, that was roughly when it started. Stopped.

Her   My diary says different.

Him   It wasn't the only factor; but it was a factor.

Her   I thought we weren't going to mention this – ?

Him   I haven't said what it was.

(*To audience.*) Sorry: something happened. But we agreed not to tell you what it was.

Her   It's not relevant.

Him   Well – I think it might be, actually; but out of respect for your privacy, we're not going to say what it was. I just think they should know that we both played a part in the initial dropping of the ball. Is that fair?

Her   I don't know; probably. I mean – who dropped it? When was it dropped? Was there even a ball to begin with?

He nods.

Whose ball was it? What do we mean by ball? Can we have our ball back – ?

Him   Eh?

Her   That's why we're here though, isn't it? To get our ball back.

Him   The truth is – I just lost the thread. And when you lose that thread, it's hard to get hold of again.

Her   Much like actual thread.

He stares at her. She looks at him: what?

Him   No more metaphors. Let's put our cards on the table: the reason we're here . . .

Pause.

Do you want to say it?

Her   I can say it . . .

Him   I don't mind saying it. I just don't want to look like I'm the overbearing guy who says everything.

Her   You don't.

Him   I feel like I'm talking a lot.

Her   Do you *want* me to say it?

Him   I don't mind which of us says it. Just as long as –

Her   We're going to have sex.

Pause. A small monkey in a waistcoat and fez cycles arthritically across the stage. (Not really.)

Her   Right?

Him   Yup.

Her   Tonight.

Him   Uh-huh.

Her   Here.

Him   Yup. Try, anyway.

Her [(*as Yoda*)   'There is no try, young Skywalker . . .']

He smiles, tight-lipped.

No – JK. There's no pressure. Just see how it goes.

He gets off his chair, possessed by a manic energy born from nervousness.

Him   But that's it: you can go to counselling and therapy –

Her   And we *have* . . .

Him   – but at the end of the day, you have to just – do it, you know? Just –

Her   Do it.

Him   'Do it.'

Her   'Just DO IT.'

Him   Like [Body Pump]. 'Do it'!

Her   'Do it.'

Him   We met at a [Body Pump] class.

Her   I thought he was gay at first.

Him   I don't mind that. I'm secure. What if I had been?

Her   Well – we wouldn't be together, would we?

Him   Homophobe.

Her   'Methinks you might be changing the subject, good sir.'

Him   'Dost thou, milady?'

Her   'I dost.'

Him   D'you remember our first proper date? At that Tudor-y place?

Her   Well – that was our second date but yes –

Him   You had red hair back then –

Her (*to audience*)   Brown, really –

Him   And you had that fringe, just like –

He makes a severe gesture across his forehead.

Her   Bangs. I had bangs.

Him   Why do they call it bangs? Who knows? Sexy though. I don't know why but bangs are sexy. And heels – you had heels on –

Her   Tottering about, like a baby giraffe.

Him   No, you looked great. She scrubs up well; she really does.

Her   Well – scrubbed up now but . . .

Him   Yes but not –

Her   Not like that, no; but I was younger then; and more of a – scrubber. Anyway –

Him   Funny thing was: I was quite pleased with myself cos I'd never been out with a redhead before –

Her   Collect the set . . .

Him   And then about six months later, she comes round and her hair's this colour –

Her   Not quite.

Him   Bangs are gone –

Her   Way before . . .

Him   – and she was like, 'You thought that was my real hair?' –

Her   Real *colour*.

Him   – and I was like 'Yes!' I had no idea!

Her   There were clues. 'Curtains and cuffs'.

Him   I know but I didn't know – ! So I hadn't been going out with a redhead at all! I was, like –

He mimes being on the phone.

'Hello? Trade descriptions?'

She smiles curtly, a little hurt.

Her   Sorry: no refunds.

Him   No, it's fine. I wasn't disappointed – I just thought, 'What an idiot!' Six months in and I didn't know your hair colour!

Her   Still don't.

He laughs at this. She makes a face: not a joke.

Him   I don't?

She shakes her head: no. Then looks at her watch.

Her   Jimmy – James – do you think maybe we should – get started?

Pause.

Him   Ok.

Pause.

Her   Like – *now-ish?*

Him   Okay. I mean – if we've set the scene . . .?

Her   I think we have . . .

Him   There's nothing else we should tell them?

Her   Can't *think* of anything . . .

Him   Nope? Ok – well: I guess we should just –

Her   – do it.

Him   Yep.

He turns to face the audience.

So – umm – I should just warn you that – whilst entirely natural; and completely consensual – what you're about to witness – may nonetheless offend certain – sensibilities; and that's not our intention. So if anyone feels like they want to leave – now would be – the time.

Nobody will make any judgements: you could be leaving for any number of reasons. Anyone (else)? Last chance . . .

All right – so: ladies and gentlemen – without further ado – my partner and I will now – sex!

A drum roll begins, insanely loud.

Hold on: stop. Stop that!

It stops.

Ok, that's not helpful. Whose idea was that? Jess – ?

She shakes her head.

Come on, guys: it's stressful enough . . .

Her   Can we have something more relaxing?

Whale song.

Ok, that's better. Is that better?

Him   It's better than a drum roll . . .

Her   Ok: just take a second.

He hits something, in faux frustration.

Him   Damn it!

Her   It's okay . . .

Him   No, you see – there was a moment there. A familiar hackling of the scrotal hairs that tells you 'You are present: you are animal; you are ready to seize the prize'. And now it's gone . . .

Her   It'll come back.

Pause.

Him   See it's easier for you; to just – do it. All you have to do is –

Her   Lie back and think of England?

Him   Or wherever. I'm not saying you'd enjoy it. But you could just *do it*. You might need some lubrication; but that can be done artificially. You can't have an artificial erection.

Her   Well . . . we've talked about that.

Him   I don't need *viagra*.

Her   There's no shame in it . . .

Him   I know there's no shame in it! I just don't need it, that's all. I don't have – erectile issues.

Her   Well –

Him   I don't! Not actual – *physiological* – !

Her   You keep saying that; but how do you know?

Him   Because.

Her   Because – ?

Him   Because I wouldn't be able to . . .

Pause.

Her   To what?

Lights on him:

Him   To masturbate! That's what I want to say. There's no problem with that. In solitude, the soldier stands steadfast. But I can't tell her that: it feels like a betrayal. This is where we are after fourteen months of celibacy: I say there's no shame but there fucking is. There's shame everywhere.

Under U/V light, the stage is revealed to be covered with stains.

We used to masturbate quite freely, back in the day. We'd do it together sometimes, shoulder to shoulder, with the sun just rising through the blinds.

Lights shift to her:

Her   Is he talking about masturbation? He is, isn't he?

Pause.

I know he does it. A girl knows the signs: the laptop ajar. Teddy facing the wall, like the Blair Witch got him. Toilet rolls out of context; their crispy white flowers blooming in baskets; relics of a cold that never was.

Pause.

I'm not saying I don't do it. He used to watch me do it. He'd ask me to. I was shy at first but then I got to like it. I mean, he got the Audrey Hepburn version; not the bum-up, sweaty, [Charlotte Church] version; but even so – the fact that he wanted to – and in his eyes, I could see myself – see what he saw; and I was . . .

Pause. Lights on him:

Him   It was just Jess, for years. We'd have sex and then I'd masturbate thinking of the sex we had; which made me want more sex. She colonised every inch of my erotic landscape. She was every penny in the wank-bank.

And then a snake crept into the garden; an apple was bitten; and I was no longer a child of nature; just some bloke, bollock-naked, in a field.

Now I masturbate like I'm at my mother's house. She must know I do it – not my mother: Jess – but she doesn't know when or how often. Not that any woman knows that. I mean, I masturbate –

He honks a horn.

– times a –

Honk.

– but I'd never give that information up willingly. No man would. You always lowball. That's the rule. And what you think of when you do it? That's like Magic Circle shit. You don't even admit that to yourself: you take that stuff to the grave.

Lights on her:

Her   He probably watches porn. They all do, whatever they say. That doesn't bother me. But who's he thinking of the rest of the time? The girl next door? The girl that got away? That fucking – [Dua Lipa] cow? Maybe all of them; in some kind of unfeasible wheel of cunnilingus. Why not? Anyone could be in there. My sister could be in there. She better not be. I've always thought he had a thing for her. He tried to get a fantasy going about me and her shagging once. I shut him right down. Dirty bastard!

Lights on him:

Him   There's no rejection in Porn Land; no crossed wires; no judgement.

And sometimes it works for me; five stupid minutes and I'm done; like farting, without the sense of achievement. But sometimes I trawl the net for hours; not for weirder porn but for little spikes of truth – a look, a gesture; something recognisable as life; something that reminds me; of Jess; and how we used to be.

Lights on her:

Her   But now we 'respect each other's privacy'. We close doors. We knock before entering. We telegraph our approach, with coughs and heavy steps. We freeze at the merest creak and listen; like rabbits in the grass.

Lights on him:

Him   We wank alone; in separate rooms; on different floors.

Pause.

And shame is everywhere. On everything.

Lights on both of them:

Him   Look, it's not a medical problem. Can you just accept my word for that?

Her   Fine.

Him   I know men say, 'Oh my penis has a mind of its own'. But that's not true. Or it's not true for me . There's only one mind and that's this one. And what's going on up *here* – is directly linked to what happens – down *there*.

Her   It's psychological. I get it.

Him   Do you though?

Her   Yes, I get it. But what am I supposed to do? I don't want a life without sex. Do you want that?

Him   Ok, fine! So I take a viagra and I get an erection. Then what?

Her   I don't know, Jimmy: lie back and think of [England]?!

Pause. He looks hurt. She relents.

I'm not being heartless: I'm just saying – maybe if you address the physical problem – the rest will follow . . .

Him   Ok. Maybe. But why bother with the potential cardiac risk of viagra? I could just tie a stick to it; like it was a tomato plant. Or better yet – I could get a strap-on! How would that suit you? Me in a strap-on just pounding like a piston from behind. And then you go 'Oh – what's that on my shoulders? Did you ejaculate? Is it semen?' and I'll go 'No, Jess – it's *tears*! Cos I'm *crying*: it's the stinging-hot tears of male emasculation!'

Her   Now you're being stupid.

Him   Why? Because I thought you might want something more *meaningful*?

Pause.

I mean don't you care, Jess? Don't you care what's happening in my head?

She sighs and looks at the audience. Pause. Lights on her:

Her   My little niece – who my Sister decided to call Poppin for some reason – she's seven; and she's literally obsessed with *Goldilocks*. Every time I'm there, she's like 'Read me Goldilocks, Auntie Jess! Goldilocks and the Bears!' Which is disappointing because, even at her age, I thought it was the most stupid story ever.

Seriously: what's it about? A little girl with presumably *fantastic* hair breaks into a family home, eats their cereal, breaks a chair and then crashes out in their bedroom. Then the family comes home – they're bears – and she screams and jumps out the window. The End.

Now, what's the moral there? Fairy tales should be little lessons that teach you something. But what does my niece learn from that? Don't take a kip in the house you've just burgled? It's *guff*.

But then: I saw this documentary, about – space or something: and it said that when a planet orbits a sun at exactly the right distance – so it's not too hot for life and not too cold – they say it's in the Goldilocks zone. And suddenly the penny dropped: every time I read Goldilocks to my niece, this is the message she's getting:

Don't be too hot. Don't be too cold. Don't be too big. Don't be too small. Don't be too hard. Don't be too soft. And – whatever you do – *never* piss off the bears.

Lights on both:

Of course I care what's happening in your head. But what is that? I can't help you if I don't know.

Him It's not any one thing. It's just that there are – *sexy* thoughts – and there are – *un*sexy thoughts –

Her Right . . . like what though?

Him I don't know – the usual stuff – Death. Racial inequality. Tax returns . . .

Her You think about tax returns during sex?

Him No but –

Her Cos that would be the *only* time you think about them . . .

He stares at her: Seriously? She dismisses him.

JK . . .

Him JK?

Her Jo-king.

Him Just kidding?

Her   Yes . . .

Him   It means just kidding. JK.

Pause.

Her   I *know*. Which means Jo-king.

Him   Who do you know that says JK?

Her   Who do I *know*?

Him   Is it someone at work? Cos that's what you do. You suddenly start saying something like JK – or 'I've no dog in the fight' – and I know you've picked it up off someone at work.

Her   I don't think –

Him   'Said no one ever'. That's another one.

Her   Lots of people say 'JK'. You don't like it; that's what you're saying?

Him   No –

Her   You don't like me saying it.

Him   I don't –

Her   You want me to stop saying it.

Him   I don't care what you say! Don't make out like I'm –

Her   So what's the problem?

Him   There's no problem! It was just an observation.

Her   Was it?

Pause.

Him   I don't know. Was it? I'm trying to be honest with myself. Why does it bother me that she said JK?

Pause.

It's a bit wanky. It's the sort of thing that makes you think 'tool'. Some tool at work, probably. But whoever it is, she likes them enough to hear them say JK and think, 'Oh yeah that's a cool thing to say: I'm going to start saying that.'

Pause.

You know what? I *don't* want her to say JK. But that's controlling, isn't it? I can't be telling her what to say; any more than I can tell her to stop wearing those fucking flip-flops in summer because they make her look like Bilbo fucking Baggins and the sound of her flipping and flopping about in them makes all human endeavour seem so fucking futile that I want to climb up on the kitchen-top and tea-bag the fucking blender!

Pause.

She didn't used to wear flip-flops. And I dropped hints in advance. I basically said: I don't know why but flip-flops disgust me. I said when I see a girl in flip-flops, however attractive, my junk rots like a time-lapse fruit bowl. But then we went on holiday to Spain and she started wearing them anyway. Maybe that's *why* she started wearing them: as an act of defiance against the patriarchy I symbolise. And look – nobody hates the patriarchy more than me; my dad was an arsehole – but then when we don't have sex for the entire holiday, she's all hurt and like, 'What's wrong? Don't you fancy me anymore?' So great: everyone loses.

He sits down. Pause.

Her   You know I heard all that, don't you?

Him   Hmm?

She points to the lighitng rig.

Her   If the light's on both of us, I can hear you. That's the rule.

Pause.

Him   Ok, listen –

Her   That's why we didn't have sex in Spain that time?

Him   No – Jess, forget all that: I was just playing to the crowd –

Her   No you weren't –

Him   I was. I was ranting. People like a ranting man. It's funny for some reason.

Her   It's fine. It's good. We shouldn't suppress these things. I just didn't know you felt so strongly about flip-flops.

Him   I don't –

Her   Clearly you do. I'll stop wearing them.

Him   No – please don't –

Her   Jimmy, it's fine. It's not like I *love* flip-flops. They were free with *Marie Claire*.

Him   Jess, please: I'm not that guy. I don't want to tell you what to wear.

Her   You're not. It's my decision. It's not a big deal: certainly not worth you destroying all the tea-bags.

Pause.

Him   Look: let's reset, ok? How about we open another bottle of wine?

Pause.

Her   As opposed to a bottle of *whine*? Which is what *you* just opened.

Him   Oh very *good*. You're like bacon tonight.

Her   Bacon?

Him   You're on a roll.

She shakes her head.

There you go, see? We can still laugh together. That's something. Girls always say that's the most important quality in a man: that he makes them laugh.

Her   Maybe. You want to feel safe, more than anything. Hard to laugh if you don't feel safe.

He gives her a glass of wine.

Him   Ok. Let's do this.

Her   Sure?

Him   Yep.

Her   Oh – did you bring any – ?

Him   Gum?

Her   No. You know . . .

Pause.

Condoms.

Him   Why?

Her   Why ? Umm –

She indicates the audience. Pause.

Him   No but aren't you on the – ?

Her   Jimmy – no: I came off that months ago. I told you.

Him   You didn't.

Her   Well, there was no point in keeping on taking it.

Him   Fine; but you didn't tell me . . .

Her   I *did*. I remember telling you.

Him   What did I say?

Her   You said it was up to me.

Pause.

Him   I have no memory of that.

Her   Well, it's in my diary.

Him   Shit. What do we do about that?

Pause. She looks at the audience.

Jess, no –

Her   Why not?

She addresses the audience:

Sorry, everyone – I know this is a lot to ask – but can anyone lend us a – ?

Him   No, wait, come on –

Her   What?

Him   You'll embarrass them.

Her   They're here to watch us have *sex* –

Him   No but it means admitting they've got a –

Her   That's not embarrassing. It's very sensible.

Him   No but it means they're –

Her   What?

Him   You know – looking for it. *Hoping* for it.

Her   Oh don't be daft –

To the audience:

Listen: Nobody's making any judgements –

Him   Jess, Jess, Jess – it's fine: it's better, actually. It's better without one.

Her   I've heard that before. Right, ladies?

Him   No, not – because of that; it's just – it's less of a foregone conclusion. And if we get there – *when* we do – then I'll just – withdraw.

Her   Withdraw?

Him   Yeah. Not a problem.

Her   You never withdraw . . .

Him   Not with you –

Her   What?

Him   I never had to. But before you –

Her   Before me?

Him   Before you I was, like – the king of withdrawal.

Her   The king – ?

She curtseys and takes his hand. They dance, in courtly fashion.

Him   Had a crown and everything.

Her   So I'm in the presence of royalty?

Him   You may kiss my ring.

She drops his hand, briefly disgusted by the innuendo.

No, not – like that –

Her   Well – if Your Highness is sure – ?

She ushers him back to his seat.

Him   But let's start nice and easy, shall we? Baby steps.

Her   Baby steps . . .

Him   Yeah. I mean – how about I just – put my arm around you? Just to begin with?

Her   Ok . . .

Him   Ok: I'll put my arm around you.

She nods. He doesn't do anything. They never touch, only talk.

How's that?

Her   Nice.

Him   Nice, isn't it? Like old times.

She nods. Pause.

Him   We should have done more of this, probably.

Pause.

That's the problem: You stop – being intimate – and soon you're not touching at all.

Pause.

But it's stupid, really. I mean, this is really fine. I'm totally at ease with this.

Her   I'm going to rest my head on your shoulder then . . .

Him   Go ahead.

Pause.

Her   Is that ok?

Him   It's good. Like being at the pictures.

Pause.

First girl I ever snogged was at the pictures. I think it was, like – *Basic Instinct* or something. I was a bit shocked when she put the tongue in. This little thing poking into my mouth. But once I'd got over that . . . I got a bit bored, if I'm honest.

Pause.

Her   You didn't – touch her?

Him   Not much to touch really. Not upstairs anyway.

Pause.

Her   What about – downstairs?

Him   No chance: you'd have needed a jack to get those knees apart.

Pause.

Her   You wouldn't need that with me.

Awkward pause.

I said you wouldn't –

Him   I remember I pulled her hair when I kissed her cos that's what Michael Douglas was doing. She didn't mind that.

Pause.

There was a lot of that in movies back then. Rough stuff: shoving girls against walls, throwing them down on beds. Tearing their clothes. It was a sign of passion.

Her   I remember.

Him   Seems creepy now but back then – it was almost an insult if you weren't a bit rough.

Like you weren't that bothered.

Pause.

Her   Changed days.

Him   Thank God.

He nods. Pause.

I was a bit rough with you now and then. I mean – not seriously but – grabbed your hair a bit. Little bitey here and there.

She nods.

You didn't seem to mind that. Did you mind that?

Her   It's all about context, isn't it?

He nods – not sure what that means. Then he stiffens (not like that) –

I've put my hand on your thigh.

Him   Yep.

Her   Is that ok?

Pause. Lights have slowly ramped up on the house.

Him   Suddenly very aware of the audience . . .

Her   They're fine: ignore them.

Him   Ok. Yep.

Her   Just rubbing it now. Just my fingers moving; small circular motions. More soothing than sexual.

Him   But advancing slightly with every rotation –

Her   But only by fractions of a millimetre –

Him   Yes – but with a clear destination –

Her   Which they never have to reach; if they're not welcome.

Pause.

Are they welcome?

Him   They're not *not* welcome . . .

The distant sound of a woman crying.

Do you hear that?

Her   What?

Louder now.

Him   Someone crying. A woman – crying . . .

Her   Are you sure?

Him   Yes –

Her   Because sometimes you've thought you heard me crying . . .

Him   No, listen: out there. In the audience.

Pause.

Why's she crying? Is it my fault?

Her   Why would it be your fault?

Louder –

Him   I don't know: did I say something ? Did I not say something I should have said? Did I do something? Did I not do something – ?

Her   Jimmy – calm down: it might be hard to believe but you are not the delta of all women's tears. Maybe she's just moved.

Louder –

Him   No – there's something wrong. What's wrong?

Her   Don't lose focus.

The crying stops.

My hand is on your thigh.

Him   Ok . . .

Her   Small rotations.

He nods.

And now my fingertips are just skirting the area . . . just lightly . . . can you feel it?

Lights on him:

Him   Don't be soft. Don't be soft. A little prayer to my penis.

She wants to feel it stiffen at her touch. I want her to feel that. I want her to feel wanted. Everything would be right in the world. Everything would be back to how it was.

She's getting closer. Don't be soft. You're pathetic when you're soft. When you're stiff, you command respect. But when you're soft – you're weak, laughable; a shivering child in a cold bath. Stand up. Be a man. Don't be soft. Twitch at least.

Lights on both. He gets up from the chair:

Him   Wait, wait –

Her   Jimmy –

Him   I just need to ask you something; and then we'll go on, I promise.

She nods.

This is a very vulnerable thing to ask; but I want an honest answer, ok?

Her   Ok.

Him   But you can't hate me for it. You can't be disgusted – all right?

Her   I'm sure I won't hate you . . .

Him   But you can't be disgusted either. For your sake as much as mine. Cos if you're disgusted, I'll feel ashamed; and then I won't be able to – do – what we came here to do. Do you understand?

Her   Jesus, Jimmy – that seems –

Him   Don't show it then. You can be disgusted but hide it. Don't make a face or go quiet or anything. Can you do that? Can you hide it?

Her   Yes. I can do that.

Pause.

Him   Ok. So – I had a girlfriend at college – Severyn – and sometimes – I'd wake up in the middle of the night in a state of – arousal –

Pause.

And Sevvy would be asleep – but nonetheless – I would just – you know –

Her   Have sex with her?

Him   Yes.

Her   And she didn't wake up?

Him   No. I mean – yes! She wasn't asleep when I – !

Her   Ok –

Him   No – Jesus – no: I wouldn't – penetrate – a sleeping woman.

Her   Good to know.

Him   She'd wake up as soon as I started – touching her. A bit startled at first but she always went with it. Got into it even. Enthusiastically sometimes.

Her   What's the question?

Him   Well – the fact remains – that I didn't *ask* – I just – *took*. So – you know – technically speaking – isn't that . . .?

Her   How often did this – ?

Him   I mean – quite often –

Her   And she never said to stop doing it?

Him   No. Never really mentioned it.

Her   And she didn't end the relationship?

Him   No. Not then.

Her   Then she was ok with it. She consented.

Him   Did she?

Her   Pretty much.

Him   No but, Jess – did she consent? Or did she *relent*? There's a difference.

Her   You're not a rapist. Ok?

Him   I'm not, am I?

Her   I mean generally it's best to stick to fully conscious women –

Him   Oh yeah: I wouldn't do that now.

Her   – but it sounds like she was ok with it.

Pause.

Him   I feel like maybe I should call her; but last I heard she'd moved back to Reading.

Pause.

You're on Facebook, aren't you?

Her   Jimmy – how does this help us?

Him   Facebook?

Her   No: how is your fretting about – whether you're a rapist or not – how does that help us here? Tonight?

Him   Because it's been on my mind. And that's not a sexy thought. Well – unless you're a rapist, I guess; in which case it might be . . .

Her   You know what? I think this is what we talked about in therapy. We could get into a big philosophical discussion about this but that's just our way of avoiding the *real* issues.

Him   An avoidance strategy.

Her   Exactly.

To an electronic riff, the two of them do the 'robot', whilst chanting in robot monotone:

Both   Avoidance strategy / Avoidance strategy / Avoy-dance! / Avoy-dance!

Avoidance strategy / Avoidance strategy / Avoy-dance! / Avoy-dance!

They stop.

Her   Exactly. So we have to stay focused. Because I'm not joking, Jimmy –

Him   JK.

Pause.

Her   If we can't do this – it's curtains for us.

Pause.

Him   Don't say that . . .

Her   It is, Jimmy. It has to be. You know this.

Him   Sooner or later . . .

Her   Then I choose sooner. Because I can't do later. It's too late for later.

Pause.

Him   That's not fair . . .

Her   Maybe not.

Him   It's cruel.

Her   Maybe. But this is where we are now.

He nods.

Him   Ok. Ok. Fuck it.

He leaves the auditorium. Blackout. When he returns, he's carrying a storm lantern, as if he were a lighthouse keeper. He addresses the audience as if he was telling a ghost story:

Ok: I know me and Jess had an agreement and I know it's not my story to tell but I'm sorry: I need you to know what this thing is that happened. Because you can't understand what I'm dealing with otherwise.

Pause.

And I'd appreciate it if we could keep the fact that I'm telling you between us. So if it comes up later – poker face. Ok?

Pause.

The short version is – I discovered – she didn't tell me – but I discovered – that Jess – had put something – on a website. Not with her own name. A pseudonym. Oldelbow; which is a craft beer she likes.

Anyway – it turns out – that one of her cousins – who was fifteen at the time – basically coerced her into – pleasuring him – on a regular basis. Not actual – penetration; but – all the other stuff.

This went on until she was fourteen; maybe six or seven incidents over that time. So these were her first sexual experiences. Eventually – when she threatened to tell – he stopped. But she carried that secret alone, up until last year.

Now imagine what that was like; to find out that had happened to your girlfriend. After nine *years*.

I get why she didn't tell me. It hurts but I get it. She felt if it was treated like a trauma, it would become one. She says she might have told me one day. Maybe.

I was as supportive as she needed me to be; which wasn't much. But between you and me, I've felt out of sorts ever since; like I've taken on the trauma in her place.

It's like when you see on the news that, like – a severed head was found on Clapham Common or something; and then they go on about whose head it was; and who might have cut it off and why. But I always think: what about the poor sod that found it? You never hear about them. How are they bearing up?

Now she's right: we didn't just stop – doing it – when I found out. But it was hard not to think about it when we did.

All my old moves started to feel wrong. I'd previously prided myself on my fingering technique; having achieved a speed and consistency comparable to one of the lower-end vibrators. But now I was getting clumsy; all scrapes and bumps and involuntary pokes. I started keeping my vest on. Sex talk turned to ashes in my mouth.

And she changed too: She wanted dimmer lighting. She kept turning on her back, forcing me into the missionary position. And she started making different sounds: not little.

Small desperate gasps.

But more like –

Longer sounds, more like sighs.

And now expressions I'd always thought were excitement looked more and more like flashes of fear; her eyes rolling white like a horse smelling death. And I'd see myself in those eyes; except it wasn't me, it was him – her cousin; her – and that was when –

Her   What are you saying?

Full lighting returns. He hides the lamp behind his back.

Him   What?

Her   What are you telling them?

Him   Nothing . . .

Her   Nothing?

Him   Well, just – stuff. About me.

Her   Are you telling them what we said we wouldn't tell them?

Him   What? No!

Her   Jimmy –

Him   I'm not!

Pause. She nods, dubious. Lights on both of them.

Her   They don't want your life story.

Him   Sorry – is this what we're doing now? Are we interrupting each other?

She shrugs.

I thought we agreed the monologues were private? Do I get to ask what you're saying?

Her   Ask what you like.

Him   Except I wouldn't. Because I respect your privacy.

Her   I know you, that's all. You go on. Some of them might have babysitters.

Him   Oh right. Well I'm sure they're grateful for your concern. [Maybe we should get a clock like the one on *Countdown*. Boop-de-BOOP-de-boop. Boop-de-BOOP-de-boop. Da-dup; da-dup; diddley-DUM!]

Her   Listen – if this isn't happening . . .

Him   It is happening. It's totally happening. But you know – to be honest – this isn't the most relaxing situation for me.

Her   Jimmy – we've tried relaxing – we've tried everything –

Him   I know. The problem's in my head. I know that. And I'm trying to work it out, Jess. I really am.

Pause.

Her   You can talk to me, you know. You can tell me anything.

Him   I could say the same to you. But you didn't did you? When you had something to tell.

Her   That was different.

Him   Why?

Pause.

Ok, fine. We can't talk about that. Where were we?

Her   My hand was on your thigh. But I feel like you weren't comfortable with that . . .

Him   I was fine with it.

Her   Have some more wine: it'll relax you.

Him   I better not.

Her   A few sips won't hurt.

Him   Jess –

Her   Ok fine: let's forget the thigh for now. How about we just – kiss?

Him   Old school?

Her   Old school. That'd be nice, wouldn't it?

Him   We stopped kissing.

Her   We did. And we shouldn't have.

Him   We pecked . . .

Her   That's right. We went from snogging to kissing to pecking.

Him   Pecking's lame.

Her   It is. Kiss or don't bother, I say. It's like when you meet people now –

Suddenly their faces contort, grotesquely. Then stop.

Him   I kissed you!

Her   You snogged me!

Him   No –

Her   That was a snog. Definitely.

Him   Sorry –

Her   No don't – it's fine. Just caught me off-guard, that's all.

Him   Sorry –

Her   Stop apologising. It was nice.

Him   Was it?

Her   Yes. Keep going.

Him   Should I?

Her   Yes but maybe –

Their faces contort again. And then –

Her   Oww – Jimmy?!

Him   What?

Her   You bit me!

Him   I didn't –

Her   You did.

Him   I nipped you.

Her   Well, don't.

Him   It was meant to be passionate. You used to like that.

Her   [Yeah, well, I used to like – Kevin Spacey. But things change.

Him   Oh Jesus . . . why would you say that?

Her   Say what?

Him   Kevin Spacey: why would you bring him up?

Her   It's just what came to mind.

Him   Yeah but why? Are you saying I'm like Kevin Spacey? A straight Kevin Spacey?

Her   That's in your mind, Jimmy. I never said that and I didn't think it.

Him   So why Kevin Spacey? Why didn't you say 'I used to like – Pot Noodle' or something?

Her   I still like Pot Noodle.

Pause.]

I'm just saying: you don't have to be rough to be passionate.

Him   But this is it, though, Jess: I don't know what's allowed any more.

Her   Allowed?

Him   Yeah, I mean – there were things we used to do. And I don't know if we can do them anymore.

Her   Like what things?

Him   Well, I don't want to say what things. Because then it'll sound like I'm asking you to do them.

Her   But that's ok: if I don't want to do them, I'll say no.

Him   But then I'll feel humiliated.

Her   But why? It's all right to do things for each other. As long as we're both ok with it.

It's nice.

Him   Is it?

Her   Well, what are we talking about? I mean – ejaculating on my face . . .?

Him (*tentatively*)   You're all right with that?

Her   No I'm fucking NOT!

Him   No! And I don't – I hate that! That's totally – demeaning. You shouldn't be all right with that.

Pause.

No, it's more – other things.

Pause.

Ok, look: the thing is – I brought something.

Her   Ok . . .

Him   Just in case I had – trouble. I thought it might – help me. But I don't know if you'll be ok with it.

She shrugs.

Ok but listen: I don't want anyone to think that I condone this sort of thing. This is not indicative of the man I am; or the man I want to be.

And I'm working every day to be that man but I'm not there yet. So as I seem to be facing an ultimatum – regrettably –

Her   Oh, Jimmy, just get on with it, will you!

Him   Ok! But please – don't mock me, ok?

Her   Ok.

Him   Promise?

Her   I promise.

From above, a costume is lowered: the tackiest naughty nurse costume ever.

Oh Jesus . . .

Him   Please, Jess – you promised.

Her   Jimmy . . . where did you find this?

Him   It was in the attic. I cleaned off the mildew. It should still fit.

To audience:

Her   Ok – I wore this once –

Him   Twice.

Her   I got it for a party; as a joke.

Him   Yeah but afterwards . . . remember? It was one of the most powerfully erotic moments of my life.

Her   Really?

Him   Don't say it like that. We're victims too, you know? We're conditioned to respond to stuff like this. We know it's stupid; but that just makes it more exciting somehow.

Her   Me looking stupid excites you?

Him   No but you don't look stupid: you look beautiful. And knowing that you're willing to –

Her   Demean myself –

Him   No to – indulge me – it makes me feel so –

Her   Dominant.

Him   No – !

Her   Masterful.

Him   No: *grateful*. It makes me feel so grateful and special and – *loved*. It's like when you get *chocolates*: think of it like that.

Her   Tell you what, Jimmy: you go to [Thornton's] in a gimp suit and then you can tell me what it's like.

Him   I'll dress up. What do you want? Cowboy? Policeman? Naval commander?

Her   All very high status, I notice.

Him   Nurses are high status. They're not paid enough, I'll grant you; but they're the backbone of any good health service.

Her   I'm not wearing this, Jimmy.

Pause. He slumps, dejected.

Him   Ok. I understand.

Her   It's just not – *me*.

Him   I know.

Her   You don't want that, do you? You don't want me to not be me?

Him   No. Course not.

Pause. He waves, petulantly, and the costume is winched back up.

Her   Jimmy . . .

Him   It's ok, Jess. Really. It's my failure; not yours.

Her   I'm not saying I'd never – dress up a bit.

He nods.

I mean, if it was something a bit less – tacky.

Him   Tacky . . .

Her   Yeah – something a bit more –

Him   A bit more – credible . . .

Her   Yeah. A bit more now.

Him   D'you know, it's funny you should say that –

Her   Is it?

Him   Because no offence, but I was a bit worried you wouldn't still fit in that one. So I brought an alternative.

Her   Another nurse . . .?

Him   No! That's what's funny: I actually thought: maybe we shouldn't look backwards.

Maybe we should try something more – progressive.

Her   Ok . . .

Him   It's hanging backstage there. Go and have a look.

Pause.

You'll definitely like it more than the nurse one.

Her   I'm sure. It's just that – when I said I might be willing to – dress up sometime – I sort – of meant – at home . . .

Him   Right. Except if we don't have sex tonight – that won't really matter, will it? Cos we'll be finished, done; according to you. Am I wrong?

Pause.

Her   It's just – costumes and things . . .

Him   I get it: you're worried you'll feel embarrassed.

She shrugs: Kind of.

Right. Cos this isn't embarrassing for me, is it? Having to perform sexually; here; now. That's not even remotely humiliating, is it?

Her   Is that what this is about? You want me to feel humiliated too?

Him   No, Jess! I want to give you what you want! I've come here and I've put my heart and my guts and my – everything – on display because I love you and I want to save our relationship! And you're not prepared to risk looking a tiny bit silly?

Well then maybe you don't want what you think you want. Maybe you never wanted this to work. Maybe you just set me up to fail.

Her   Yeah, well – maybe I didn't!

Him   Or maybe you did.

Her   Or maybe you did.

Him   Maybe I did what?

Her   Maybe you've set *me* up to fail!

Him   How have I set you up to fail?

Her   Because – if I don't put your stupid costume on – then you can say 'Oh well I tried but you refused to help me' and then we spend another – fourteen sexless months and by then we'll be so dead inside that we'll end up doing jigsaw puzzles and complaining to the BBC about – too much rhino shagging in the nature programmes; because any hint of sex will make us feel all coughy and awkward and remind us of the vast canyon of misery and regret that we'll eventually just DIE in!

Pause.

So fine! I'll put your costume on! But then I want SEX, do you hear me? Not excuses, not more bleating about your male guilt – SEX! Ok?

Pause. He nods.

Him   Yup.

Her   Fine!

She stomps off stage, leaving him there.

Pause.

Him   Awkward . . .

Pause. He clears his throat.

Might take a while to get into, actually. Probably quite tricky.

A long wait. His nervousness builds. He swigs back a whole glass of wine. He adjusts himself. Eventually, she appears . . .

Her   Oh good choice, Jimmy –

She is dressed in a cheap Wonder Woman costume.

Wonder Woman? Seriously?

Him   What? She's modern –

Her   She's not actually –

Him   She's high status.

(*To audience.*) See – she looks good, doesn't she? Doesn't she –

Jess *grabs his hair, pulling his head back and kissing him so forcefully, he ends up on the floor with her on top of him.*

Her   Now I snogged *you*!

Him   I thought you didn't want to be rough –?

Her   I thought you did.

Him   Well I –

She kisses him again, roughly.

Ok listen –

Her   What? I'm Wonder Woman: I take what I desire.

Him   Yeah but no – the whole point of Wonder Woman – is that she's strong – and powerful – but without sacrificing her – feminine qualities – Compassion. Empathy. Sensitivity . . .

Her   Oh fuck you, Jimmy. You get me to dress up as Wonder Woman and now you're telling me to be less strong?

Him   No – but that's her strength. Her strength is her femininity.

Her   Bollocks! Her strength is in her ability to tear your fucking head off. That's the only strength that matters. Ask fucking – Goldilocks!

Him   Goldilocks?

She pursues him around the stage.

Her   We live with bears, Jimmy. Women live with bears. We've been living with them for centuries. So of course we're *sensitive* and *compassionate*. Those aren't feminine qualities imbued by the fucking gods! They're survival tactics.

Him   Ok, right. And I'm a bear, am I?

Pause.

See this is what I've said all along –

Her   What, Jimmy? What have you said all along?

Him   That you're angry; that you're angry with men. And all that anger gets directed at me, and I get to feel like a Nazi! And not even a main Nazi; not even a Hitler; one of those background Nazis in the big coats; and that's even worse! And God knows I'm not perfect – nobody knows that better than me – but there's got be some nuance, Jess: there has to be!

She hits him with a pillow.

Her   Nuance! Nuance! What nuance do I get? Naughty Nurse or Wonder Woman? That's your privilege, right there: you think you're entitled to nuance!

Him   Fine! We're all pigs: I agree! But at least I'm trying not to be; and all I get is shit for it!

And I hate the things that happened to you, Jess, but I didn't do them! Sometimes it feels like I did but I didn't! I'm not your cousin, I'm not a –

He stops dead, realising. Pause.

She looks at the audience. A lack of confusion. She interrogates an audience member, asking if he has told them her secret. Sometimes they cover for him; sometimes they don't. In either case:

Her   You told them!

Him   What?

Her   I knew it! I knew you told them! You are so transparent!

Him   Come on, Jess: I had a right to tell them –

Her   You had a right to tell them my story?

Him   Yes! Because it's my story too!

Pause.

Because I care about you, Jess, so it affects me. I've a right to say how it affected me.

Her   But nobody cares, Jimmy! Nobody cares how *you* feel about *you* being told what happened to *me*.

Him   That's not true: I think some people care. I would be interested in that.

Her   Of course *you* would – !

Him   And anyway – I wasn't told. You didn't tell me. That's interesting, don't you think?

After nine years? That I had to see it on your laptop –

Her   And look what happened! Fourteen months of enforced celibacy!

Him   Maybe if you'd told me there wouldn't have been – !

Her   Oh right – ok: you want me to tell you? I'll tell you, Jimmy.

Him   Bit late now . . .

Her   Oh do you think that's it, Jimmy? Do you think there's no more stories to tell?

There's always more stories.

Him   No, you know what, Jess – I'm done with this –

Her   No but there's a prequel. I'll tell you – !

Him   Why don't you tell them, Jess? Maybe they won't make the mistake of giving a shit.

He walks out of the auditorium again.

Her   Coward!

He's gone. Pause.

Ok . . .

Pause. Lights on her:

Her   So my mum left my dad when I was nine years old. She left him for our local vet; a heroic-looking Australian man called Zip who'd murdered most of my pets.

Weirdly, women get a pass on affairs. If a man leaves his wife, he's a philandering bastard; but when women leave their husbands, it's seen as a liberation; a grand voyage of personal discovery. I suppose that's nuance.

Anyway – my mum moved to Australia so me and my sister stayed here with Dad; which was fine by me. I was a daddy's girl.

Pause.

Jimmy?

Pause.

Jimmy, I know you're there.

Pause. From off stage:

Him   What?

Her   I want you to hear this.

Pause.

It's about you.

Him   Me?

Her   In a way.

Pause. He comes back in and sits down.

So that summer, my father took us to France. His brother had a house outside Paris and it was so sunny: it was perfect.

Every morning, I'd run into my dad's room and jump up on the bed and wake him up. Probably quite annoying; but he didn't show it. He'd stay in bed, and we'd laugh and sing and I'd bounce up and down on him.

That's important: he didn't bounce me. I was the one bouncing. And it was the morning, remember; and he was a young man back then; younger than I am now. So it was understandable what happened; biologically; it was natural.

I don't think I knew what I was feeling; something hard under the sheets; but I knew it felt nice to bounce against it. And I think I knew that I shouldn't but I didn't know why: why would I not do something that felt nice?

He didn't do anything. He didn't act weird; he didn't encourage it. I remember when he stopped it.

Pause.

I was bouncing as usual; but there was something different. He was quieter. He wasn't smiling. And that was the one time he held me in place.

And then suddenly – he was angry, like a bear, and I didn't know why. He told me to go; to let him sleep.

And the next morning, when I ran to his room – the door was locked. I banged on it and shouted 'Daddy, let me in!' But he didn't. And he never did again; not even back at home. That door stayed locked for ever.

I can't say for certain what happened that morning. Did he ejaculate under the sheets? Or did he just have the thought? Was he angry with himself? I don't know.

What I'm sure of – is that he was a truly good, decent man, my father; and he loved me unconditionally. And it breaks my heart to think he might have felt sick or guilty with himself.

But at the time, all I knew – was that I'd done something wrong; and Daddy wouldn't bounce me anymore.

Pause.

Him   Jess – I'm sorry –

He goes to embrace her; but as he does –

Her   Oh . . .

She steps away from him, surprised.

Him   What?

She's looking at his crotch. He's sporting a very prominent erection, tenting his trousers. He looks down and sees it.

What the – ?

Her   Ok . . .

Him   Jess – !

He looks horrified.

Jess, I swear – you've got to believe me: This is in no way related to that story you told – !

Her   Ok –

Him   No but honestly: I wasn't remotely turned on by any of that, I swear!

Her   I believe you.

Him   I didn't even feel it happening – Maybe it has got a mind of its own . . .!

Her   Jimmy, it's ok.

Pause.

But – maybe we shouldn't look a gift horse in the mouth . . .?

Him   What?

He looks at his erection. Then at her.

No – Jess –

Her   What do you mean 'no'? We had a deal, Jimmy – remember? Sex –

Him   Yes but not with – *this*!

Her   Not with your penis?

Him   It's tainted, Jess: it's ill-gotten gains!

Her   How? You said it wasn't my story; and I believe you –

Him   No but – what if it was?

Her   You'd know if it was –

Him   But what if it's subconscious? What if subconsciously – hearing that – gave me this?

What would that make me, Jess? What kind of man would that make me?

Her   You're over-thinking it. Let's just – put it to use –

Him   It's the porn, Jess. It's all the porn I've watched. It has to be – !

Her   The porn – ?

Him   Yes! It's pathetic but – since we stopped – I've had recourse to pornography – and it's got out of hand, Jess – it's warped my brain!

Her   How much have you watched?

Him   It doesn't matter how much: it's what I've been watching!

Her   What have you been watching?

Him   No not – nothing illegal. But *things*, Jess. Things I'd never have thought to watch. Things I never thought I'd see!

And I realised – in the right circumstances – there's virtually nothing I can't – respond to. Do you see?

Her   Not really . . .

Him   It means I can't be sure! I can't be sure your story – your sad, painful story – didn't give me an erection. I can't say with any certainty that I'm not capable of rape or abuse or even murder! All I can say – is that I haven't done it *yet*.

Pause.

Her   But that's good enough, Jimmy. That's all anyone can say.

Him   But that's terrifying, Jess. It's terrifying!

Her   No, Jimmy – it's just life.

Pause.

Him   Then life is terrifying.

Pause.

Why won't this thing go down?! It's like I've taken – !

Pause. He looks at her. He looks at the wine.

Jess . . .?

Pause.

No no no no no – Jess –

He goes to the wine and smells it: inspects the glass –

Tell me you didn't . . .?

She shifts awkwardly.

Oh. My. God. You did! You spiked me! You spiked me with Viagra!

Her   It won't harm you . . .

Him   You don't know that! You're meant to see a doctor before you take it! I could have an undetected heart condition or something!

Her   I asked you, Jimmy! I asked you – for me; for us – just to try it – !

Him   And I said no! No means no, doesn't it?!

Her   But it's just vanity, Jimmy! You just don't want to feel old! And you don't want the girls at the chemist's to think you're impotent!

Him   I'm not impotent!

Her   No – just with me, it seems. But why, Jimmy? Because you know what it feels like? It feels like I'm being punished. Like you're punishing me!

Him   For what?

Her   I don't know: I thought, at first, for not telling you. But now I think you didn't *want* to know, not really. Because now you've got that thought in your head and it disgusts you, like those – flip-flops –

Him   Of course it disgusts me! That someone would do that to you – ? And now your father – ?!

Her   My father didn't *abuse* me, Jimmy! Didn't you hear a word I said?

Why are you so desperate for me to be a victim? So you can be sure that you're the good guy? That they're the villains and you're the hero? So you don't have to question yourself?

Him   Jesus Christ, Jess: all I *do* is fucking question myself – !

Her   That's right! That's *all* you do! And it's fucking useless! Give me something I need, Jimmy – !

Him   Don't turn this round on me! You just spiked me with Viagra! Imagine if I'd done that to you? I'd be burned at the stake!

Her   I know, Jimmy! It's bad! It's bad and I'm ashamed! But this is what it's come to! This is how desperate I am!

Him   This is what I *made* you do?

Her   Just tell me what you want, Jimmy! Just for one second stop lying to yourself and tell me what you fucking WANT!?

Him   I WANT – for things to be all right again, Jess! That's all I want! For things to be back – how they *were*! For you to be the girl I – !

Pause.

Her   The girl you fell in love with?

Pause.

Him   Is she gone, Jess? Is she just gone for ever?

Her   No, Jimmy. She's here. But she's different now.

Pause.

Can you be all right with that? Can you let me be different?

Pause.

Him   It's painful, Jess.

Her   I know. But we can work it out –

Him   No, I mean – the erection –

Her   Oh . . .

Pause.

Him   I see how it works now. Your mind's telling you no; but your body's telling you yes.

Her   I am sorry. I don't know what I was thinking.

Him   It's ok.

Pause.

Don't get me wrong: I feel violated on a deep level. But at least I know you're invested.

Pause. He looks down at his erection.

Him   Look – I suppose we could just . . . do it. It would be rewarding bad behaviour; but I could – think of [England].

Pause.

Her   Here? Now?

They climb back on the chairs. She looks out across the audience, the tension rising. Pause.

You know – I've actually got a headache.

He nods. Pause. they both look tired out.

Him   Thank you, Jess.

Her   For what, Jimmy?

Pause. He shrugs.

Him   For loving me.

Pause. He reaches across the table to her and she reaches to him, but it's slightly too far and only their fingers touch.

They squeeze briefly, in a gesture of comfort that only they – knowing fully the hell they've created – can offer each other.

After a while, they sit up straight again, as if to start over.